**WITHDRAWN**

Morality and the Meaning of Life 9

# MORALITY AND THE MEANING OF LIFE

Edited by:
Professor Albert W.Musschenga (Amsterdam)
Professor Paul J.M. van Tongeren (Nijmegen)

Advisory Board:
Professor Frans De Wachter (Louvain)
Professor Dietmar Mieth (Tübingen)
Professor Kai E. Nielsen (Calgary)
Professor Dewi Z. Phillips (Swansea)


In this series the following titles have been published:

1  Michael Moxter
   Güterbegriff und Handlungstheorie:
   eine Studie zur Ethik F. Schleiermachers
   ISBN 90 390 0042 5

2  Bert Musschenga (ed.)
   Does Religion Matter Morally?
   A Critical Reappraisal of the Thesis of Morality's Independence
   from Religion
   ISBN 90 390 0404 8

3  Philippe van Haute & Peg Birmingham (eds.)
   Dissensus Communis
   Between Ethics and Politics
   ISBN 90 390 0403 x

4  Hub Zwart
   Ethical Consensus and the Truth of Laughter
   The Structure of Moral Transformations
   ISBN 90 390 0412 9

5  Ina Praetorius
   Essays in Feminist Ethics
   ISBN 90 429 0590 5

6  Göran Möller
   Ethics and the Life of Faith
   ISBN 90 429 0699 5

7  Stephen Theron
   The End of the Law
   ISBN 90 429 0725 8

8  Joke J. Hermsen & Dana Villa (eds.)
   The Judge and the Spectator
   Hannah Arendt on Thought and Action
   ISBN 90 429 0781 9

# GIFTS AND INTERESTS

Antoon Vandevelde (ed.)

PEETERS
2000

The research on which this book is based has been funded by the research program "Human Sciences" of the Flemish Community (Belgium)

© 2000 — Peeters, Bondgenotenlaan 153, B-3000 Leuven, Belgium
D.2000/0602/19
ISBN 90-429-0814-9

All rights reserved. No part of this publication may be reproduced, stored in a retrieval system, or transmitted, in any form or by any means, electronic, mechanical, photocopying, or otherwise, without the prior permission of the Publisher.

# Table of Contents

Introduction . . . . . . . . . . . . . . . . . . . . . . . . . . . . . . . . VII

Toon Vandevelde, Towards a Conceptual Map of Gift Practices . . . .   1

### PART 1: MAUSS AND HIS CRITIQUES

Jacques T. Godbout, Homo Donator Versus Homo Oeconomicus . . . .  23

Alain Caillé, Gift and Association . . . . . . . . . . . . . . . . . . . .  47

Jean-Luc Boilleau, On Meteors: Considerations Touching upon the Agon, in which Questions Concerning Gifts and Love Are Tackled .  57

Christian Arnsperger, Gift-giving Practice and Noncontextual Habitus: How (not) to be Fooled by Mauss . . . . . . . . . . . . . . . . . . .  71

### PART 2: COMPARATIVE AND HISTORICAL PERSPECTIVES

Chris A. Gregory, Value Switching and the Commodity Free Zone . . .  95

Ilana F. Silber, Beyond Purity and Danger: Gift-Giving in the Monotheistic Traditions . . . . . . . . . . . . . . . . . . . . . . . . . . . 115

Camille Tarot, Gift and Grace: A Family to be Recomposed? . . . . 133

Raymond Corbey, On Becoming Human: Mauss, the Gift and Social Origins . . . . . . . . . . . . . . . . . . . . . . . . . . . . . . . . . . 157

### Part 3: THE PHILOSOPHY OF THE GIFT

Christian Roy, Transpositions of Mauss' Theory of the Gift in the Personalist Social Critique of Arnaud Dandieu (1897-1933) . . . . . . . 177

Marin Terpstra, Social Gifts and the Gift of Sociality Some Thoughts on Mauss' The Gift and Hobbes' Leviathan . . . . . . . . . . . . . . 191

Aldo De Martelaere, Personal Obligations in Personal Relations . . . . . 209

# Introduction

"Why are the Graces three in number and why are they sisters, why do they have their hands interlocked, and why are they smiling and youthful and virginal, and clad in loose and transparent garb. Some would have it appear that there is one for bestowing a benefit, another for receiving it, and a third for returning it; others hold that there are three classes of benefactors – those who earn benefits, those who return them, those who receive and return them at the same time. But of the two explanations do you accept as true whichever you like; yet what profit is there in such knowledge? Why do the sisters hand in hand dance in a ring which returns upon itself? For the reason that a benefit passing in its course from hand to hand returns nevertheless to the giver; the beauty of the whole is destroyed if the course is anywhere broken, and it has most beauty if it is continuous and maintains an uninterrupted succession. In the dance, nevertheless, an older sister has especial honour, as do those who earn benefits. Their faces are cheerful, as are ordinarily the faces of those who bestow or receive benefits. They are young because the memory of benefits ought not to grow old. They are maidens because benefits are pure and undefiled and holy in the eyes of all; and it is fitting that there should be nothing to bind or restrict them, and so the maidens wear flowing robes, and these, too, are transparent because benefits desire to be seen."

SENECA, De Beneficiis, Bk I, iii, 1-5, translated by J.W. Basore, Harvard University Press, Cambridge Mass., 1935, pp. 13-15.

# Towards a Conceptual Map of Gift Practices

Antoon VANDEVELDE (Institute of Philosophy, K.U.Leuven)

The gift may be omnipresent in contemporary society as well as in bygone ones; nevertheless, it seems ungraspable for the theoretician who is interested in conceptualizing it. The problem is that the issue of the gift interferes with the issue of the foundations of every human community. One need not be surprised, then, that it takes great pains to find that the multiformity of the gifts one empirically identifies can be situated within one single paradigm. In this introductory text I will contrast the logic of the gift to that of market exchange. Subsequently, I will explore the possibilities of drawing a kind of conceptual map of the gift component in economic and social contemporary life. Finally, after a brief presentation of the various contributions to this volume, I will conclude with some remarks on the relation between the logic of the gift and the idea of reciprocity.[1]

**Gifts and Commodities**

Let us start with the crux of the matter. All the social sciences, including the economic sciences and virtually all of social philosophy, including a substantial part of the literature on the gift, are haunted by the question: why are we not in the state of nature? Why do our societies know at least a semblance of order? Why is it that we do not live in chaos or anarchy — at least not all the time? How is it possible that a certain coordination can be established between people, and that their projects are not systematically thwarted? Hobbes' description of the state of nature is actually even more pessimistic: according to him, life in the state of nature would be solitary, nasty, brutish and short. Without the constraining intervention of a Leviathan there would be a lack of not only coordination but also cooperation. However, many people do not accept this ultrapessimistic diagnosis: they are not under the impression of continuously living in sordidness, in a situation in which no one can trust anyone, and in which opportunism infiltrates into every social relation. Of course there is not as much cooperation as we would wish for, but there is certainly more than Hobbes and the vulgar advocates of 'homo homini lupus' allow for.[2]

---

[1] I thank Professor Howard Caygill for his valuable comments on an early version of this text.
[2] This is not a universally shared opinion. Robert Bellah reports a survey of his students at the University of California which reveals that more than two thirds of them approve of the proposition

In the course of the history of philosophy and of the social sciences many answers have been given to the above questions. Most economists tend to privilege the role of market exchange in the explanation of social coherence. Mauss, on the contrary, together with those he inspired, tends to privilege the logic of the gift. It must be granted that gifts and commercial exchanges have something in common: the reference to the notion of reciprocity. The existence of this common element undoubtedly explains the reductionist attempts of Maussians as well as economists. Both pretend to be capable of explaining the essential characteristics of the rival model.

Nevertheless, there are very distinct differences between the logic of the gift and that of the market, between gifts and commodities, and between the kind of reciprocity that is implied in both models. Market exchange is founded on a very strict notion of equality and on an immediate reciprocity. Rights and duties of the parties concerned are scrupulously fixed in advance, and in the event of one of the contractants not keeping his engagements, the aggrieved party can press charges in court. On the other hand, the reciprocity required by the logic of the gift is not strict, not immediate and unintentional. One who would immediately return the gift he received, would in doing so indicate that he is incapable of receiving: such is the case with Timon of Athens in Shakespeare's play. Every gift incites a countergift, but only at the appropriate juncture: some period of time must have elapsed, not in order to mask the interest calculation as the "objective truth of the gift", as Bourdieu[3] suggests, but rather as a sign of accepting to enter into relation with the donator.

Moreover, the logic of the gift demands that one is not to give with the intention of receiving countergifts, possibly increased with interest. As Jacques Godbout has rightly remarked, the donator often even has the tendency to devaluate the value of his gift, explaining it is not worth as much as the donatee imagines, and that, hence, there is no call for the latter to be particularly grateful.[4] That is why in receiving a countergift, one uses more or less stereotypical formulae to mark one's surprise. A philosopher easily recognizes in this ritual the desire for authentic social recognition. We are not interested in receiving a gift that is merely given out of duty, for instance as a couterpart of a previous gift. We greatly enjoy receiving a present, honours or thank-yous,

---

according to which "most people are not trustworthy". A quick survey of my own students — last year economics students — reveals that only one third of them approves of this assertion. Sociologists confirm that the latter figure corresponds more or less to the results of surveys on the degree of mutual confidence which prevails in the population of most European countries. This percentage seems to me incredibly high still for people who will have no difficulties at all finding a job, and of whom the greater part will belong to the well-to-do classes of the population.

[3] P. Bourdieu, *Le sens pratique (Practical Sense)* (Minuit: Paris) p. 105.

[4] See J. Godbout's text in this volume.

provided they are spontaneously given. A gift is worth nothing if it does not reflect an authentic appreciation of our personal qualities and of the value of our friendship or our social bond. This social recognition will be destroyed, due to its very own nature, if we try to manipulate it, to extort it from our partners or to buy it on the market. Love, friendship and social recognition are either given freely or utterly worthless.

This characteristic structure of human relations explains why the external point of view on the gift, which highlights the matter of reciprocity, is so deceptive. True enough, one can calculate the equivalences and the interest rates between exchanged gifts a posteriori. One may even be capable of predicting the next move in the gift game, but from an internal point of view this game requires indetermination, risk and uncertainty, surprise and wonder. Moreover, generosity very often proves to establish a good reputation and to serve our long-term interest. It not only supplies us with countergifts, but also with honour and gratitude. Owing to it, we are more often elected as a commercial partner, friend or guest.[5] Nevertheless, it is not, as Adam Smith observed in his *Theory of Moral Sentiments*, because an act serves our interest that it has been performed *with a view to* this interest.

As long as one is confined to a theoretical comparison between the sheer logic of the gift and the pure model of economic exchange, things are crystal-clear: there is a plain opposition between those two ideal types of social relations. In the real world, however, things are much less evident. Not every gift can be perfectly classified within the logic of the gift which I pictured above. Moreover, there is less opposition between gift and interest than there is between gift and market. Even when starting from the point of view of the pure logic of the gift, I can quite indisputably claim to be interested in love, in friendship, in honour or in a reputation engendered by my generosity, but of course, for the above reasons, this preoccupation or this interest will never cause me to engage in a manipulatory action with a view on controlling my partners. Every direct strategy aiming at captivating the desire or the appreciation of the other would be otiose. Which means that the interests do not explain the ins and outs of the gift, but that they are not entirely absent either.

One of the most attractive characteristics of Marcel Mauss' model of the gift is that it is situated beyond the opposition between egoism and altruism, or between interest and disinterestedness. The actual practices of the gift mostly refer to an enormous variety of motivations which can only be disentangled with great difficulty. Take, for instance, the social relations in a neighbourhood.

---

[5] R.H. Frank, *Passions Within Reason — The Strategic Role of Emotions* (New York, London: W.W. Norton, 1998).

There are people who devote themselves to withdraw from the exchange of gifts. They prefer to spend considerable sums of money to buy an expensive tool that they will need only once in a lifetime, rather than lend it from a neighbour who wishes nothing more than to do them a favour. They are not necessarily disagreeable people. When asked, they may be willing to help others, but they prefer to keep distance. They seem to loathe the idea of being indebted to others. They live in a commodified world. If everyone would behave similarly, every sense of community would quickly disappear from the neighbourhood.

On the other hand, other people will voluntarily engage in the game of the gift. Suppose you asked your neighbour's daughter to keep an eye on your children for an hour. On returning you intend to give her some pocket money, and if she refuses you will insist on her accepting it. But suppose the daughter is not in, then her mother might replace her. At this juncture things become more complicated. It is out of the question to pay your neighbour: this will not do. She will refuse your offer indignantly, which means that you cannot but accept her gift and your debt towards her. Undoubtedly you will have to render her a countergift in the fullness of time. But why exactly will you do this? Possibly to make sure that in a future case of emergency you will still be able to appeal to her. In that case you have a kind of implicit insurance policy. Even family relations often obey such logic. It is also possible that you want to avoid a bad reputation in your neighbourhood at all costs. You may want to point out clearly to your neighbours that you most certainly do not want to take advantage of their goodwill. This explains why neighbours often return gifts and services with a certain margin: they give more than the simple equivalence between gifts and countergifts requests, not so much in order to gain social prestige, but to indicate that they are in no way enclined to maximize their interest at the expense of others. Sometimes the motivation to give may in the first place be altruistic: there is a more or less continuous flux of small gifts and countergifts that are not directly interrelated.

**Models of the Gift**

Is it possible, starting from the empirical confirmation of the enormous variety of existing gifts, to draw a kind of conceptual map of the gift component in economic and social life? The cartographer can make an inventory of many different issues.

1. From the point of view of the donator or the benefactor one can reveal various *motivations to give*. A good example of such a study is André Masson and Pierre Pestieau's analysis of the different motivations to bequeath a

heritage. They distinguish, amongst others, altruistic, accidental, strategic, paternalistic, retrospective and capitalistic inheritances.[6]

2. One can reveal the different interpretations of the gift by the *beneficiary* as well. Will he be grateful or, quite the reverse, humiliated? What is the exact nature of the obligation of gratitude? What is the foundation of the distinction between rights and favours or between justice and generosity?[7] Can thank-yous or symbolic countergifts suffice to respond to a material gift, or need gift and countergift be part of approximately the same register? Even if the element of surprise may be essential in choosing the countergift, this does not prevent the whole procedure from being a game with rules that can easily be made explicit.

3. A third possibility is to concentrate on the *significance* of the gift. In doing so, one focuses on the interaction between donator and beneficiary. As the significance of the gift depends on the social context, there will be an infinite variety of forms of gift. Which means that we would like to impose more structure on our comprehension of the practices of the gift.

4. This is exactly what the objectivistic perspective of science promises to do, for instance by introducing rational choice theory. Here, the structure of opportunities, coupled to some relatively simple postulates on human motivations, explains the social interaction. The practices of the gift will, for instance, be analysed as a variation of Axelrod's 'tit for tat'. I do not want to reject this kind of thought experiment as a whole, even though it certainly starts from a point of view that is external to the actors, and even though it neglects what is, hermeneutically speaking, essential to understand the gift. Moreover, the classical methodology of science is problematic because it postulates the existence of universal laws. This modus operandi is hardly compatible with social sciences, even if it is only because knowledge can modify the behaviour of the social actors, or because history always conceals unknown events. As a consequence, the explication of past or present social phenomena does not necessarily permit the prediction of future events on the basis of analogous antecedents.

5. This situation must incite social sciences to be modest, but it does not necessarily condemn them to impotence. Only a more supple and more pragmatic methodology has to be found. Since its goal is to gain a better

---

[6] A. Masson, P. Pestieau, 'Bequest Motives and Models of Inheritance: A Survey of the Literature', in G. Erreygers, T. Vandevelde (eds.), *Is Inheritance Legitimate? — Ethical and Economic Aspects of Wealth Transfers* (Berlin: Springer Verlag, 1997) p. 54-88.

[7] See, for instance, F.R. Berger, 'Gratitude', in *Ethics*, 85 (July 1975); Ph. Pettit, R. Goodin, 'The Possibility of Special Duties', in *The Canadian Journal of Philosophy*, 16: 4 (Dec. 1986) p. 651-676; J. English, *Having Children* (Oxford: U.P., 1979); J. Rachels, *Morality, Parents and Children,* in H. Lafollette (ed.), *Ethics in Practice — An Anthology,* (Oxford: Blackwell, 1997) pp. 195-206.

understanding of the existing practices of the gift, it is useful to simply accumulate the theoretical models of the gift without paying much attention to their origin. Whether these social models or logics are inspired by game theory, by functionalism, by sociobiology, by hermeneutic analyses, by the narration of historical sequences or by the reading of novels is of no importance as long as they add to our understanding. These models more or less function like the 'mechanisms' Elster talks about in the beginning of his *Nuts and Bolts in the Social Sciences*, except that Elster still privileges too much the causal explanation.[8] To take up one of his examples, one cannot predict whether a particular person will prefer an accessible option, or whether his desire will be fixated on an inaccessible object, that is to say, whether he will be subject to adaptive or counteradaptive preferences. The skillful eye of the scientist, nevertheless, easily recognizes the mechanisms which preside the formation of preferences, and this knowledge will eventually help him to tinker up explications of more complex phenomena. According to this methodology, the progress in science chiefly consists in an extension of the questionnaire used for surveying social phenomena. To that purpose, therefore, one has to construct and to develop a list of topoi, of commonplaces, of causal or narrative sequences, of theoretical models that allow one to understand, for instance, the real practices of the gift.

Anyway, chance would have it that Elster's methodology was inspired by Paul Veyne's study on *evergetism*, the ostentatious gift which was customary in Greek and Roman antiquity. Veyne tries to explain evergetism using the economic theory of collective goods, using the Aristotelian theory of magnificence, using the Keynesian theory of investment and multiplicator, using Veblen's theory of ostentatious consumption, using Mauss' theory of the gift and Polanyi's theory of redistribution. He compares evergetism with Christian charity, with Maecenatism and with the contemporary welfare state. Each time he concludes that, on the one hand, these endeavours to explain and these comparisons teach us something, but that, on the other hand, they fail in part. Nonetheless, these models do not function like somewhat vague analogies: it is only in revealing their specific difference that the author succeeds in improving our comprehension of the analysed phenomenon.[9]

Elster's methodology and Veyne's example suggest that the unsophisticated opposition between the logic of the gift and the logic of the economic exchange

---

[8] J. Elster, *Nuts and Bolts in the Social Sciences* (Cambridge: Cambridge University Press, 1989). See also, by the same author: *Explaining Technical Progress* (Cambridge: Cambridge University Press, 1983).

[9] P. Veyne, *Le pain et le cirque — Sociologie historique d'un pluralisme politique (Panem et Circenses – Historical Sociology of a Political Pluralism)*, (Paris: Le Seuil, 1976). See also by the same author: *Comment on écrit l'histoire (How History is Written)* (Paris: Le Seuil, 1971) and *L'inventaire des différences (The Inventory of Differences)* (Paris: Le Seuil, 1976).

which I outlined in the beginning of this article, is much too simplistic. The logic of the gift I dealt with in the above is important, even if it were only because it is rooted in a fundamentally human desire: the desire for social recognition. But it does not explain the vast variety of practices of gift one discovers for instance in a neighbourhood. Besides, even if it were possible to explain every practice of the gift starting from one single logic, it would still be useful to try and make more subtle distinctions. Even in Mauss' *Essay sur le don (Essay on the Gift)* one distinguishes different conceptions of the gift, and it is far from certain that all these conceptions can be reduced to a single concept. Let us bury our reductionist temptation for the time being, and let us endeavour to construct a more refined taxonomy of the practices of the gift.

1. First of all there are *instrumental or strategic gifts*. These gifts particularly aim at promoting the interest of the donator. Take, for instance, elderly people who let the size of their future legacy depend on the number of visits, on the attention and the care each potential heir spoils them with. Needless to say that as you sow, so shall you reap. The strategic behaviour is reversible: the law of reciprocity will impose itself, and it can be expected that each potential heir will make the number of his visits and the quality of his care dependent on the expected size of his inheritance... However, there are much less grudging versions of instrumental gifts. The models of implicit insurance merely allow for a partial explanation — and only from an external point of view — of the solidarity within families or in traditional social relations. Even altruistic gifts often have an instrumental side. One looks after one's elderly and sick parents, not only out of a sense of duty or gratitude, but also hoping that one's own children will follow this good example later on, or more exactly, because one can count on being neglected by one's own children if one neglects one's parents. It has to be pointed out that even Kant does not condemn every form of instrumentality: only a behaviour by which others are *exclusively* or essentially treated as a means to increase one's own interests, is morally despicable and unworthy.

2. Opposed to strategic gifts, there are purely *altruistic gifts*. These gifts exclusively aim at the well-being of others. However, this motivation can go hand in hand with a considerable paternalistic dimension. Instead of looking for a present that would please the beneficiary, one intends to improve the behaviour of the beneficiary by choosing a present with educational value: altruism is not always sympathetic, and it certainly does not exclude instrumentalism. Especially within the well-to-do classes many people save up, not for themselves, but for their children. This altruistic behaviour is not necessarily opposed to egoistic motivations: often enough people do not in the least distinguish between their own interest and their children's. Anonymous gifts, for instance the gift of blood, or gifts to the

deceased,[10] come closest to the ideal of a totally disinterested sacrifice. Nevertheless, because in the latter cases every reciprocity is by definition excluded, they are forms of gifts which — more than instrumental gifts — escape from the logic of the gift as formulated in the beginning of this article.

3. The *expressive gift* embodies a feeling, an identity or an already existing social relation. It distinguishes itself from strategic or altruistic gifts insofar as it emanates from a frame of mind which distinguishes means and ends. The difference between expressive gift and *symbolic gift* is minute. The latter does not express an existing relation, it establishes or constitutes the social relation itself. In the symbolic gift no trace whatsoever of utilitarianism subsists. Most often it takes place on the occasion of a ritual ceremony. A good example is the wedding ring, which symbolizes the very presence of the other in his physical absence. Another example is the armour or the ceremonial war costume, which the Chiefs of War often receive in traditional or primitive societies, and which inconveniences them more than it helps them on the battle field.

4. The *agonistic* gift, the best known example of which is the potlatch, is equally close to the symbolic gift. In agonistic relations, the identity of the social actors, their dignity and their honour are at stake, which means that their identity is not fixed but subject to alterations and repeated challenges.[11]

**Mauss and his critics**

What is the place of Mauss' theory in this landscape of the gift? At first sight, Mauss particularly analyses the agonistic gift and the logic of honour to which this gift is related. If such is the case, the principal merit of Mauss' theory would be that it reminds us of the fact that the patterns of ancestral behaviour and thought undeniably keep a certain validity in our contemporary societies. One can show that the agonistic subsists in sports, and that it explains certain aspects of economic and political life. One also suspects it behind the challenge which the self-destructive behaviour of certain terrorists or hard drug users launches at the established society. The agonistic reveals the precariousness of every established order and of every form of community life. It would be dangerous to neglect this aspect of things, but from the normative point of view it decidedly is not this kind of motivations or interactions that should be stimulated. The point is rather to neutralize their violent potential and to canalize these energies towards socially desirable objectives.

---

[10] S. Kierkegaard, *Kjerlighedens Gjerninger (Acts of Love)* (Copenhagen, 1852) 2nd part, Ch. IX.

[11] J.L. Boilleau, *Conflit et lien social — La rivalité contre la domination (Conflict and Social Bond — Rivalry Versus Domination)* (Paris: La Découverte/M.A.U.S.S., 1995).

The ambivalence of the quest for honour too, is evident. It engenders cycles of vengeance as well as the pursuit of an incorruptible moral integrity. It may inspire a very remunerative strategy in a world in which most partners strive to maximize their immediate gain — that is why the Mafia is more successful in New York than in Palermo — but it can equally inspire unfailing loyalties which reflect the most elevated moral stature. This way one can demonstrate that solidarity with elderly people is not to be explained away exclusively by the pursuit of personal interest. If this solidarity is so robust, it is just because it is linked with a notion of honour. Even in circumstances in which a more and more restricted number of active people has to contribute increasingly important sums to the pension systems of the nonactive, solidarity with the elderly remains a taboo subject in the political debate. If a political party so much as gave the impression of wanting to break down the intergenerational solidarity, this would immediately ruin its credibility.

On a more fundamental level, Mauss formulates a *logic* of the gift, that is to say, he most certainly makes no attempt to explain isolated examples of the gift or of the reasons that could inspire altruism, but he starts from the presupposition of the social nature of man, and he tries to understand how and why gifts ensue from each other. Mauss' originality lies in his attention for the dynamical aspect of the game of the gift, in which every action invites another. The suggestion that there is a spirit in the thing which impells the receiver to render it, is undoubtably not very illuminating, except that it indicates a religious foundation of the social bond. But there are more concrete and more interesting suggestions in the *Essai sur le don*. For instance that in the triple obligation to give, receive and render, the latter is the most important. True enough, one could argue that from the human point of view the obligation to give is itself already derived from the obligation to render. There is the gift of life itself, of our talents, of our physical and intellectual capacities, of language, of the technical universe and of culture. He who refuses to take the initiative to give, places himself in the margin of the human community. He can be considered as being ungrateful, at least if he is not particularly disadvantaged by nature or by want of affection during his childhood. In a way every gift is already a countergift. Plato has exemplified this truth in books VI and VII of *The Republic* using the image of the sun: it gives without asking for immediate compensation, and in doing so it incites the philosopher to imitate it and to share his knowledge with the ordinary mortals.

Most articles in this book have been presented at a colloquium on *Gifts and Interests*, organised at the University of Leuven in april 1998. We asked the authors to assess the actuality of Mauss' famous essay on *The Gift* and to make a contribution to our project for a conceptual map of gift practices. Let us summarize briefly the results of this quest. J.T Godbout, A. Caillé, J.L. Boileau and C. Tarot belong to a French group editing *La Revue du M.A.U.S.S.*, the review of the so-called Anti-Utilitarian Movement in the Social Sciences. For more than fifteen years now they have been publishing a series of very heterogenous, but also very imaginative texts out of which slowly emerged a kind of Maussian paradigm for the social sciences. Although some of the more radical members of the group tend to think that social science is simply impossible and that, consequently, there is no need to construct new paradigms within it, a clear presentation of what the core of such a paradigm could be can be found in the texts of Jacques Godbout, Alain Caillé and Jean-Luc Boileau in this volume. In the first part of our book we grouped these texts together with the article of Christian Arnsperger which contains a fierce criticism of Mauss'essay and of the theories of the French Maussians. The central theme of this group of essays is the relationship between the logics of gift and market, or in Godbout's terms Homo Donator and Homo Oeconomicus.

Godbout revolts against the paradigmatic privilege of rational choice theory in the social sciences, which he considers to be a reflection of the increasing influence of individualism and neoliberalism in social and political life. Many sociologists and anthropologists on the contrary defend a holist or relational paradigm, which emphasizes strongly the fact that human beings borrow their identity from their fellowmen and that they have 'internalized' social norms. However, neither the homo oeconomicus with his purely instrumental rationality, nor the homo sociologicus who is more or less blindly 'pushed' by social norms and customs look very attractive to the author. Mauss' logic of the gift, insofar as it is linked to the desire for recognition, transcends both paradigms in that it reconciles freedom and obligation: without freedom, no value can be attached to the actions and reactions of our fellow human beings. Hence, Godbout argues that the basic postulate of self-interest, on which rational choice theory is founded, should be complemented by the postulate of the gift. Only the presupposition of mutual trust or of a natural tendency to give explains why in situations that can be modelled as a prisoner's dilemma, much more cooperation actually occurs than is predicted by game theory. Also recent research in the field of child psychology and ethology equally confirms the presence of altruism and compassion in very young children and animals. Therefore, instead of investigating how society has been able to restrain people's spontaneous tendency to maximize their self-interest, we should rather inquire into which social dispositions prevent them from excessive giving. This leads the author to reject any conception that links the logic of the gift too closely to the notion of reciprocity. Furthermore, he presents a classification of various models of the gift which cannot be explained within the framework of instrumental rationality. Here he strongly emphasizes the relationship between gift and debt. Someone who enters into the logic of the gift accepts his indebtedness towards the other. This also explains some of the legitimation problems of the welfare state in a highly individualized society. From the point of view of the beneficiaries, welfare systems easily turn into unilateral gifts that cannot be returned. Probably the only way to cope with such a humiliating situation without yielding to feelings of envy and violent reactions, is to convert the gift into a legal right.

After having carefully summarized the paradigm of the gift and its main conceptual distinctions, Alain Caillé, the chief-editor of *La Revue du M.A.U.S.S.*, explains how associative life can be understood as a gift practice. The author defines the association as a more or less permanent pooling of material means, knowledge and activities for a purpose other than that of sharing profit. Whether the convention at the basis of such an association is tacit or explicit, written or unwritten, formally protected by law or informally sanctioned by social norms and custom, is less important. Associations are voluntary initiatives. Personal contacts are of paramount importance for realizing their functional objectives. Associational life transcends the well-known opposition between *Gemeinschaft* and *Gesellschaft*, between community and society. Strict contractual reciprocity does not apply here, neither does unconditional love or violent threat. Associations are based upon trust, which means that every member is willing to devote his energy unconditionally to the common good and that he will continue to do so unless too many other participants refuse to cooperate. Smoothly functioning associations thus involve a mutually positive indebtedness. Finally, as has also been noted by Robert Putnam in another context,[12] a dense network of associations is a precondition for sustaining participatory democracy, for stimulating civic virtue and the invention of new forms of solidarity, and for enhancing the legitimacy of a highly redistributive welfare state.

In his essay *On Meteors: Considerations Touching upon the Agon in which Questions Concerning Gifts and Love Are Tackled* Jean-Luc Boileau starts off by distinguishing three closely intertwined components in gift giving. These practices can be described as quasi-contractual exchanges, as revealers of interhuman solidarity and as attempts to prove one's superiority. However, it is the latter aspect of gift giving that puzzles the author most. We find agonistic gifts not only in archaic or primitive societies, but also in contemporary sports for instance. Boileau emphasizes the basic equality of all competitors, united as they are by the consciousness of their dependence on chance and of the ephemeral character of their triumphs. For a brief moment they emerge from obscurity and then vanish again for ever. Someone who is susceptible to the agonistic universe, will sympathize with all forms of life that struggle against their slipping into indifference. In agon there is no fixed reality, no deeper truth, only appearance, diversity and novelty. The world of agon is

---

[12] R. Putnam, *Making Democracy Work: Civic traditions in Modern Italy* (Princeton, Princeton University Press, 1993).

crowded with gods and 'meteors'. Here even love is not just harmony, agapè or exchange, but also conflict, rivalry and seduction.

Christian Arnsperger criticises Mauss and the French 'Maussians'fiercely in his *Gift-Giving Practice and Non-Contextual Habitus — How (Not) To Be Fooled By Mauss*. The gift practices described by Mauss and especially those highlighted by Boilleau, are mainly characterized by mutual defiance, distrust and the desire to dominate the beneficiary. For Arnsperger this may be a fairly good description of the logic of the gift as it was predominant in past societies and as it continues to function latently in contemporary society, but it is difficult to understand how attractive normative propositions or a call for more generosity could be derived from this factuality. Mauss starts from a Hobbesian view of the gift and ends up with an anti-Hobbesian ethical call: this is blatantly inconsistent. Still Arnsperger looks for a way to safeguard Mauss' ethical call. This boils down to the question of how one should interpret the combination of freedom and obligation that is so typical of Mauss' logic of the gift. Pierre Bourdieu's famous analysis of this topic runs as follows. Due to the work of time the agents never become totally aware of the constraint of reciprocity that is prevalent in the game of gift-giving; therefore they can keep up the appearance of spontaneity and freedom. This way Bourdieu strongly relativizes the possibility of a self-conscious subject that would be totally transparent to itself: human behaviour is governed by a set of internalized norms, a habitus determined by the social and historical context. Arnsperger, however, prefers the philosophy of Emmanuel Levinas to Bourdieu's sociological approach. Levinas joins Bourdieu in his rejection of the primacy of the autonomous subject, but in doing so he refers to the ontological situation of the subject that comes into being through the request emanating from the 'face' of the other. In this view generosity is not socially, culturally or historically determined. It emerges out of a 'non-contextual habitus' through the confrontation with radical alterity. The gift too, is not a functional device intended to nourish the social bond, but it originates from the trauma of the sudden appearance of the other. For Levinas freedom is finite: it is constrained by the other who urges me to take on my responsibility. However it is not an illusion, as Bourdieu and Mauss, at least in Arnsperger's interpretation, seem to think.

In the second part of this volume we grouped a certain number of essays exploring the comparative and anthropological aspects of Mauss' work. In the essays of Chris Gregory, Ilana Silber, Camille Tarot and Raymond Corbey Mauss' claim to produce a general theory of the gift applicable to all recorded societies is questioned. C.A. Gregory's essay *Value Switching and the Commodity Free Zone* is based on recent empirical research in Central India and it presents itself as a reappraisal of the value-perspective developed in his well-known book on *Gifts and Commodities*. He draws up a list of all the terms people use in Halbi, a local dialect, to denominate various ways of mobilizing labour. Of course, the translation of these terms and the classification of the types of exchange they denote, raise a problem all anthropological studies are confronted with, namely that one is obliged to use general terms borrowed from the language and culture of the researcher. This runs the risk of obscuring the specificity of exchange- and gift-practices in nonwestern cultures. It is not easy to escape the trap of ethnocentrism without yielding to the easy solution of extreme relativism. Gregory shows that classical and neoclassical economic theories look at the world from a single and fixed point of view. They focus on objective relationships of equivalence and they try to explain them either from the perspective of the wage labourer, as determined by quantities of abstract labour, or from the perspective of the consumer, equalizing marginal utility into all directions. Until recently, anthropologists tended to privilege another fixed perspective, namely that of the family, or that of its male members, the father and brothers. Gregory refuses all reductionism: people are producers, consumers, members of a family, neighbours, friends, etc. They are able to switch quickly and easily from one value regime to another. Only from the very general point of view of ordered human relationships is it possible to distinguish various types of commodity-free zones.

Silber and Tarot's essays *Beyond Purity and Danger: Gift-Giving in the Monotheistic Religions* and *Gift and Grace: A Family to be Recomposed* are fascinating reconstructions of the place of the gift in Rabbinic Jewish and Christian culture. Ilana Silber points out that research on religious gift giving, especially in the context of the great monotheistic traditions, Judaism, Christianity and Islam, is still underdeveloped. Because he tries to unveil the logic of the gift as a universal phenomenon, which is closely linked to reciprocity, Mauss is partly responsible for this state of affairs. He seems to have seriously neglected the asymmetry which is so typical of religious gifts. Silber points for instance to an interesting Indian example: some gifts to the Brahmans are considered to embody the sins of the donor. Hence no reciprocity at all is desired. One cannot say that these gifts are totally disinterested, but the donor surely does not want his generosity to be rewarded by the (immediate) recipient of the gift. Silber wants to inquire into the specificity and multiplicity of religious gifts. She distinguishes between 1) gifts to the gods, 2) 'cultic' gifts, i.e. gifts to religious institutions or to specialists and 3) charitable gifts to the poor and the needy. Cultic gifts seem to be predominant in Indian religions, charitable gifts in the monotheistic religions — although important exceptions can be cited and various odd combinations can be observed. The author stresses the need for a non-monolithic approach to gifts, reciprocity and disinterestedness and she illustrates this with the example of the Jewish tradition of the Zedaka.

Camille Tarot explores the difficulties of constructing a theory of divine grace from the point of view of the anthropology of the gift. Doubtlessly the

Maussian theory provides a better heuristic framework to understand grace than the paradigm of self-interest. However a more thorough inquiry into the subject shows that the differences between divine grace and the logic of the gift as it functions in archaic societies are considerable. For instance, grace is absolutely free: God is not submitted to any obligation to give. Also, human beings may be confronted with the impossibility of reciprocity or reversibility. Moreover, as a supernatural gift, grace does not have the ambiguous and somewhat dangerous character of purely human gifts. The former creates righteous persons, the latter create honour and welfare. Tarot rejects the sociological conception of the theory of grace as an ideology. Rather he suggests that one cannot understand the social reality of religion without grasping some of the fluxes within it. Conflicts between various religious traditions, but also between various currents of Christianity or between Judaism and Christianity happen to be about the meaning and the economy of religious gifts, about the prohibition of some gifts and exchanges with pagans, about the proper attitude towards grace and fate, about the importance of gifts to priests, poor people or co-religionists.

Raymond Corbey's essay *On Becoming Human: Mauss, the Gift and Social Origins* develops an evolutionary perspective on the origin of humanity. Starting from Mauss' intuitions he suggests some extremely thought provoking hypotheses in line with the theories of Hobbes and Rousseau on the state of nature and the means of getting out of that situation. To interpret the various theories of social contract as historical hypotheses or as archaeological theories on how animals evolved into humans may seem somewhat odd to philosophers who are in the habit of considering theories of the state of nature as merely normative devices destined to assess the legitimacy of existing social and political structures. However, the problem of what it means to become and to be human is an interesting one. For Mauss and Durkheim the development of exchange and gift relations is the key to understand the transition from an animal to a human stage in evolution. Corbey sees this as a variant of the 'release of proximity' stressed by many contemporary researchers of the genesis of human social organisation. However, he criticizes the implicit dualism inherent to this conception. The idea that social organization is superimposed on a brutish, impulsive animal nature that had to be restrained in order to make civilization possible is refuted by recent research in the field of (socio-)biology. Hence a plea for integrating natural and biological factors in Mauss' 'totalizing' approach, without however slipping into an equally untenable reductionist naturalism. With this in mind Corbey emphasizes the continuity between symbolic behaviour and earlier forms of communication on the one hand, and action based upon incorporated routines, habits and skills on the other. Finally, he points towards Habermas' theory of communicative action as the most exhaustive philosophical and non-utilitarian account of the origin of normativity, subjectivity and rationality.

The third part of this volume gathers the texts of Christian Roy, Marin Terpstra and Aldo De Martelaere, three essays inquiring into some philosophical implications of Mauss' theory. Roy highlights an interesting but little known episode in the reception of Mauss' theory of the gift. Arnaud Dandieu, one of the founding fathers of French personalism in the early 1930's, seems to have conceived a very original blueprint of a new type of society that would give free rein to the potlatch practices described by Mauss. Dandieu derives a dichotomic organization of society from a dualistic anthropology. Human beings have to fulfill some physiological needs, but much more important is their desire for social recognition, honour and prestige. The sphere of material production should be mechanized as much as possible. Every progress in automation that can diminish the need for undifferentiated labour is welcome. Like Georges Bataille, Dandieu is much more radical than Mauss: he rejects the very idea of wage labour. Repetitive labour tasks that cannot be eliminated should be equally divided among all citizens as a kind of civilian service in exchange for a guaranteed basic income. The whole society should be organized in such a way as to permit a maximal expansion of the sphere of free creativity. It is within this realm that people can escape the narrow utilitarian calculation and that the potlatch gains normative value: a basic income permits everybody to engage in entrepreneurship and to take creative risks. These ideas have profoundly inspired the well-known work of André Gorz in the 1980's. Another interesting aspect of Dandieu's thought lies in his interpretation of the development of credit within an international financial system. He sees it at the same time as a manifestation of the logic of the gift — credit presupposes the gift of trust — and as a facilitating factor for potlatch-like gambles, which however by-pass the concrete act of human exchange in real time to replace it with abstract speculation on an impersonal scale.

Terpstra's essay *Social Gifts and the Gift of Sociality* shows how both Mauss and Hobbes analyze the noncontractual, 'symbolic' or 'political' dimension of human interaction. In the primitive and archaic societies which Mauss describes, social cohesion is relatively unproblematic: social order and peace may be threatened, but war seems to be no more than a temporary crisis which does not lead to the breakdown of an economy structured by the famous threefold obligation to give, to receive and to return. However, the beginning of Modernity causes a much more fundamental crisis of obligation. Hobbes thinks that normal social life can only be sustained by a distinct political power. In modern society individuals are unable to eliminate all uncertainty by purely intersubjective agreements. The existence of rights and obligations, the very possibility of contracts and markets, depends upon a preliminary transfer (a gift) of all individual rights to the sovereign. This way people hope to receive in return the gift or grace of sociality, although they do not have any formal (or contractual) guarantee to this effect.

Demartelaere's essay *Personal Obligations in Personal Relations* is typical of a recent shift in attention in the Mauss reception, also attested in Boilleau's essay in this volume, from the formal and structural properties of the gift to their affective correlates in sentiments of pity, sympathy, superiority, shame, love and gratitude. De Martelaere analyzes the exchange of gifts in the sphere of personal relations, i.e. relations characterized by mutual love. He shows the peculiarity of obligations of love by distinguishing them from moral obligations, role-bound obligations and promises. He challenges the classical moral theories insofar as they claim to apply to personal relations. Even virtue ethics is off the mark here. Doubtlessly what we do out of love is a free gift. This means that no one can be obliged to love all persons in the world, nor to reciprocate the love dedicated to him. The author emphasizes strongly the element of spontaneity in authentic personal relations and he contests that Mauss' doctrine of the three obligations applies to the requirements of love.

**Gifts and reciprocity**

A very puzzling question arising in many contributions to this book is the role of reciprocity in gift-giving. In the structuralist reading of Mauss' essay by Claude Lévi-Strauss for example, the formal properties of the logic of the gift were very much stressed. Also *No Free Gifts* is the shortest possible summary of Mauss' *Essay on the Gift*. It is also the title of Mary Douglas' *Foreword* to the English translation of this essay. Douglas' devise has a normative meaning: "there should not be any free gifts"[13], because charity wounds its beneficiaries. A free gift does not enhance solidarity among people. A second possible reading of the same motto can be found in Derrida's texts on the gift[14]: purely free gifts are litterally inconceivable. From the moment on that one is aware of one's own generosity, one gets already some gratification: one's self image gets dressed up and one feels a warm glow inside. Consequently pure disinterestedness may be possible, but only on condition that nobody, not even the benefactor himself, notices it.

However in this volume the central role of reciprocity is contested in some way or another by Godbout and Tarot as well as by Arnsperger, Silber, Demartelaere and to some extent even by Corbey and Terpstra. This is a moot point. In some cases gifts are required to restore some form of reciprocity, in

---

[13] M. Douglas, *No Free Gifts, Foreword* to *The Gift*, by Marcel Mauss, (New York and London, W.W. Norton, 1990), p vii.

[14] J. Derrida, *Donner le temps I (Giving Time I)* (Paris, Galilée, 1991) and *Donner la mort (Giving Death)*, in J.M. Rabatè, M. Wetzel, (eds.), *L'éthique du don — Jacques Derrida et la pensée du don, (The Ethics of the Gift — Jacques Derrida and the Gift)*, Colloque de Royaumont (Paris,Métailié, 1992).

other cases they seem to be necessary because no reciprocity at all is possible. In addition to this, there are a lot of intermediate situations. In the final paragraph of this text we try to rank the various relationships people get involved in according to the degree of reciprocity and the type of gifts they allow or require.

1. In situations where a strict or completely balanced reciprocity is possible, there is no need for gifts. Insurance systems for instance imply a transfer of means from people with good luck to people having bad luck, but this is only a very thin form of solidarity: it is the quasi-automatic result of contracts to which all parties concerned agreed freely. Here the logic of the gift does not apply, at least insofar as problems of moral hazard can be minimized. In informal systems of insurance one relies on the interiorization of social norms and on informal sanctions against those who do not comply with the social norm of reciprocity. In these cases there is often a time dimension implied, so that a diffuse gift of trust is required. When I help you to build your house on condition that later on, you will help me in the same way, the mutual services that are expected are so similar that the gift-dimension is rather thin. It is still thinner in recurrent situations, such as mutual help in harvesting, in which case individuals themselves are able to sanction eventual free-riders. Honouring a contractual agreement or fulfilling a promise is not really considered to be a gift, at least not in these examples.

2. Sometimes strict and immediate reciprocity is utterly undesirable: you do not return to your friend on his birthday the bottle of wine you received from him on yours. In situations where strict reciprocity is impossible or inappropriate, the logic of the gift has to play a role. This is for instance the case in large-scale insurance systems, in which serious problems of moral hazard arise. Therefore, we should qualify the last statement of the former paragraph: intuitively most of us will agree that honouring a contractual agreement or fulfilling a promise in cases where non-compliance will certainly not be detected, *does* imply a gift-dimension. Even more important is the fact that human relations can seldom be fully based upon purely contractual agreements. Fully comprehensive or totally explicit contracts are unthinkable. Recently, economists have discovered that asymmetric information and uncertainty about the quality of the exchanged goods and services or about the trustworthiness of partners in business or in ordinary life are ubiquitous. Even when they take all possible precautions, employers can never be completely sure that their employees are not shirking. Moreover, such a permanent control would be very costly. Historical research has shown that slavery was a very inefficient way of organizing production. Besides, it is difficult for the owners or the shareholders of a firm to make sure that the managers they have appointed serve the interests of the former instead of their self-interest. In both

instances there is evidently a problem of trust. Inspired by the principal agent theory, economists have tried to elaborate refined systems of payment and detailed types of contract, but it is clear that one can only reduce but never eliminate the gift component which is so typical of all social relations in which commitment or loyalty is required. Therefore, many firms pay higher salaries than the market clearing equilibrium wage, hoping that their gift will be reciprocated in the form of employee loyalty. In personal relations between persons of roughly equal status, some form of (non-strict) reciprocity applies, although it is seldom consciously intended. In common life, when someone offers us a gift, it is hard to refuse it or not to reciprocate it. Certainly, we feel an obligation to do so, although we will sometimes be wayward enough to refuse to live up to the expectations of our partners. In addition to this, empirical sociological research has shown that most people follow the norm of reciprocity in their common behaviour.[15] This external description of human relations nevertheless does not exclude that on a more fundamental level asymmetry applies. This is Levinas' thesis and he offers attractive arguments for it.

3. In some instances there is so much asymmetry that no reciprocity at all is possible or that gift and countergift become completely heterogeneous or almost totally disconnected. These gifts can hardly be subsumed into the Maussian logic of the gift. Apart from the religious gifts, which are discussed by Tarot and Silber, there is the whole domain of intergenerational relations. We can make efforts for the preservation of the environment in which our children, grandchildren and future generations will have to live. We can refrain from polluting air and water, from exhausting easily accessible sources of energy or raw materials, from causing irreversible harm, but future generations can do nothing similar for us. Moreover, we never asked for life and we will never be able to compensate our parents and the anterior generations for the gift of life. Only by passing on life — and the debt associated with it — to our children can we show that, after all, what they did was not that bad. Clearly, there is a large degree of incommensurability between the gift of life itself and the care we eventually provide for our parents when they have aged. We may hope that we will be treated by younger generations in the same way as we treated our parents and grandparents, but certainly, the reciprocity we expect then has to come from other donators than the beneficiaries of our care. Recently, the development of an ethics of care has made us aware of the fact that we are (relatively) autonomous only during half of our existence. Children, persons who are ill, aged or disabled depend on the care provided by others. Mostly, dependent persons do not pay, or at least not directly, those who take care of them, and relations of care can certainly not be conceived

---

[15] E. Fehr, S. Gächter, Reciprocity and Economics: The Economic Implications of Homo Reciprocans, in *European Economic Review*, 42, 1998, pp. 845-859.

according to the contractual model. Even when the intervention of medical professionals, social workers or educators is aimed at restoring the autonomy of their patients and clients, this is clearly a gift that cannot be fully compensated.

4. He who refuses to give, to receive or to render is ungrateful. He wrongs the cosmic order, the law of reciprocity and his benefactors. Mauss has strongly insisted upon this theme. But what happens if one is incapable of rendering? In principle, one is always capable of rendering gratefulness, but very often situations in which one can only respond to a gift by being grateful, are considered as humiliating. They oblige us to admit our inferiority. Even if the donor has no mischievous intentions whatsoever, unilateral gifts are generally taken very badly. They engender feelings of rancour, envy and hatred rather than gratitude. This profound Maussian intuition explains why a welfare state which creates dependence and passivity of its beneficiaries arouses so many frustrations. It also explains the weariness of life of chronic patients, the frustrations of people with few marketable capacities, the rancour of many people in the Third World and in relatively backward areas like Wallonia, the south of Italy or former East Germany. Here a task for a Mauss-inspired social science undoubtedly takes shape: to imagine systems of social security, a social assistance and a worldwide solidarity organization which make countergifts possible. Godbout has rightly emphasized that the way in which social assistance and aid is presented (as a right or as a gift) is very important. We think that the context is equally important. From our perspective, the welfare state should not only confer rights to, but also impose duties on its members. It could enhance its legitimacy in the eyes not only of the taxpayers, but also of the beneficiaries by asking a contribution from them. Stimulating people to accept a job or to do something useful for other people does not necessarily mean that we reduce the overall level of social protection or that we engage in a movement of social regress. Still more research should be done on this topic. It remains unclear why unilateral gifts are considered as humiliating in some cases and not in others. Youngsters seem to revolt when they have suffered from a lack of attention and care on behalf of their parents and the rest of society, but also when they have been overprotected. Maybe in both cases they were refused the gift of freedom...

5. A last puzzling question: are there societies that are not founded on the gift? Maurice Godelier has formulated the hypothesis that "there can be no society (...) if there are no bench marks, no realities that are (temporarily or lastingly) drawn from gift exchanges or market exchanges."[16] He suggests that the identity of a society depends more on the number and the type of goods that are inalienable or sacred than on the economy of the circulation of gifts and commodities. This gives rise to the problem of the exact connection between

---

[16] M. Godelier, *L'énigme du don* (*The Enigma of the Gift*) (Fayard, Paris, 1996), p. 16.

the logic of the gift and the religious foundation of society. Moreover, the recent revival of nationalism has made us susceptible to another type of problems concerning societies without gift: the problem of communities which are obliged to live together by destiny or historical chance, sometimes even communities joined together by hatred. It remains to be seen whether the negative reciprocity that often characterizes this type of societies, complies with a kind of reverse logic of the gift, or whether it necessitates entirely different analyses.

**Bibliography**

F.R. BERGER, 'Gratitude', in Ethics, 85 (July 1975)

J.L. BOILLEAU, Conflit et lien social — La rivalité contre la domination (Conflict and Social Bond — Rivalry Versus Domination) (Paris: La Découverte/M.A.U.S.S., 1995)

P. BOURDIEU, Le sens pratique (Practical Sense) (Minuit: Paris) p. 105

J. DERRIDA, Donner le temps I (Giving Time I) (Paris, Galilée, 1991) and Donner la Mort (Giving Death), in J.M. Rabaté, M; Wetzel, (eds.), L'éthique du don — Jacques Derrida et la pensée du don, (The Ethics of the Gift — Jacques Derrida and the Gift), Colloque de Royaumont (Paris, Métailié, 1992)

M. DOUGLAS, No Free Gifts, Foreword to the Gift, by Marcel Mauss (New York and London, W.W. Norton, 1990), p. vii

J. ELSTER, Explaining Technical Progress (Cambridge, Cambridge University Press, 1983)

J. ELSTER, Nuts and Bolts in the Social Sciences (Cambridge: Cambridge University Press, 1989)

J. ENGLISH, Having Children, (Oxford: U.P., 1979)

E. FEHR, S. GÄCHTER, Reciprocity and Economics: The Economic Implications of Homo Reciprocans, in European Economic Review, 42, 1998, pp. 845 - 859

R.H. FRANK, Passions Within Reason — The Strategic Role of Emotions (New York, London: W.W. Norton, 1998)

M. GODELIER, L'énigme du don (The Enigma of the Gift) (Fayard, Paris, 1996), p.16

S. KIERKEGAARD, Kjerlighedens Gjerninger (Acts of Love) (Copenhagen, 1852) 2nd part, Ch.IX

A. MASSON, P. Pestieau, 'Bequest Motives and Models of Inheritance: A Survey of the Literature', in G. Erreygers, T. Vandevelde (eds.), Is Inheritance Legitimate? — Ethical and Economic Aspects of Wealth Transfers (Berlin: Springer Verlag, 1997), p. 54-88

Ph. PETIT, R. Goodin, 'The Possibility of Special Duties', in The Canadian Journal of Philosophy, 16:4 (dec. 1986), p. 651-676

R. PUTNAM, Making Democracy Work: Civic Traditions In Modern Italy (Princeton, Princeton University Press, 1993)

J. RACHELS, Morality, Parents and Children, in H. Lafolette (ed.), Ethics in Practice — An Anthology, (Oxford: Blackwell, 1997), pp. 195-206

P. VEYNE, Comment on écrit l'histoire (How History is Written) (Paris: Le Seuil, 1971)

P. VEYNE, L'inventaire des différences (The Inventory of Differences) (Paris: Le Seuil, 1976)

P. VEYNE, Le pain et le cirque — Sociologie historique d'un pluralisme politique (Panem et Circenses — Historical Sociology of a Political Pluralism), (Paris: Le Seuil, 1976)

# MAUSS AND HIS CRITIQUES

# Homo Donator versus Homo Oeconomicus

Jacques T. GODBOUT (Université du Québec)

## A Paradigmatic Privilege

There exists today a dominant paradigm: neoliberalism. In the social sciences it assumes various names: rational choice theory, instrumental rationality, methodological individualism, utilitarianism, homo oeconomicus, neo-classical economic theory. These different designations point to different aspects of the paradigm, but there is a common core to all of these theories. They intend to explain the system of production, and especially the circulation of goods and services in society, on the basis of notions like interest, rationality and utility.

Though rather modest at the time of Mandeville and Adam Smith, this theory enjoys phenomenal importance today, to such a point that a modern individual can no longer think about what circulates in society without using these notions and this model. As Abell states, "rational action theory is the necessary starting point with which to compare other types of theory", thus giving this theory what he calls a 'paradigmatic privilege'.[1] What does this expression mean? On the one hand, it means that this paradigm is taken as a premise, that one spontaneously resorts to this explanatory scheme in order to give an account of a social agent's behaviour; on the other hand, it means that any other premise is not legitimate, that it must be demonstrated. It is this paradigmatic privilege that I would like to question here.

What is contained by this model? There are numerous variants, but two ideas are fundamental, that of preference and that of optimization. According to the first idea, an individual acts according to his preferences and he is the only one who knows what those preferences are. The word 'preference' is a way this paradigm indicates interests, values, ends, needs, and passions.[2] How

---

[1] P. Abell, 'Is Rational Choice a Rational Choice of Theory', in J. Coleman and T. J. Fararo (eds.), *Rational Choice Theory: Advocacy and Critique* (London: Sage, 1992), p. 186, (pp. 183-206).

[2] Note that interest should not be confused with utility in the strict sense. Preferences come in many different kinds, and they do not have to be useful. What is not useful is even the privileged domain of the market when one compares it with the public economy. The gadget, products in various colours, appearance — all this is legitimate for the market. Indeed, the market has progressively displaced its field of activity from the useful to the useless (the useful does not augment GDP sufficiently). It lies in wait for the lesser "passions" in order to satisfy them, especially those that are rejected by official social norms, thus giving it a "monopoly". Market reasoning adheres to Hume's principle: "reason is, and ought only to be, the slave of the passions" (cited in J. Elster, 'Rationalité et normes sociales: un modèle pluridisciplinaire' ('Rationality and Social Norms: a

are one's preferences determined? That is not a problem for this theory, which is content with posing the following question: how does an individual make decisions once his preferences have been fixed? The answer to this question is provided by the theory of instrumental rationality, with the notion of optimization as its core concept. Instrumental rationality is a rationality of means in relation to ends. It says practically nothing about ends however. The theory of rational choice "contains one element that *differentiates* it from nearly all other theoretical approaches in sociology. This element can be summed up in a single word: *optimization*. The theory specifies that in acting rationally, an actor is engaging in some kind of optimization. This is sometimes expressed as maximizing utility, sometimes as minimizing cost, sometimes in other ways. But however expressed, it is this that gives rational choice theory its power: It compares actions according to their expected outcomes for the actor and assumes that the actor will choose the action with the best outcome. At its most explicit, it requires that benefits and costs of all courses of action be specified, then postulating that the actor takes the 'optimal' action that maximizes the difference between benefits and costs".[3] This idea of optimization applies to both the individual and the collective level, since the model of *homo oeconomicus* maintains that when each person optimizes its individual interest, the members of a society produce an optimum collective welfare.

**Positive aspects**

The opponents of this model tend to overlook what makes it attractive, thus weakening their criticisms. It is undeniable that interest exists and plays an important role, and this point of departure is a good way of guarding against taking human beings to be something they are not, which constitutes a good means of protection from totalitarian utopias. As for the notion that private interests lead to public goods, and that being egoistic is sufficient to discharge our debt to the rest of society, who would deny that it is a seductive idea? It implies that if we are to rein in passions and disorder, and make society function for the greatest happiness of the greatest number (Bentham), then we can dispense not only with the appeal to virtue, but also with authority, tradition, etc. With the idea of the sovereignty of preference, neutral with respect to the

---

Pluridisciplinary Model'), in L. André, G. Varet and J. C. Passeron, *Le modèle et l'enquête. Les usages du principe de rationalité dans les sciences sociales* (*The Model and the Survey. The Uses of the Principle of Rationality in the Social Sciences*) (Paris: Éditions de l'École des Hautes Études en Sciences Sociales, 1995)). The passions, in every sense, make up a part of our preferences and the market refrains from judging them.

[3] J. Coleman and T.J. Fararo, *Rational Choice Theory: Advocacy and Critique* (London: Sage, 1992) p. xi.

ends, the market is in possession of a structure which contains a certain amount of respect for the values shared by everyone. Such respect is invaluable in modern society, which is no longer situated within a communitarian framework (Tonnies' *Gemeinschaft*) but in a context where the individual is invaded by an incredible number of social relations — a phenomenon well described by Simmel. A member of modern society is locked in a struggle with an impressive number of authorities who try to tell him what his values and preferences should be, and who try to tell him what is good for him. Often it is the authorities external to his community that he tends to regard as illegitimate. This refusal to judge values, contained in the concept of preference, is well adapted to non-communitarian, pluralistic societies where it is precisely people's values and norms that differ sharply. In other words, this model liberates us from unwanted social relations, which are numerous in a pluralistic society. Without preventing us from obtaining what we want from the others, we are nevertheless freed from having to maintain a personal relationship with them. What we all spontaneously admire about the market is this freedom. It is the ease with which we can leave a relation that we do not like, and go and look elsewhere. It is the availability of the 'exit'-option.[4]

How is such freedom possible and on what is it based? It is founded on the *immediate and permanent liquidation of debt*. The market model aims at the absence of any debt in social relations. On this model, every exchange is clear and complete. By virtue of the law of equivalence, every relation is punctual. It is without any future, and therefore does not enclose us within a system of obligations. This type of relation, which seems so natural to us, is in fact quite unusual. It is neither more nor less than the invention of a previously unknown social link, as Karl Polanyi has shown.[5] This is the best sociological definition of the market: a social link that aims to escape the normal obligations that are inherent to social links. It is the essence of modern freedom. "In the infinite circulation of equivalences, being an individual comes down to not owing anything to anyone".[6] Modern freedom is essentially the absence of debt. "The pair consisting of individualism and neo-classical economics attempts to found the ethics of having no debt towards anyone, which establishes this theory's claim to be recognized as the discourse of freedom".[7] In short, this model

---

[4] A.O. Hirschman, *Exit, Voice and Loyalty: Response to Decline in Firms, Organizations and States* (Cambridge: Harvard University Press, 1970).

[5] K. Polanyi, *The Great Transformation: The Political and Economic Origins of our Times* (Boston: Beacon Press, 1957).

[6] G. Berthoud, 'L'économie: un ordre généralisé? Les ambitions d'un prix Nobel' ('Economics as Knowledge of a Generalized Order? The Ambitions of a Nobel Price), in *La Revue de MAUSS semestrielle, Pour une autre économie* (Paris: La découverte, 1994) p. 53.

[7] A. Insel, 'Une rigueur pour la forme' ('Formal Rigour'), in *La Revue de MAUSS semestrielle, Pour une autre économie* (Paris: La découverte, 1994) p. 88.

derives its power from the fact that it constitutes an alternative to the imposed hierarchy, that it contains a fundamental principle of autonomy and freedom so well described and defended by Hayek, one which classical orthodox Marxism has never wanted to recognize. It is indeed a quite limited social relation, a weak link, as we shall see. It also brings in its wake exploitation, injustice, exclusion, etc. No one would deny that. But any time someone claims not only to know better than ourselves what is good for us, but also claims to have the authority to impose it instead of trying to persuade us, the market is to be preferred. The market is an antidote against all those who would pretend to know what is good for us.

## Limits and weaknesses

There is, however, another side of the coin, for this social relation that humanity is nowadays prepared to globalize has, until quite recently, not only been an object of fear but also of scorn. This is proved by anthropology as well as by the history of the West. Need we recall that one of the worst insults directed at Ulysses during his famous voyage occurs when the son of Alcinoos, whom he is visiting, takes him for a merchant. "Ulysses steals, plunders, kills, but does not trade!"[8] There must be some reason for such a negative attitude. There are in fact several reasons, and I would like to insist on one of them.

## The paradigm of growth

Let us reexamine the postulate of preferences. As we have seen, it is a theory of the means of taking a good decision whatever may be the person's ends or values. This model, then, is theoretically neutral with respect to values. But the market adds a condition of functioning which affects its neutrality to values: whatever those values may be, they must be able to be transformed into merchandise, they must take the form of products on the market, they must become 'commoditized'. Freedom is total, on the condition that all values, beliefs and passions be translated into consumer goods or services. However, to say "neutral, provided you consume, provided you are inscribed in the producer-consumer model", is in fact not neutral at all. This is what is hidden by the so-called neutrality of preferences.

Why is this condition necessary? Because there is a single basic value: that of growth. Modern man possesses all freedoms with respect to social links, but

---

[8] D. Temple and M. Chabal, *La réciprocité et la naissance des valeurs humaines (Reciprocity and the Origin of Human Values)* (Paris: L'Harmattan, 1995) p. 188.

he does not have the freedom not to contribute to GDP growth, to production. This model, then, tends to generalize one single value — the value of *production*. If we are liberated from our social links as a result of modernity, we become more and more dependent on our goods, our products, and particularly on the necessity of always producing more. In other words, what had been the means (the product) now becomes the end. There is a reversal of the means-end relationship. What was initially defined as being in the service of everyone's preferences — production — ends up by being the highest value, the goal. How is this possible?

**The means contaminate the end**

Such a consequence is possible precisely because this entire model of instrumental rationality is based on the means-end distinction. More specifically, this model is based on the watertight distinction of two orders, means in relation to ends. The fundamental problem however is that this means-end distinction is untenable. The means contaminate the end. How many times does a means towards an end become itself an end, to such a degree that the end becomes secondary. This is a common phenomenon of everyday life. Even in business life — i.e., in that social sphere that almost invented and developed the rational model, the sphere from which the rationalization of the world originates — a sociologist as solemn as Crozier could write: "What matters is not so much the precise objective one aims at, but the path, the development, the way to be opened".[9]

We know that this linear view of the relation between means and ends has led utilitarians, following Bentham, to propose happiness as an end and to apply the means-end model to it. But human wisdom has always affirmed the opposite: in order *not* to attain happiness, the surefire method is to seek it directly. This is illustrated by the paradox of the unfortunate egoists. A psychology professor recently asked his students to draw up a list of ten people that they know well, stating whether these people are happy or not and also mentioning whether they tend to be generous or egoistic. Out of a sample of 1988 lists, the result was clear: people who are considered to be happy are perceived as being generous in 41,6 % of cases, while those considered to be unhappy tend to be egoistic. The author's conclusion is this: "The findings represent an interesting paradox: selfish people are, by definition, those whose activities are devoted to bringing themselves happiness. Yet, at least as judged by others, these selfish people are far less

---

[9] M. Crozier, *L'entreprise à l'écoute: apprendre le management postindustriel (The Firm Listening: to Learn Post-Industrial Management)* (Paris: InterÉditions, 1989) p. 200.

likely to be happy than those whose efforts are devoted to making others happy."[10]

This rational choice model, which seems so natural, in fact seldom corresponds to the reality of decision making. It is hardly an adequate model of human action. It does not take account of the fact that means and ends continuously influence each other by way of emotions, feelings, and the results of the preceding action. This social phenomenon should not be analyzed using a model of a linear hierarchy, as the theory of rational choice does, but rather within the context of what Hofstadter calls an 'overlapping hierarchy'.[11] Each decision is an adventure and a surprise, but the model of instrumental rationality aims to eliminate this dimension of decision making. "By its very structure, the theory only applies to closed worlds, worlds in which neither regrets nor surprises can figure".[12] One ends up by submitting individuals, in the name of freedom, to a mechanical, deterministic model that leaves no room for the unexpected. In order to give an account of real behaviour, we need to reflect on the link between ends, intentions and means. We need a theory of the relation between means and ends, a theory that does not exist within rational choice theory.

**The other paradigm**

Despite all the attractions of this paradigm, which have been described above, it will easily be admitted that instrumental rationality is not without problems, and one should not be surprised at the presence of another significant paradigm in the human sciences. This other paradigm is holism, and it has been developed mainly by sociologists and anthropologists.[13] Here, the term designates in a broad sense any theory that begins from society rather than the individual. We can illustrate this holistic paradigm by briefly describing the socio-economics movement. In 1988, the American organizational sociologist Amitai Etzioni published a work entitled *The Moral Dimension*,[14] and the following year he launched a movement called 'socio-economics' (SASE, the Society for the Advancement of Socio-Economics). This movement criticizes the monopoly exerted by neo-classical economics and presents itself as an alternative to the utilitarian paradigm. Without

---

[10] B. Rimland, The Altruism Paradox in *Psychological Reports*, 51, 1982, pp. 521-522.

[11] D. R. Hofstadter, *Gödel, Escher, Bach: an Eternal Golden Braid* (New York: Vintage Books, 1980).

[12] G. Varet, L. André and J.C. Passeron, *op. cit.*

[13] L. Dumont, *Essais sur l'individualisme (Essays on Individualism)* (Paris: Seuil, 1983).

[14] A. Etzioni, *The Moral Dimension, Toward a New Economics* (New York: The Free Press, 1988).

denying the importance of interests in explaining the behaviour of social agents, this 'new paradigm' (the title of the book's first chapter) wants to break out of the individual's isolation and situate him in the context of his social relations. This is what Etzioni calls the 'I & we paradigm' (following Baldwin), which means that the individual has a sense of identity that is shared with others. Etzioni employs strong formulations to express this relational paradigm: "the society is not a constraint, not even an opportunity, it is us" (p. 9). It was this sense of community that also led him, a few years later, to establish the Communitarian Network, with the journal, *The Responsive Community*.

More particularly, Etzioni wants to reintroduce the moral dimension, as the title of his book suggests. Social agents do not only act in function of their interests, but also in function of norms and values. It is this moral nature of acts that removes social agents from the paradigm of neo-classical economics. Morality, as defined by Etzioni, has various characteristics that oppose it to the paradigm of instrumental rationality. For instance, "moral acts (...) are intrinsically motivated and not subject to means-end analysis"; "they repudiate the instrumental rationality which includes consideration of costs and benefits. (...) Indeed the 'instantaneousness' of such decisions is used by several researches as an indication that a non-deliberate commitment is made" (p. 42). In addition, however, he also states that moral behaviour is distinct from the search for pleasure. Etzioni tends to assimilate pleasure with utilitarianism. He opposes pleasure to moral action and to a sense of duty.

This inclusion of pleasure within the dominant utilitarian model and the insistence on duty expose the socio-economic model to criticism from the adherents of the dominant paradigm, in the name of freedom. Indeed, Etzioni admits that this sense of duty is not a constraint external to the individual. They are rather 'internalized' norms. He defines internalization as the process of socialization whereby a person learns to "conform to rules in situations that arouse impulses to transgress and that lack surveillance and sanctions" (p. 45, Kohlberg's quotation). Nevertheless, it is a matter of conforming, of obeying rules.

Socio-economics attempts to show that interest does not explain everything, that there are also norms, rules, values, morals, duty. But these norms tend to be conceived as external obligations, as constraints on the individual. This, in turn, leads to a tendency to want to liberate the individual from these constraints, and to return to the dominant paradigm. It is the classic sociological problem of the internalization of norms. Socio-economics thus runs up against the most important problem posed by sociological models confronted with the dominant paradigm: how to think freedom in the context of social control.

## Why in the world would anyone ever make a gift?

By sticking with these paradigms, one is led to believe that the social sciences are faced with the following alternative: either our behaviour is free, in which case it can only be susceptible to the model of instrumental rationality, or else our behaviour is more or less constrained or determined by norms, by obedience to rules. Within the framework of interests, then, the phenomenon of the gift can only be amenable to two sorts of explanation: either one gives in order to receive, out of interest, in which case the phenomenon is explicable by the dominant paradigm; or it is not out of interest, in which case one is socialized, one learns to give, one internalizes norms which incite us to give, for why in the world would we make gifts if there is no interest served in doing so? In other words, since the only 'natural' motor for human action is interest, the gift must defer to an interest, otherwise it necessarily pertains to the other paradigm in social science: holism.

I would like to show now that neither of these two paradigms can adequately explain the gift.

## The gift does not correspond to the market model

A primary feature of any gift system is the fact that social agents seek voluntarily to distance themselves from any equivalence. This does not mean that the gift is unilateral. It may be so, but that is not an essential characteristic of the gift. To the contrary, in general there is a gift in return, often one that is more significant than the original gift, but this is not the aim. The linear means-ends model is applied, wrongly, to the gift by reasoning as follows: he received after having given, therefore he gave in order to receive; the end was to receive and the gift was a means to that end. The gift, however, does not function in such a way. One makes a gift, one often receives something more in return, but the relationship between the two is much more complex than the linear model of instrumental rationality is capable of explaining.

Why is there this voluntary distancing from the means-ends model and from the search for equivalence? For this reason: although the market is founded on the liquidation of debt, as we have seen, the gift, to the contrary, is founded on debt. One can see as much both in primary relations such as those of kinship as well as in gifts to strangers such as organ donations.[15]

A debt entered into voluntarily is essential to the gift, just as the search for equivalence is an essential tendency in the market model. The partners in a gift

---

[15] J. T. Godbout, J. Charbonneau and V. Lemieux, *La circulation du don dans la parenté (The Circulation of the Gift in Kinship Relations)* (Montréal: INRS-Urbanisation, RR 17, 1996)

system are in a positive or negative state of debt. If it is a positive state, this means that each person believes he owes a great deal to the others. This is not a conception borrowed from accounting. The gift system, as a result, is situated at the opposite extreme from the market system, not because it is unilateral, but because what characterizes the market is, as we have seen, the punctual transaction, without any debt.

**Non-correspondence with the holistic paradigm**

It will be objected that, if this system maintains obligation within the relation, in the form of debt, then it belongs to the holistic model. We assert, however, that the holistic paradigm cannot be applied to the gift either. It can neither be applied in general, nor in the form of the socio-economic model that we have briefly presented, because of the following additional characteristics of the phenomenon of the gift.
1) Agents value the pleasure of the gift. A gift made out of obligation, out of obedience to a norm, is considered to be of inferior quality. We saw that the morality of duty was fundamental to socio-economics, but it is secondary with the gift.
2) More generally, the gift's relation to rules distances it from both the holistic paradigm and the individualist model. Indeed, the members of a gift system have a very peculiar relation to rules. In the first place, the rules of the gift must be implicit. It would, for instance, be in bad taste to leave the price tag on a gift, or to make any allusion to the price. In addition, there is a general tendency among agents to deny any obedience to rules in the gesture of giving. Of course, in certain areas such as gifts to strangers, the gift has more of a tendency to obey a moral norm. And there are many types of giving behaviour that obey a rule or a social convention. But where personal relations are concerned, such gifts are viewed by the social agents as of an inferior quality. The 'true' gift is one whose meaning is not conformity to a social convention or rule, but rather the expression of a relationship with the person.
3) This tendency goes so far as to deny the importance of the gift itself. This is, at first sight, one of the most strange types of gift behaviour: the negation of the gift's importance by the giver. Mauss remarks that, in the *kula*, "one gives as if it were nothing".[16] "The giver exhibits an exaggerated modesty", says Mauss. But there is no need to go even this far. Our formulas of politeness have the same meaning: *de rien, di niente, de nada,* my pleasure — all expressions used by the giver to assure the one who gives thanks for the gift

---

[16] B. Karsenti, *Marcel Mauss. Le fait social total (Marcel Mauss: The Total Social Fact)* (France: Presses universitaires de France, 1994), p. 28.

received. Why? We thus arrive at the conclusion that, in this way, they diminish the obligation to give something in return, and make any return gift uncertain. They make the other free to give in return. If what one has given is nothing, then the recipient is under no obligation to give in return, but is free to give, and if he then gives me something it will also be a true gift. In this way, the recipient is given the possibility to make a true gift instead of having to obey the obligation to give in return. As Lefort has so shrewdly noted, "one does not give in order to receive; one gives so that the other will give". Thus we can see that the agents in a gift system voluntarily and permanently introduce uncertainty, indetermination and risk into the appearance of the return gift, in order to take as much distance as possible from the contract, the (social or market) contractual engagement, and from the rule of duty — in short, from every sort of universal rule. Why is this? Because the latter all share the property of obligating the other independently of his 'feelings' towards me, independently of the connection that exists between the other and myself.

So there is indeed freedom in the gift,[17] and a relation that is very different from the 'moral dimension' of which Etzioni speaks. But this is not the same kind of freedom as is found in the market. The freedom we are uncovering here is not accomplished by liquidating debt, and does not consist in the agent's ability to exit from the relation. On the contrary, it is situated inside the social connection and consists of making this connection itself more free by multiplying the rituals that aim to diminish the weight of obligation on the other, within the relation itself. The gift is a continual play of freedom and obligation. The majority of the gift's characteristics can be understood if one interprets them in light of this principle of the freedom of the agents.

## The gift and sociological models

This social system is different from both the dominant paradigm and the holistic model. In fact, this valuation of the other's freedom makes it different even from the majority of sociological models. To illustrate this, we will take the example of strategic analysis, a system of action that is well known in organizational sociology. Let us briefly compare the two social systems: gift and strategic analysis.

In the framework of strategic analysis, each agent, in order to increase his power and control over the organization, is seen as attempting to reduce what

---

[17] This claim is shown, in particular, by the behaviour of physicians during the transplant of kidneys between living subjects. They prefer not to take the kidney and risk the person's life rather than have doubts about the freedom of the gesture, thinking that it might be the result of social (family) pressure.

is called his 'zone of uncertainty'. For a sociologist like Michel Crozier, people are endowed with a 'strategic instinct' which incites them to reduce uncertainty in interactive situations, with the aim of increasing their power.[18] Reducing the zone of uncertainty means reducing the other's freedom to increase his. But observations of gift circulation lead us to believe that a social agent, in certain social relations, is also led not so much to reduce, but rather to create and maintain zones of uncertainty between him and the other, with the aim of increasing the value of the social connections in which he is involved. In a gift relation, the agent does not aim to limit the freedom of others, but to increase it, for it constitutes a precondition for the value that will be ascribed to the other's gesture. We are saying that he tends to increase uncertainty because he tends permanently to reduce any feeling of obligation on the part of the other, even if the obligations are always present in other respects. The agent in a gift system tends to maintain the system in a state of structural uncertainty so as to allow trust to appear. This is why norms, whatever they may be (justice, equality, etc.), must continually be transgressed, changed, overcome. Something unpredictable must be produced in what is obligatory. We are here confronted with two logics: that of strategic analysis which incites the agents to reduce the freedom of the others, and that of the gift which tends to increase it. These are not individual characteristics, but those of two different social systems. Moreover, it has frequently been observed that it is the same people in both cases who adopt one model or the other according to the system of action in which they are situated with the other agents. But one does not find the properties of gift systems in the logic of strategic analysis, nor in the systems of action that it studies. All such systems, of course, are ideal types and any analysis of a concrete social system will exhibit a varying mixture of these different models.

## The gift as a system of action

Sciulli asserts that "the great strength of rational choice theory is that as its proponents endeavor to account for social order and group solidarity, they resist as long as possible appealing to actors' supposed internalization of shared norms."[19] Just like rational choice theory, the gift model is suspicious of obligatory norms imposed on agents being used as explanatory factors. From this perspective, the gift has an obvious kinship with rational choice

---

[18] E. Friedberg, *Le pouvoir et la règle (Power and the Rule)* (Paris: Seuil, 1993) p. 210.
[19] D. Sciulli, 'Weaknesses in Rational Choice Theory's Contribution to Comparative Research', in J. Coleman and T. J. Fararo (eds.), *Rational Choice Theory: Advocacy and Critique* (London: Sage, 1992) p. 161.

theory and methodological individualism. Yet at the same time, it is quite far from these theories, since it takes freedom to be ultimately more important than in the economic model itself, for the gift model is the only system of action that incites its members to increase the freedom of the other members. In addition, it remains fundamentally different from the rational choice model since it is based on debt.

The gift model, consequently, belongs to neither of the two dominant paradigms. Non-equivalence, spontaneity, debt and the uncertainty that is sought at the heart of the social relation are all opposed to rational choice theory and contract theory. Freedom and the pleasure of the gesture, however, are opposed to the morality of duty and to the internalized norms of the holistic model. The gift requires us to discard the holistic and individualistic paradigms, and seek out something else. This is why one might advance the idea that the gift poses problems for the two main paradigms in the social sciences. In the words of Elster, one could say that the gift brings to light the 'vices' of the two traditional paradigms: "if the economist's vice is that of understanding everything in function of interests, the sociological vice is to see human beings as passively carrying out social norms."[20]

But can we go a step further? We have seen that one of the two paradigms enjoys a paradigmatic privilege. I would like to suggest that not only can the gift not be explained by the two existing paradigms in the social sciences, but that it also throws into question the privilege of one of the two paradigms, that of rational choice theory. Why is this so?

**The postulate of the gift**

With individualism and holism, we seem to have two explanatory principles of human action at our disposal: interest and the internalization of norms. But are there really two principles? Why is it absolutely necessary to postulate that those behaviours which are not driven by interest must be learned, internalized? In posing this question, we return to the problem of the interest model's paradigmatic privilege. For if we must assume that all behaviour not ruled by the model of *homo oeconomicus* must be internalized by social agents, this is ultimately because we make the assumption that only interest is natural, only interest does not need to be learned, only interest has no need of explanation. In fact, it turns out that the paradigmatic privilege enjoyed by *homo*

---

[20] J. Elster, *op. cit.*, p. 144. This problem of the two approaches has been discussed by many authors, among whom the most well known is probably D. Wrong, 'The Oversocialized Conception of Man in modern Sociology', in *American Sociological Review*, 26 (1961), with his "oversocialized conception of man in modern sociology".

*oeconomicus* and the fact that the other paradigm is condemned, as it were, to viewing the social agent as "passively carrying out social norms" (Elster) are one and the same thing. It is because they recognize only a single 'spring' of human action — interest — that every model beginning with interest is confronted with the insoluble problem of the internalization of norms, since they cannot be natural. Only interest enjoys the privilege of being natural in the social sciences.

Yet the gift model is satisfied neither with the postulate of interest nor with the interiorization of norms. Which is why the gift not only poses questions, but in its most radical form also throws into question interest's paradigmatic privilege and leads to the necessity of postulating another psychological spring for human action, one which has the same rights as those enjoyed by interest. Every theory of society requires a psychological postulate.[21] But the current paradigmatic privilege of rational choice theory forces all sociological theories into the straightjacket of one single psychological theory. I am personally more and more convinced that the lure of profit as the only motor of human action is in no way obvious, and that the notion of the lure of the gift is not such a farfetched postulate. In order to subscribe to such a postulate, it would be necessary to reverse our habitual way of thinking and to entertain the idea that if we feel compelled to believe that all gift behaviour is the result of learning, of internalized norms, it is perhaps because we have been socialized into thinking in this way because we are inhabitants of modernity. Try to imagine, as Temple says, that "producing in order to give is a different motor than producing in order to accumulate."[22] In addition to interest, and the 'lure of profit', the analysis of the gift leads us to postulate a 'lure of the gift'; in addition to *homo oeconomicus, homo donator*.

I would now like to turn to a discussion of these two points before looking into the consequences of this postulate for the study of the gift.

**Interest as the only postulate: is it obvious?**

There is nothing obvious about interest being the only natural motor of human action,[23] not even within the economic world. By way of illustration, we could

---

[21] J. Coleman and T.J. Fararo, *Rational Choice Theory: Advocacy and Critique* (London: Sage, 1992). Moscovici has devoted a work to this topic (see S. Moscovi, *La machine à faire des dieux* (*The Machinery to Make Gods*)(Paris: Fayard, 1988)).

[22] D. Temple and M. Chabal, *op. cit.,* p. 5.

[23] The two paradigms present themselves as applying to the domain of human action, i.e., the domain where there exists a minimum amount of freedom, not entirely determined. In addition, there are uncontrolled, animal passions, or also reflexes. The result, according to Gérard-Varet and Passeron, is that on the one hand there are actions to which the notion of rationality can be

mention the literature about trust that is currently being developed and whose conclusion is that trust, while being necessary for economic exchange, cannot arise between individuals who only act in function of their own interest. Very few authors connect this theme of trust with the gift (Fukuyama, for instance,[24] says not a single word about gifts). There is nevertheless one recent work devoted to this topic.[25] The author sets out to demonstrate two propositions. Let us examine the first of these. It intends to show the insufficiency, even for individuals who pursue their interest, of "the hypothesis of the rational and egoist individual and the theorem of the invisible hand" (p. 4). "The thesis ... is that individual interest is insufficient to provide the principle of exchange ... Somewhere or another, economic exchange counters individual interest ... Even when the motive for exchange is interest or the lure of profit, one must first know how to give up or lose something in order to subsequently obtain what one desires. It is the very movement of exchange that wills this" (p. 8). " ... the dilemma one discovers in market exchange ... is played out ... between interest, profit or individual utility which provides its motor, and the obligation to cooperate which constitutes the process of (and which leads to the agent's) putting his interest in play" (p. 9). "Certain economic situations require agents to rationally give up their economic rationality in order to attain their economic ends" (p. 11).[26]

To demonstrate this thesis, the author utilizes the prisoner's dilemma. First off, he notes that the economic model, by "focusing on the principle of equivalence" (p. 16) — itself entirely regulated by competition, "the prerogative of the market" (p. 17) — exhibits a tendency to empty out the course of exchange. The invisible hand, price mechanisms — in short, the 'self-regulating market' as Polanyi would say — does not even pose the question regarding the way in which real exchange takes place. It introduces a mechanical model. It *is* true that this model does correspond to more and more real exchanges that are made under a certain form, i.e., precisely in cases where machines are concerned: vending machines, automatic tellers, etc. Yet this does not eliminate the necessity of explaining other sorts of exchanges among

---

applied, and which have as "a common point always to assume that a *choice* has been offered to the agents", while on the other hand there is a domain of human action where the notion of choice does not apply, is irrelevant. A behaviour can be instinctive, impulsive, a reflex, repetitive, etc. — in short, *constrained* by all sorts of determinations (1995, p. 17, my emphasis).

[24] F. Fukuyama, Trust. The Social Virtues and the Creation of Prosperity (New York: The Free Press, 1995).

[25] L. Cordonnier, *Coopération et réciprocité (Cooperation and Reciprocity)*(Paris: Presses Universitaires de France, 1997).

[26] This is what we have called the Dale Carnegie paradox (in *L'Esprit du don*) (*The Spirit of the Gift* (Paris, La Découverte, 1992)). Carnegie advises those who want to reach their (individualistic) objectives to become interested in others, and — here comes the paradox — to do it with sincerity: "make the other person feel important and do it sincerely" (p. 11).

human beings in which something else is taking place, and which remain absolutely fundamental, even in economic life. The author believes these other exchanges — the most important kind — can be grasped on the basis of the prisoner's dilemma, which constitutes the archetype of non mechanically regulated market exchanges. By pursuing their interests alone, on this model, agents come up with a less interesting solution than if they had taken the other's interests into account. The prisoner's dilemma counters Mandeville's fable of the bees. By egoistically pursuing our own individual happiness, we do not attain happiness for the greatest number. The prisoner's dilemma attacks the very basis of political economy. It is "the archetype of situations in which individual interest frustrates all cooperation ... and frustrates all individual interest" (p. 59). Interest would dictate that one deny all assistance, but in denying assistance one attains a less desirable solution than if one had cooperated. This is every liberal economist's nightmare.[27]

So much for the theoretical level. But what happens when one tries out this experiment on real subjects (p. 83)? It turns out in fact that individuals cooperate quite frequently (p. 84-87), and for reasons which are foreign to individual economic rationality. "It may be that they cooperate because the other cooperates, which is not an economically rational way to play" (p. 86). The author concludes: "Elements foreign to the principle of economy become grafted onto the relations between persons, so that even in situations where the nature of the game is clearly economic, regulation or fulfillment of the relation appeals to principles of action oriented more towards the quest for reciprocity" (p. 87-88). If the postulate of a single motor for human action can be put in question at the very heart of economic relations, one can conclude that it is not as obvious as is normally supposed for the totality of human behaviour.

## Is the postulate of the gift farfetched?

Cordonnier's reasoning illustrates the weaknesses of the postulate of interest as the sole motor of human action. He thus establishes the need for another postulate. But why the gift? Is it not too idealistic, even farfetched? It is, unfortunately, impossible to develop this point in a sufficiently satisfactory manner within the limits of such a brief text. We can do no more than to evoke certain paths and mention certain elements in favour of introducing this postulate, so scandalous for moderns who believe that the gift must be explained socially and cannot, therefore, be posed as a postulate. In order to establish the 'natural' character of the gift (in the same sense that the interest is natural, remember),

---

[27] The model of the "pure" gift probably leads to the same dilemma, as is clearly shown by the story of the two altruists who never succeed in crossing the door's threshold.

we could cite a recent work that brings to light altruism among animals.[28] In Chapter 8, which deals with altruism and compassion (which he distinguishes from Dawkin's selfish gene, where help is given to one's progeny or siblings in order to propagate one's own genes), the author provides numerous examples of animals giving help not only to unrelated animals, but even to members of different species. Numerous studies in child psychology are also adduced which tend to show that the need to give exists in the child from the moment of birth. "Rather than being the result of a long period of learning, as classical theories of development would have it, giving is a very precocious activity found in babies".[29] In sum, one might think that sociologists have always felt a certain malaise when faced with this problem of the internalization of norms, which has turned them into defenders of social control and a closed community confronting the economic model and its putative 'monopoly' on freedom. But they have not ventured to propose the postulate of the gift, which would lead them to adopt the postulate of *homo oeconomicus* in order to solve the problem of social constraint. One can wonder whether the current dominance of rational choice theory in sociology is not partly the result of sociologists' efforts to find a suitable psychological theory. Since they had no other psychological motor of action at their disposal than the problematic internalization of norms, the solution which gradually imposed itself was that of importing the psychological theory belonging to economic theory and then generalizing it. From Homans to Blau to Coleman, this can explain the contemporary success of the idea of 'social capital'. In any case, it was explicitly for this reason that Coleman proposed this idea in his 1988 article, thus transforming the social bond into a means, a resource for something else. Nevertheless, the majority of sociological models are evolutionistic, always presenting human societies as originally composed of members enclosed within a community where everything belongs to everyone, hence much closer to a kind of 'primitive gift' model than to an interest model. On this model, freedom has emerged progressively; it is in fact a conquest of modernity itself. If freedom and individual identity have emerged out of a constraining social bond with the community, then the fear of losing one's identity will appear as a good fundamental reason not to give. But inversely, could we not just as well conclude from this that social thought contains an implicit postulate, namely that there could be a natural tendency (dangerous in other respects, as everyone knows) in human individuals to sacrifice themselves, to lose themselves for the sake of society, and that for this reason the postulate of the gift is not so farfetched?[30] In that case, the modern

---

[28] M. Masson, J. and S. McCarthy, Quand les éléphants pleurent. La vie émotionelle des animaux (When Elephants Weep. The Emotional Life of Animals) (Paris: Albin Michel, 1997).

[29] Le Goff and Garrigues,

[30] Yet it has clearly lost its inoffensive character.

individual would be the result of a conquest of this natural tendency: the conquest of personal interest as a legitimate end (Hirschman), and even positive for the collective, A. Smith would say.

## Consequences of our study of the gift

Let us recapitulate. The theory of rational choice (optimization of preferences) which currently dominates the social sciences led us to examine the gift, specifically to the question why anyone would make a gift. What could the reasons be for giving, since if one assumes the postulate of interest — i.e., the natural tendency to receive rather than to give — there is no *a priori* reason. This approach leads to a classical dilemma in sociology, that of the internalization of norms, and to the idea that a minimal dose of holism is necessary in order to found any theory of the gift. The gift, on this view, requires an explanation, a social explanation.

We found ourselves compelled to question this postulate and to propose the postulate of the gift, i.e., to propose the existence of a natural tendency to give, a sort of gift drive, in addition to the tendency to receive. In this context, 'natural' signifies something like an 'externality', as economists say with respect to values and norms — all that is subsumed under the notion of preferences that are 'already there', 'given', or like the famous 'natural' tendency to exchange postulated by A. Smith. Polanyi shows convincingly, following Mauss,[31] that nothing could be less obvious.

This frees us in a way from the dominant model. The gift is no longer regarded as something that does not quite fit in the framework of a model that was not made for it, that was made against it, in a certain sense. The new postulate has some significant consequences for the study of the gift. We would now like to briefly present three such consequences.

### *1) Good reasons not to give*

In the first place, we are led to turn around the question that is customarily asked. If the gift has the status of a postulate, then the question to be posed is no longer the one that is asked ordinarily: what makes us give despite the fact that we are fundamentally egoists, receivers, and fundamentally motivated by the lure of profit? The question is turned around and becomes: what prevents us from giving? Why is it that a certain number of people do not give, or give very little? Why is it that under certain circumstances we do not give, while under other circumstances we are more inclined to give? What are good reasons not to give?

---

[31] M. Mauss, *The Gift* (New York and London: W.W. Norton, 1990).

This reversal of the question is not so innocent, it seems to me. If I may venture an analogy, allow me to recall what happened in the science of physics when people stopped wondering why bodies moved. For centuries, scientists wondered what the force might be that made bodies move despite what was believed to be their natural tendency towards inertia, to be immobile. They moved in spite of that, so there must be a force that makes them move. For centuries, the question was posed in this fashion, but one day some physicist turned the question around, hypothesizing that the bodies had a tendency, once they were in motion, to pursue such motion *ad infinitum*, assuming nothing stopped them. This led him to pose the opposite question: what is it that stops motion? What resistance do bodies encounter that makes them stop moving? It was by turning the question around that the laws of motion were discovered. Similarly, by postulating the lure of the gift instead of the lure of profit, the same sort of reversal is carried out and the question then becomes: what is it that prevents the members of a society from giving? What impedes the lure of the gift? What makes people resist the gift, what makes them hold onto things instead of allowing them to circulate? Research in progress on the subject of organ donation has led us to answer this question in terms of identity. The main 'good reason' for not entering into the cycle of the gift (whether as giver or receiver) is the threat to identity. In other words, insofar as the gift can constitute an essential ingredient in the construction of identity, it can also constitute a threat to identity, such that it is preferable to substitute it with a different principle of circulation: the law or the market.

## 2) *Reciprocity is secondary*

A second consequence: the postulate of the gift requires that we reject any conception of the gift based on reciprocity. This consequence is just as difficult to accept as the postulate itself. Reciprocity has always been at the very centre of discussions about the gift, particularly since Mauss and as a result of the influence of anthropological reflections on thinking about the gift. We should recall that Gouldner made the norm of reciprocity a kind of postulate, in the sense we would like to establish for the gift, when he said that it was a norm as strong and generalized as the incest taboo. Reciprocity is important, but it is not what is essential about the gift, and it inevitably leads back to the dominant paradigm. It is only by the presence of the gift principle that the norm of reciprocity is not absorbed by the principle of equivalence. When one tries to model the gift on the basis of reciprocity, one sees it only as the positive face of vengeance: vengeance and gift are seen as two symmetric forms. Yet in so doing, one forgets that what puts an end to vengeance, to the unending symmetry of vengeance, is a non-reciprocated gift, a 'true' gift. Gouldner himself recognizes this in a little-known text that appeared after *The Norm of Reciprocity*, significantly entitled 'The importance of something for nothing', where he shows that there is nothing specifically Christian about this, and that it is as universal as the norm of reciprocity (Confucius, Buddha, Lao-Tze, Plato, Socrates and Aristotle).[32] The big mistake made by models based on reciprocity derives from a confusion between the observation of a return gift and the will or intention to give in return. This is the main paradox of the gift, as Gouldner admits: "The paradox is this: there is no gift that brings a higher return than the free gift, the gift given with no strings attached. For that which is truly given freely moves men deeply and makes them most indebted to their benefactors."[33] This is the reason why, as M. Douglas says, there is a grave violence in the unilateral gift, the gift that refuses any return: "There should not be any free gift. What is wrong with the so-called free gift is the donor's intention to be exempt from return gifts coming from the recipient". We should note that Douglas[34] does not define the unilateral gift by the absence of return, but by the absence of an intention to return, more precisely by the refusal of any return. The confusion between an observation of what circulates and the meaning of what circulates is the greatest source of misunderstandings in the theory of the gift.[35]

It is these two dimensions of reality that get confused and this leads not only to basing the gift on reciprocity, but also to proposing reciprocity as a principle superior to the gift. This confusion can be explained by the importance of anthropology in the entire reflection on the gift. Anthropology most frequently suffers this confusion, more or less voluntarily, because it centres its reflections on the 'objective' circulation of things (the quantity, the time and the rituals that accompany it in one direction or the other), without going into the meaning or the reasons for this circulation, thus implicitly (and often explicitly) endorsing the postulate of reciprocity. Mauss must bear a large responsibility for this. One could illustrate this point by citing, once again, the work of Cordonnier. Since he does not really propose the postulate of the gift, Cordonnier is unable to overcome the model of equivalence because he refers to the model of the archaic gift developed by anthropologists, a model that is based on reciprocity when it is not based on long-term equivalence. However, it is the idea of the 'first gift', as Simmel would call it, that resolves the prisoner's

---

[32] A.W. Gouldner, The Norm of Reciprocity, in *American Sociological Review*, vol. 25, n° 2, 1960, pp. 161-178; A. W. Gouldner, 'The Importance of Something for Nothing', in *For Sociology. Renewal and Critique in Sociology today* (New York: Basic Books, 1973) p. 283.

[33] Ibidem, p. 277.

[34] M. Douglas, *No free gifts*, foreword to M. Mauss, The Gift (New York and London: W.W. Norton, 1990), p.vii.

[35] On this subject, cf. my text, 'Is there an intention to give?', in *The Gift: Theory and Practice* (International Conference: Trent University, 1996).

dilemma, not reciprocity. By definition, the first gift is not reciprocated. It engenders the system. "The first gift is given in full spontaneity; it has a freedom without any duty, even without the duty of gratitude (...) To do it follows from a psychic imperative (...) We *cannot* return a (first) gift; for it has a freedom which a return gift, because it is *that,* cannot possibly possess."[36] Gouldner is even more precise: "To use a crude analogy: the norm of beneficence is an ignition key that activates the starting engine (the norm of reciprocity) which, in turn, gets the motor — the ongoing cycle of mutual exchanges — to turn over."[37]

Reciprocity as the principle norm of gift systems must be rejected. This is the upshot of the analysis of the gift in our societies. We have demonstrated this important point elsewhere,[38] based on research into gifts made to strangers and gifts within networks of kinship. These systems are not based on reciprocity, even when there is return, a return that is often more significant than the original gift. To simply distinguish between an immediate return and a return with delay is not sufficient, although this does not mean that reciprocity does not exist, nor that there is no actual return. Fundamentally, the gift is not a model of equivalence, not even in the long term. This can of course happen, but it is not the model.

## 3) *Models of the gift*

Finally, the third consequence of introducing the postulate of the gift: if reciprocity is not central, what replaces it? Certainly not a unilateral gift, as we have just seen. These are the two models that have always been opposed to each other: interest, and the pure gift (in the sense of unilateral), even if neither of the two seems appropriate when one observes the meaning of the gift in our societies. A third consequence of this postulate, then, is the need to elaborate models of the gift on the basis of this postulate, referring to models suitable for the circulation of goods within the framework of the gift, rather than in a framework of instrumental rationality.

There are five models in the course of being developed,[39] all based on the role of debt, since we have just seen that this is what fundamentally distinguishes the gift from the market.

— Solidarity: this model is the closest to a circulation of goods by the state,[40] in which debt is assimilated with what is owed.

---

[36] G. Simmel, 'Faithfulness and Gratitude', in K.H. Wolff, *The Sociology of Georg Simmel* (New York, The Free Press, 1950) p. 392-393.

[37] A.W. Gouldner, *The Importance of Something for Nothing*, p. 275.

[38] J. T. Godbout, J. Charbonneau and V. Lemieux, *op. cit.*

[39] Each model will be the focus of a chapter in a work I am currently preparing.

[40] J.T. Godbout, 'Is there an intention to give?', *op. cit.*

— The agonistic gift between equals: on this model, debt is assimilated with equality and reciprocity plays the most important role.[41] Reciprocity plays an important role on the condition that there is a system of equals — a necessary but not sufficient condition, for some systems of equals are not based on reciprocity, but on mutual positive debt.
— The hierarchical gift between non-equals (clientelism, patronage): an important system of the gift in which the debt is *structurally* unequal.[42] The relation is initially founded on a gift of life on the part of the patron, for which the recipient will be eternally indebted.
— The gift to strangers: one gives to a third party, without any primary link between giver and recipient.[43] This model's particularity lies in the fact that the debt refers to a third party rather than reverting to the giver. This distinguishes it from both the primary relations and the model of the *hau* put forward by Mauss: it does not have to revert to the giver.
— Mutual positive debt: a model found primarily in kinship and primary relations,[44] but also in gifts to strangers. One could say that a state of positive debt is attained when the desire to give (or the gratitude) that each partner feels towards the other is directed not only to what was received from the other, but to the other as such. This important distinction was made by Simmel and Gouldner with respect to the gift. "… we do not thank somebody only for what he does (…) We are grateful to him only because he exists, because we experience him (…) Here gratitude consists not in the return of a gift, but in the consciousness that it cannot be returned."[45] When this consciousness is present in both partners, we are in the presence of the mutual positive debt model. According to Gouldner, there is a movement away from the norm of reciprocity and closer to what he calls "something for nothing" when "the donor gives because of what the recipient *is*, not because of what he *does*".[46]

All of these models are defined in relation to debt, to the status and the role of debt within the model. They all contain mechanisms for maintaining the debt, and norms for the non extinction of the debt. This is what fundamentally *distinguishes* them from the market model based on the liquidation of debt, as we have seen. In addition, each model possesses a certain freedom with respect to the rules and, finally, in each model it is important to notice how identity is simultaneously reinforced and nourished by the gift, as well as how it can be threatened by the gift.

---

[41] J.L. Boilleau, Conflit et lien social. La rivalité contre la domination (Conflict and Social Bond. Rivalry against Domination) (Paris: La Découverte, 1995).

[42] M. P. D. Lanna, A Divida Divina Troca e Patronagem no Nordeste Brasileiro (Campinas: Editora Unicam, 1995).

[43] J.T. Godbout, 'Is there an intention to give?', *op. cit.*

[44] J. T. Godbout, J. Charbonneau and V. Lemieux, *op. cit.*

[45] G. Simmel, *op. cit.*, p. 389 and 392.

[46] A.W. Gouldner, op.cit., p. 270 (Gouldner's emphasis).

## Conclusion

All of the gift models, including that of the unequal gift, imply a reference to debt among all the partners. The wish not to incur a debt is, in a gift system, a wish to dominate the other, an attack on his or her identity. In such a situation, the passage from gift to law constitutes an essential improvement. This can also be observed in sectors such as volunteer work: in an ongoing study of the beneficiaries of volunteer work, it was observed that when they could not or did not want to return the gift, their identity was threatened and they tended to adopt the model of the law in their relations with the volunteers. They considered the volunteer system to be an extension of the state. But why would the move to a frame of reference such as that of rights constitute less of a threat to identity? Because the law establishes a debt on society's part to those having rights. Then, the giver no longer gives, but rather returns, and returning is no threat to identity.[47]

The most common negative image of the gift is 'to be taken in'. Ultimately, perhaps, it is the most benign form of the dark side of the gift. 'To be taken in' means losing — or not receiving — possessions, which are the most external layer, the primary layer of our identity. More profoundly, it is to lose trust in someone, it is to lose a social bond. More profoundly still, it is to lose one's identity. The danger of receiving is the major reason not to give, and the best reason for justifying replacement of the gift system by a system of rights or a market system. "To accept something from someone is to accept something of his spiritual essence, his soul. The conservation of this would be mortally dangerous"[48] (Mauss, p. 161, 254). Mauss makes these comments regarding *hau*, the most controversial idea in Mauss. In so doing, he has understood the essential point of the good reasons not to give, i.e., the impossibility of giving in return. Not to be able to give in return is to become what one has received, it is to be transformed in one's identity, as organ donation shows. In the film 'Ghost Dance', by Ken McMullen, Derrida claims that ghosts, for Freud,[49] are a metaphor for the failure of mourning, a symptom of an unsuccessful mourning. The work of mourning normally results in the interiorization of the deceased, who is made to live again through us. If this work of mourning fails, instead of interiorization, one speaks of incorporation, in which case death lives in us as a ghost and threatens our identity. The negative gift is the gift's ghost, the ghost of a positive gift. This is exactly the alternative confronting recipients of organ donations: interiorization of the other's organ, which becomes part of oneself, or incorporation of the other, who becomes a ghost within.

---

[47] On the condition, of course, that this right is recognized as legitimate by the members of society.

[48] M. Mauss, *op. cit.*

[49] For this, see N. Abraham and M. Torok, *L'écorce et le noyau (The Cortex and the Core)* (Paris: Flammarion, 1987).

Such a ghost also haunts relations between the West and the Third World. Humanitarian gifts exhibit a general feature of the system of gifts to strangers: the fact that the recipient is considered as acquired, that no one asks his opinion.[50] Much more than through the market, it is through gifts not returned that subjugated societies end up *identifying* with the West and losing their souls, as Serge Latouche has shown in *L'occidentalisation du monde*: "the vehicle of this 'conversion' (to Western values) cannot be open violence or pillage disguised as 'unequal' market exchange; it is the gift. It is by giving that the West acquires the power and the prestige that engender real cultural destructuration" The West "keeps itself out of reach and continues to give without accepting anything. It takes over, if need be, but never recognizes any debt nor receives advice from anyone"[51] (p. 69).

This is exactly what Mary Douglas says in her preface to Mauss: "There should not be any free gift. What is wrong with the so-called free gift is the donor's *intention* to be exempt from return gifts coming from the recipient"[52] (1990, p. vii, my emphasis).

**Bibliography**

P. ABELL, 'Is Rational Choice a Rational Choice of Theory', in J. Coleman and T. J. Fararo (eds.), *Rational Choice Theory: Advocacy and Critique* (London: Sage, 1992) pp. 183-206.

Q. ABRAHAM and M. TOROK, *L'écorce et le noyeau* (Paris: Flammarion, 1987).

R. BERTHOUD, 'L'économie: un ordre généralisé? Les ambitions d'un prix Nobel', in *La Revue de MAUSS semestrielle, Pour une autre économie* (Paris: La découverte, 1994) pp. 42-59.

J.L. BOILLEAU, *Conflit et lien social. La rivalité contre la domination* (Paris: La Découverte, 1995).

J. COLEMAN and T.J. FARARO, *Rational Choice Theory: Advocacy and Critique* (London: Sage, 1992).

L. CORDONNIER, *Coopération et réciprocité* (Paris: Presses Universitaires de France, 1997).

M. CROZIER, *L'entreprise à l'écoute: apprendre le management postindustriel* (Paris: InterÉditions, 1989).

M. DOUGLAS, *No free gifts*, foreword to M. Mauss, The Gift (New York and London: W.W. Norton, 1990).

L. DUMONT, *Essais sur l'individualisme* (Paris: Seuil, 1983).

J. ELSTER, 'Rationalité et normes sociales: un modèle pluridisciplinaire', in L. André, G. Varet and J. C. Passeron, *Le modèle et l'enquête. Les usages du principe de*

---

[50] D. Fairchild, 'Don Humanitaire, don pervers' ('Humanitarian Gift, Perverse Gift'), in *La Revue du MAUSS semestrielle, L'obligation de donner (The Obligation to Give)* (Paris: La Découverte, 1996) pp. 294-300.

[51] S. Latouche, *L'occidentalisation du monde (The Modernisation of the World)* (Paris: La Découverte, 1992

[52] M. Douglas, *No free gifts*, foreword to M. Mauss, The Gift (New York and London: W.W. Norton, 1990).

*rationalité dans les sciences sociales* (Paris: Éditions de l'École des Hautes Études en Sciences Sociales, 1995).

A. ETZIONI, *The Moral Dimension, Toward a New Economics* (New York: The Free Press, 1988).

D. FAIRCHILD, 'Don Humanitaire, don pervers', in *La Revue du MAUSS semestrielle, L'obligation de donner* (Paris: La Découverte, 1996) pp. 294-300.

E. FRIEDRICH, *Le pouvoir et la règle* (Paris: Seuil, 1993).

F. FUKUYAMA, *Trust. The Social Virtues and the Creation of Prosperity* (New York: The Free Press, 1995).

G. VARET, L. ANDRÉ and J.C. PASSERON, *Le modèle et l'enquête. Les usages du pricipe de rationalité dans les sciences sociales* (Paris, Éditions de l'École des Hautes Études en Sciences Sociales, 1995).

J.T. GODBOUT, 'Don et solidarité', in MIRE, *Produire les solidarités. La part des associations*, ( Paris: MIRE, 1997).

J. T. GODBOUT, 'Is there an intention to give?', in *The Gift: Theory and Practice*, (International Conference: Trent University, 1996).

J. T. GODBOUT, J. CHARBONNEAU and V. LEMIEUX, *La circulation du don dans la parenté*. Montréal: INRS-Urbanisation, RR 17, 1996).

A. W. GOULDNER, 'The Importance of Something for Nothing', in *For Sociology. Renewal and Critique in Sociology today* (New York: Basic Books, 1973).

F.A. HAYEK, The Road to Serfdom (London: Routledge & Kegan Paul, 1976).

A.O. HIRSCHMAN, *Exit, Voice and Loyalty: Response to Decline in Firms, Organizations and States* (Cambridge: Harvard University Press, 1970).

D. R. HOFSTADTER, *Gödel, Escher, Bach: an Eternal Golden Braid* (New York: Vintage Books, 1980).

A. INSEL, 'Une rigueur pour la forme', in *La Revue de MAUSS semestrielle, Pour une autre économie* (Paris: La découverte, 1994) pp. 77-94.

B. KARSENTI, *Marcel Mauss. Le fait social total* (France: Presses universitaires de France, 1994).

M. P. D. LANNA, A Divida Divina Troca e Patronagem no Nordeste Brasileiro (Campinas: Editora Unicam, 1995).

S. LATOUCHE, *L'occidentalisation du monde* (Paris: La Découverte, 1992).

S. MOSCOVI, *La machine à faire des dieux* (Paris: Fayard, 1988).

M. MASSON, J. and S. McCarthy, *Quand les éléphants pleurent. La vie émotionelle des animaux* (Paris: Albin Michel, 1997).

K. POLANYI, *The Great Transformation: The Political and Economic Origins of our Times* (Boston: Beacon Press, 1957).

B. RIMLAND, 'The Altruism Paradox', in *Pschychological Reports*, 51:

D. SCIULLI, 'Weaknesses in Rational Choice Theory's Contribution to Comparative Research', in J. Coleman and T. J. Fararo (eds.), *Rational Choice Theory: Advocacy and Critique* (London: Sage, 1992).

D. TEMPLE and M. Chabal, *La réciprocité et la naissance des valeurs humaines* (Paris: L'Harmattan, 1995).

F. TONNIES, *Community and Society* (East Landing: Michigan State University Press, 1964)

D. WRONG, 'The Oversocialized Conception of Man in modern Sociology', in *American Sociological Review*, 26 (1961)

# Gift and Association[1]

Alain CAILLÉ (Université de Nanterre - Paris)

To enter into an association is, first of all, to give of one's time and one's person. An evident link exists, therefore, between the question of the meaning of a gift and that of the status of the associative action. We propose here to assemble in a cursory and schematic fashion certain elements which allow us to specify this link, first of all by exposing the main lines of a "paradigm of gift" as it is being sketched for some years now around *La Revue du Mauss*, then by asking ourselves what implications it is likely to have for a sociology of association.

## The Paradigm of Gift[2]

*Definition*. To fix ideas, let us first specify what we mean by gift: 1) *A sociological definition:* every allowance of goods or services made without a guarantee of return, with a view to creating, maintaining or regenerating the social bond. In the relationship of gift, the bond is more important than the good.[3] 2) A *general definition*: every action or allowance made without expectation, guarantee or certainty of return, and which, because of this fact, has a dimension of "gratuity". The paradigm of gift insists on the importance, positive and normative, sociological, economic, ethical, political and philosophical, of this type of action and allowance.

*Origin*. Always and everywhere there has been reflection on the gift. Its crystallisation in the social sciences goes back to the famous *Essai sur le don* of Marcel Mauss.[4] We insist on the fact that this essay begins with what is

---

[1] This article is an abbreviated and slightly modified version of an address given on the 6th March 1997 during a symposium organised by MIRE on the theme "Associations and Solidarity". A slightly different version has been published in the *Revue des études coopératives, mutualistes et associatives*, no. 265, 3rd quarter (1997).

[2] I summarise here the kernel of arguments which I have developed in several texts but particularly in 'Ni holisme ni individualisme. Marcel Mauss et le pardigme du don' (Neither Holism nor Individualism: Marcel Mauss and the Paradigm of the Gift), in La Revue de M.A.U.S.S. semestrielle, *L'obligation de donner. La découverte sociologique capitale de Marcel Mauss (The Obligation to Give: Marcel Mauss' Main Sociological Discovery)*, 8, 2nd semester (1996).

[3] Or, in other words, the value of the bond is more important in it than the use value or the exchange value. It is this definition which inspires *L'Esprit de don* (*The Spirit of the Gift*) (La Découverte, 1992) of J. Godbout (in collaboration with A. Caillé).

[4] But there are many antecedents, without even mentioning the ethnological material assembled by Mauss. Georg Simmel can be considered the co-founder of what we call the paradigm of gift.

presented as a discovery of the first *empirical* order, that of a certain universality — in archaic societies — of what Mauss terms *the triple obligation to give, receive and return*. Because this triple obligation constitutes, if we are to believe (and we should believe) the first sociological and anthropological law, the most general law of the archaic social order, the gift is presented there as a total social phenomenon. Let us understand: even when made by private individuals (persons, rather), it concerns the entirety of dimensions of the action and resonates in the flesh of all society. Let us translate: it is symbolic *par excellence*. It is the symbol *par excellence* which animates the whole of symbolic activity.

*A paradigm?* Let us assume that there exist two principal paradigms recognised by the social sciences, two main ways of questioning and responding. Individualism (methodological) attempts to derive every action, rule or institution from calculations, more or less conscious and rational, carried out by individuals, assumed as the only reals. Holism (culturalism, structuralism, functionalism, etc.) assumes on the contrary that the action of individuals (or groups, classes, orders, etc.) can only express or actualise an *a priori* totality, which pre-exists it, and which, thus, appears in its turn as the only real. Let us note that the gift is incomprehensible within these two paradigms; the first dissolves it in "interest" and the second in obligation. The paradigm of gift does not deny the existence of either of these two moments, of individuality or of totality, but refuses to take them as givens. Starting from the interrelation of persons, and asking itself how the two opposed moments are engendered, concretely and historically, the paradigm of gift makes of gift (of symbol, of the political) the privileged or, better, specific operator of the creation of the social bond. To its way of seeing, individuals and social totality are not undecomposable and unquestionable givens, the only reals, but the result of a myriad of intertwined gifts at every level. They are not givens but given.

*A typology of action.* Each of the two paradigms rests on an uni-dimensional and reductionist theory of social action. Individualism brings everything back to individual interest. Holism relates everything to one or other form of obligation (of constraint, debt, etc.). The paradigm of gift does not deny the existence of these moments of action but dialecticises them by suggesting how they ought to be thought through within the framework of a multidimensional and paradoxical theory of action. One already clearly presented by M. Mauss. The triple obligation to give, to accept and to return is, in effect, an obligation of freedom (of spontaneity). And, in this framework, action is at the one time, and in ever variable and unstable proportions, "interested" and "disinterested" — it being understood that interests of glory, of prestige, of being, hierarchically dominate, positively and normatively, instrumental interests, of possession, of having. In the final analysis, human action and symbolism develop at the intersection of two main oppositions, infinitely declinable and translatable:

that of death (the absolute master, the absolute constraint) and that of life, that of war (of rivalry) and that of peace (of alliance). The first translation: the opposition between obligation and freedom (creativity) is intensified as an opposition between personal interest, self-interest, and the interest of the alliance or of friendship, the interest in others (*alias* disinterest). There are therefore four dimensions to action, which are irreducible to each other.

*The gift, again.* The gift, then, is in no way disinterested, in a sense. Simply, it privileges interests of friendship (of alliance, of affection, etc.) and of pleasure and/or creativity over instrumental interests and over obligation or compulsion. The determination of religions or of many philosophers to find a wholly disinterested gift is therefore futile. It arises, moreover, from a confusion between disinterestedness and disinterest. The gift should not be considered without interest (instrumental) or outside of it, but against it. It is the movement which, for the purposes of the alliance or of creation, subordinates the instrumental interests to the non-instrumental ones.

*The historicity of gift.* Contrary to the two inherited paradigms, which it seeks to go beyond, the paradigm of gift in no way prejudges, in an a-historical or dogmatic manner, the respective weights of obligation or of interest. In effect, it has not an answer to everything but a question for everything. The importance to accord to the four motives of action (obligation or freedom, instrumental interest or friendship) can only be decided empirically and historically, because the combination between them is infinitely variable.

*Gift and politics.* Within the framework of small societies, let us assume that the agonistic gift is that through which the alliance is made with the enemies of yesterday. Who risk besides becoming the enemies of tomorrow, hence the profound ambivalence of gift, noted by M. Mauss. It constitutes, therefore, the political act *par excellence* which institutes the frontier between friends and enemies, the interior and the exterior. In the interior, between neighbours or relatives the sharing gift dominates. In fact, these frontiers are porous, since relatives and neighbours are made from allies and strangers. There is, therefore, the *agôn* in the sharing and sharing in the agôn. We note simply that in the context of the small society, founded on everyone knowing each other, the gift and politics coincide. It is not the same thing at all in the big society where the alliance is established beyond inter-personal relationships. Politics, which is the mastery of this alliance generalised beyond the interpersonal, functions as an *analogon* of gift (each one, in giving himself to everyone, gives himself to no-one). It keeps its spirit but is not reduced to the gift of person to person, to the gift which one could call primary. We can conclude: the paradigm of gift and of symbolism is equally a paradigm of politics.

*The gift today — primary sociality and secondary sociality.* It would be false to think that the discovery of Mauss only concerns archaic societies and that the anthropological gift only existed today as a relic. Let us term *primary sociality* the type of social relation in which the personality of people matters more than the functions which they accomplish (which does not prevent the functions from existing and being important). And *secondary sociality* the type of relation submitted to the law of impersonality (as in the market, in law or in science), in which the functions carried out by people matter more than their personalities. *Hypothesis no.1*: under a transposed form, the triple obligation continues to structure the sphere of primary sociality, that of interpersonal networks (family, neighbourhood, friendship, associations where people know each other). *Hypothesis no. 2*: it continues working strongly at the very heart of secondary sociality. No enterprise, private or public, no scientific undertaking, would function if it did not mobilise for its purpose the primary networks cemented by the law of gift. *Hypothesis no. 3*: modernity sees the development of an unusual form of gift, the gift to strangers[5] (Godbout), which no longer serves to bring to birth or consolidate stable interpersonal relations, quasi communitarian, but feeds networks potentially open to the infinite, very much beyond the concrete knowing of each other.

Having assembled some elements of the paradigm of gift, let us try to evaluate what would constitute a reflection on the associative fact.

**The Paradigm of Gift and the Associative Fact**

From now on, we will be even more shorthand in style and present not theses or hypotheses so much as sketches of hypotheses. A sociology of the associative fact ought, we believe, to determine itself with respect to seven types of problems. To begin with, let us start with the definition of associations in the French law of 1901, which sees there a grouping of means, brought together but not for financial gain and protected by law.

*The problem of the sociological topic*. The specific register of association does not allow it to fall easily into any of the big orders of social action distinguished by existing sociological topics. Its proper domain is not that of private or public economics, nor that of the political-administrative sphere, even if there are big organisations or big bureaucracies which intervene in these fields in the name of an inspiration or ideology of an associative type. Or again, the associative act as such is not the concern of secondary sociality. Even while associations assign themselves functional objectives, what is properly theirs is to propose to attain them while subordinating the functional exigence to a principle of personalisation, resorting in this way to typical modalities of the primary sociality. However, they escape from the dominant register

---

[5] Already defended by all the big religions, notably Buddhism. What is new in our modernity is particularly the laicisation of gift to strangers.

of the primary — dominant notably in the family and in the neighbourhood of a traditional type —, the register of a communitarian type, in this that they rest on a principle of active socialisation, deliberate, facultative and revocable. Let us assume, then, that the associative act develops at the interface[6] of the primary and the secondary, of the organic community (*Gemeinschaft*) and the contractual society (*Gesellschaft*). Or, better, that it brings about an intermixing or transformation of opposed logics, allowing it to accomplish functional tasks under the form of personalisation, or to form alliances on a big scale, alliances proper to the large society, without renouncing the form of the small society. And, to say it in terms of other theoretical references, the association fashions what one could call primary public spaces (resting on knowing each other). Private public spaces in summary.[7]

*The problem of the motives of action.* Between the unveiling of hidden interests and the apology for all-consuming dedication, the paradigm of gift remains *a priori* neutral, since it does not need to prejudge the respective parts, among the motives of action, played by material interest, moral duty, affection or pleasure. Without the duty of examining itself for the degree of purity of intentions of benevolent militants, it is sufficient for it to recognise the possibility of non-profit action enterprises, or those which subordinate profit to other, non-instrumental considerations. It is also possible, taking inspiration from the insistence put by Monstesquieu on the principles which direct the different political regimes, to reason as follows: there where the market economy rests on the principle of the interest and freedom of private individuals, there where the political-administrative sphere rests on the principle of the public (or collective) interest and the necessary constraint to put it into practice, the association, like the gift according to Marcel Mauss, rests on a principle of closely intertwined freedom and obligation through which common interests are realised. Another formulation: there where obligation encourages the discharging of a debt, there where market and instrumental interest pushes one to leave the register of debt by balancing at each instant rights and duties, debits and credits, the gift and associative action encourage one to enter into the cycle of the circulation of debt which, while it functions well and confidence reigns, creates a mutually positive indebtedness (Godbout[8]). It is by this state

---

[6] "The paradox of the association then is its ability to be a matter, at the one time, of the societary principle and the communitarian principle", writes Jean-Louis Laville ('The association, a freedom proper to democracy', resumed in J-L. Laville and R. Sainsaulieu (eds.), *Sociologie de l'association (Sociology of the Association)* (Paris: Desclée de Brouwer, 1997).

[7] The Italian sociologist, Pierpaolo Donati, for his part, speaks of the "privato sociale" (cf. *Teoria relazionale dell società* (Milan: Angeli, 1996)).

[8] Cf J. Godbout, 'De l'état d'endettement mutuel' and A. Caillé, 'Tout le monde gagne', in *La Revue du M.A.U.S.S. semestrielle*, no. 4, 2<sup>nd</sup> semestre (1994), 'A qui se fier? Confiance, interaction et théorie des jeux' (Who to Trust? Trust, Interaction and Game Theory).

of mutual positive indebtedness, alone in overcoming the apories of individualist rationalism which are highlighted by the prisoner's dilemma or the free rider problem, that the benefits proper to the associative register are explained. If everyone feels indebted to everyone, it is because in this set-up everyone gains.[9]

*The problem of the definition*. One feels it, many of the points we have just made have a sociological significance that far exceeds the juridical and formal definition of the association. From a strictly empirical point of view, it seems possible to restrict the reflection to associations declared to be in conformity with the law of 1901, which refers to "the convention by which two or more persons pool, in a permanent manner, their knowledge or their activity for a purpose other than to share a profit". But how do we assure the comparison with the associations of other countries, governed by other texts? Or with other times? Nothing allows us to state that nothing existed before the adoption of the law which resembled an association or that there doesn't exist, still today, what are very much *associations in fact*[10], but unhampered by any juridical formalism. It is tempting, therefore, to consider the juridical definition given by the law of 1901 as an important but nevertheless particular case of a more general definition of association, which could be something like this: "The convention, tacit or explicit, conforming to a law or not, written or unwritten, by which two or more persons pool, in a more or less permanent manner, their material resources, their knowledge or their activity for a purpose which is not principally that of sharing the material profits".

*The problem of the typology*. The empirical variety of associations defined by the law of 1901 is already considerable. If one widens the definition, as we have just done, the risk becomes great of finding oneself confronted with a practically infinite and totally heterogeneous universe. The need to orient oneself by being able to use typologies resting on clear principles makes itself felt in a still more pressing way. A first series of criteria ought allow us to distinguish between associations understood in the *largo* or *stricto* (law of 1901) *sensu*: is the convention, by definition always voluntary, tacit or explicit? Sanctioned by law, custom, or nothing? Can one, or can one not, leave the association, and on what conditions? A second series, evident, looks to the objectives (economic, cultural, pedagogic, sporting, etc.) of the association. A third to its scale. A fourth to its recruitment. A fifth to its degree of autonomy with respect to other organisations and to the degree of democracy (autonomy/heteronomy) at its heart coupled with its degree of self-referencing (is it

---

[9] But some more than others ... This inequality in material or symbolic gains which causes envy and division, threatens at every moment to change the status of a co-operative game to that of a zero-sum game, even to dissolve the game.

[10] Without counting juridical forms which do not come from the law of 1901 but contain, nevertheless, the associative form and spirit. What about cooperatives, for example, or parties?

turned in on itself or out towards the exterior?). Finally, it is possible to distinguish between associations which are secondarised, primarised, or in balance between primariness and secondariness (the essential criterion here being the respective parts of volunteers and of waged workers). Not counting, of course, the pseudo-associations, the screen or Mafiosi associations.

*The problem of the place of an associative fact from the general sociological point of view.* What good — no doubt more than one reader will ask — what good is it to have delayed, probably excessively, the general definition of the association if it is only to multiply in this way the *distinguos*? Our sole justification is of a general theoretical order. It seems, in effect, necessary to us to suggest how the concrete associative fact will not be fully comprehensible unless one conceives the association in its greatest generality, as *ad-sociation*, an active movement towards the sociation (*Vergesellschaftung*, to put it in Simmel's terms). In a sense, there are only two main ways of making society, of creating a social bond there where only separation or hostility existed: superior violence or *ad-sociation* (cf. the definition *supra*), every combination of the two being evidently conceivable. The gift is the means by which the associative pact is tied. Because the latter cannot be born in the unconditionality of the violence which commands unconditionally, nor in the unconditionality of love which speaks in the name of the unconditioned, nor — contrary to what all the theories of the social contract would have us believe — in the name of an impossible unconditional conditionality (contractualised). It can only be formed in the register of the *conditional unconditionality*,[11] that in which each one undertakes to give unconditionally to each one but is also ready to withdraw from the game, at each instant, if the others are not playing it.

*Association and democracy.* One of the reasons why this question of the associative modalities for engendering the social bond has remained rather obscure is that, until a little while ago, the weight of inherited society and sociality on the one hand, and that of violence, constraint and domination on the other, were so great with respect to that of voluntary initiative that the question could seem rather marginal. Let us note, however, that the same thing has been true of democracy for a long time. It is only a short while ago that modern societies were recognised as the autonomous producers of their own norms, and as only existing thanks to an incessant movement of democratic invention. Curiously, the irreducible autonomy of this moment of collective invention of society by itself, that by which "all give themselves to all", will have been recognised well before the irreducible autonomy, however much more evident

---

[11] Cf. A. Caillé, 'De l'inconditionnalité conditionnelle', *La Revue du M.A.U.S.S. semestrielle* no. 7, 1st semester (1996), *Vers un revenu minimum inconditionel? (Towards an unconditional Minimum Income?)*.

*a priori*, of the moment of the common associative invention, that by which, in forming conventions, certain individuals, or some, give themselves to certain individuals (or some others). Let us take from this the existence of a privileged bond between association and democracy. That, like the gift and the political, they are one and the same thing, but on a different scale. This hypothesis is of the sort that brings the inquiry about the place of democracy in our societies into new fields. Because the fate of democracy is not settled only on the level of the tacit collective pact, the level of politics; not only on the level of instituted politics, on the level of what one could call the *secondary public spaces*; it is settled also, and perhaps first of all, from day to day, in the heart of these primary public spaces which are the associations.

## Conclusion: Gift, Association, Solidarity And Democracy

We have left aside until now the question of solidarity. This solidarity which, in its modern and restrained sense, is understood as a redistribution of goods, material or symbolic, carried out by those who have more in favour of those who have less. Traditionally, solidarity unfolded in the heart of the primary sociality, in the context of everyone knowing everyone, and it was assured under one or other form of an asymmetric gift (Christian charity or aristocratic largesse). These different forms, often profoundly modified, remain resilient today. But what is characteristic of modernity is to have systematically substituted an impersonal, functional, public and statistical (insurance-based) solidarity for a solidarity of one person to another, a personalised one. The dominant form of solidarity is assured by a public system of redistribution (Polanyi), putting into practice a mechanical and impersonal gift which one could term a *secondary* (or secondarised) *gift*.

One knows that this public system of redistribution, on which the whole welfare state rests, has entered into deep crisis for many reasons. The principal one being the crisis of the wage-earning group which, by dint of the granting of subsidies to non-contributors, irremediably destabilises the whole. The question of solidarity is then posed in all its width. It is no longer possible to be in solidarity with others, anonymously and without giving of oneself, while limiting oneself to insure oneself and one's own future. We are going to have to reinvent new forms of solidarity, therefore. While not forgetting that the first step in solidarity is that by which people recognise themselves as members of the same society, the same *politie*, and owe each other something under this title. Faced with the crisis of work, the most urgent measure of solidarity, it seems to us, must pass through a reformulation of the central political pact, taking account of changes in the world of wage-earners, and refusing to restrict the right of active common citizenship solely to stable and full-time workers. From this perspective, three series of measures[12] seem necessary for the spawning of new forms of solidarity: 1) reducing working time[13] and organising an active redistribution of employments; 2) encouraging juridically, symbolically and financially the expansion of associative activities and notably those which contribute to the dynamism of a "third sector" or of the "social economy"; 3) encouraging the risk of confidence on the part of all towards all, of the better endowed towards the worst endowed and reciprocally, of all towards the State and of the State vis-à-vis the population, by granting those who do not dispose of at least this level of resources a minimum income helping "insertion" but without presenting this as an obligation, and which can be added to other resources averaging certain fiscal measures.

In one word, and more simply, instead of dreaming only of dismantling the welfare state and replacing it with workfare, the obligation to work, is it not high time to rebuild it with a generous interpretation of the minimum income guaranteed to everyone[14] and to reaffirm in this way a first strong principle of solidarity? These objectives are, surely, strongly interdependent, since the reduction of working time and the certainty of being able to benefit from a minimum income both constitute powerful incentives to associative involvement. Solidarity in our societies ought to begin by taking seriously the democratic exigence, and democracy only takes itself seriously when it favours the profusion of associations. It is beyond public solidarity, and in a necessary complementarity with it, that solidarity in action is practised.

---

[12] It is on these three series of measures that 35 authors or personalities with very different outlooks, since joined by many authors, agreed in an *Appel* published in *Le Monde* of 28th June, 1995, and used as a constitutive document by the association created in June, 1996, the AECEP (Appel européen pour une économie et une citoyenneté plurielles/ A European Call for a Pluralist Economy and Citizenship, 21 bd de Genelle, 75015). For example, Guy Aznar, André Gorz, Guy Roustang, Jean-Louis Laville, Claus Offe, Marco Revelli, Steven Lukes, Jean-Pierre Dupuy, Jacques Robin, Dominique Méda, Robert Castel, Yoland Bresson, Claude Alphandéry, Jean-Michel Belorgey, Patrick Viveret, Jean-Marc Ferry, Roger Sue, etc.

[13] Including in this that the lost salary is not entirely compensated for, beyond a certain threshold. The first form of solidarity that can be envisaged.

[14] In France, the RMI, Revenue Minimum d'Insertion, is the basic social assistance payment. It is instituted by a law that affirms, in conformity with the spirit of its first defenders, a double right — to a minimum income and to insertion — and not a minimum income in exchange for a largely imaginary obligation of insertion.

# On Meteors

## Considerations touching upon the *agon*, in which questions concerning gifts and love are tackled

Jean-Luc BOILLEAU (Sociologist and philosopher, member of the MAUSS-group)

Can one still find traces of the agonistic gift in our contemporary societies? And what is the link between an agonistic and an altruistic gift? And between gifts and love? These are the questions I shall try to answer in the following text. Do not expect a scientific discourse. The *agon* does not fit in with the kind of science that straightjackets the cosmos and chases the gods. Where the *agon* is concerned no logical rigour whatsoever can make sense. Still, in order to talk about gifts, about the *agon*, about altruism and love, I need to give in to at least some requirements for coherent discourse, and define what I mean exactly by *gift*, by *agonistic gift* and by *altruistic gift*. I will talk about *love* later on.

### The gift

I am a Maussian and I consider the gift to constitute the human bedrock on which all societies are built. The gift makes social life in all its components. I distinguish at least three 'ingredients' in the gift: I call them *exchange, sharing*, and *agon* (or, in other words, rivalry). From this point of view the gift always unfolds, simultaneously and in the same way, a triple relation between the actors concerned. First of all, there is a kind of quasi-contractual relation between human beings, between equals that is, because the actors recognize each other mutually, here and now, as equal human beings, fundamentally, i.e. susceptible to complete interchange; moreover, there is a relation of human solidarity, because the donator shares what is his with the donatee; and finally, there is a relation between actually differing and competing actors, because the donator wants to show that he disposes of something the donatee lacks, because the donator wants to distinguish himself from the donatee, from the other human beings.

The *agonistic gift*, then, is the kind of gift that privileges this last relation, a relation in which the other is regarded as different, be it without eliminating solidarity and equality. In the same way the *sharing gift* (or *altruistic gift*) puts to the fore the communality, the relation of solidarity, without annihilating the quasi-contractual and agonistic relations. In the same way the *exchange gift* underlines the quasi-contractual relation between equals, without excluding the two other kinds of relation, of course.

This explains why the relations of exchange, sharing and *agon* are always entangled and intricate, and one cannot untie the strong bonds between them without severing them with a butcher's cleaver, a surgeon's scalpel or a poet's alexandrine metre. Such a cleavage would mean one is no longer dealing with the gift as a living reality, or, as a matter of fact, with a gift at all. Consequently, when I give, the other becomes real at the same time and in the same way: he is my equal with whom I — effectively or almost — enter into contact, he is my neighbour with whom I share everything, and he is the 'very other' from whom I keep my distance, to whom I show my difference, with whom I compete.

It is understandable that the common logic, which simplifies and fixes relations according to certain views, has trouble explaining the gift, because the neighbour can in fact be far away, and the other can in fact be quite the same, at the same time, and without there being any perspective of dialectically bypassing the opposites. Let us say that the gift unites proximity and remoteness, equality and difference, as well as — we shall come to that — appearance and disappearance, regardless of the principle of contradiction.

## Sports and gifts

Let us take a closer look at the agonistic gift now. I was asked whether some traces of the agonistic gift are still left and continue to exist in our societies. This question is a trap. It suggests that the agonistic gift, the gift that privileges the *agon*, would in fact be something belonging to a remote past, a relic, a kind of relation between 'savages', which we no longer have been for quite some time now.

Not so long ago, I myself had the tendency to consider the *agon* as something residuous indeed. I regarded the modern sports, for instance, as manifestations of the still living agonistic gift. However, one moment I thought that sports seemed threatened with eradication, the next I considered them as a kind of agonistic cyst or abscess, that is inextirpable, but located and besieged by anti-agonistic forces. The agonistic hearth, then, had no power at all to spread itself. According to this point of view, the *agon* should unquestionably be considered as indestructible, but at the same time as incapable of infesting the social body.

Today, I no longer take this view. The agonistic gift seems to me to be very present indeed, very much alive, and on its way to irrigate all contemporary social life.

As the intellectuals — those fierce opponents of sports — have come to realize very well, sports as the expression of the agonistic gift are no longer a marginal phenomenon in our societies. Two billion human beings have watched the broadcasting of the appointment by lot of the 1998 World Cup Football. Billions of men and women watch the Olympic Games. In a country like France, for instance, 13 million people are licenced for some sport or other. This means that quite a crowd shares the vision of the sports enthusiast.

It has been suggested that the modern sports would be intrinsically fascistic, that they would be tantamount to, amongst others, militarism, racism, the worship of command and of natural hierarchies, and fetichization of the flag. Sports would be the opium of the lower classes, and as such would contribute everywhere to the legitimation of the powers that be. Sports would symbolize the submission of the weak to the strong. And, finally, sports would stand for the reign of money and business in being a purebred product of capitalism and mercantilism. I find these truisms very unsatisfactory.

If billions of people are interested in sports, this is not necessarily or only because it is in the interest of certain financial groups or certain governments. Nor is it because those people want to be dominated or worship fascism. It is perhaps most of all only because they simply adore sports, and that their freedom resides therein, as Johan Huizinga claimed. From this point of view, the tradesmen, the statesmen and the fascists would invest in sports because 'it works'.

Let us have a look now at how sports can be associated with the agonistic gift. Sportsmen, competitors, are spendthrifts: they give everything they have got, they work themselves to the bone because they strive for glory, prestige and recognition. In competition they use an abundance of energy, of subtlety, of ingenuity, of beauty, in order to excel their opponent. One has to offer an incomparable appearance and top performances in order to make oneself recognizable. Rivalry is, of course, at the very heart of the relationships between competitors. Competition means constant challenge; it means fighting the other. One has to eclipse one's antagonist as it were, and to flabbergast one's environment and the public with the strength one exhibits. But the will to surpass the other is never unilateral; it is reciprocal. Moreover, a competition is not to be regarded as a relationship between two people or between two teams. There is always a third, a fourth, a fifth party (or even more) equally involved in this kind of relationship. Not to mention the groups the competitors belong to. The rivalry in sports is characterized by the fact that power is subject to change and continuous exchange. On the platform there are three competitors today. Tomorrow there will still be three of them. But not necessarily the same. And even if they were the same, they will not necessarily be standing on yesterday's step. The reciprocity rules out the permanent domination of whoever. Sports competitions resemble potlatches in which winners are always obliged to put their title at stake. This prevents whoever from being permanently the best.

Obligation to work oneself to the bone, to challenge, to fight.
Obligation to accept challenges.
Obligation to return challenges, etc.

It has to be added that if in sports, as in the agonistic gift, one chooses conflict in order to emphasize the way in which one differs from the other (from the others), one also acknowledges the fact that, in principle, all human beings are susceptible of participating in competitions. This way a certain basic equality is underlined. Moreover, these agonistic relations develop a certain harmony, a comradery, a brotherhood, a sharing of each other's joy and sadness, a sympathy, a solidarity between all competitors.

Look at the famous traditional sculpture from Burkina Faso representing the three Gourmantché combatants. These wrestlers are literally united in combat. If the three Graces incarnate the gift (give, receive, render), I think the three Gourmantché combatants, who are perhaps more ancient than the three Graces, and even — who knows? — more ancient than the three Greek Charites, incarnate the agonistic gift. These wrestlers give, receive and render goods as well as kicks and grabs in an agonistic way. They distinguish themselves permanently, but they are also equal and solidary men. Look at the way they fight. Nevertheless, they sometimes need each other to recover their equilibrium. *You'll never walk alone.*

These three Gourmantché combatants remind one of the platform in sports. One moment the competitors were fighting one another, the next they embrace one another. We have all witnessed such scenes, in the Olympic Games for instance. Today they have their place on the steps, but tomorrow? Everything can change. Other competitors could be on the platform, others with whom all the combatants will have to tie new bonds, in rivalry.

And if there is one amongst them who shows himself as very, very strong, and who seems likely to become a permanent fixture on the upper step of the platform, one must be aware of the fact that the day after tomorrow that competitor will be old, will be dead. Everything goes round in circles anyway: the victories, the defeats, the gifts and everything else.

In *agon* everything emerges, everything changes, everything vanishes. Nothing can be preserved forever. There are no immutable beings. Only memories tend to last for some time.

Sports are an authentic, living, contemporary manifestation of the agonistic gift. But they are not the only one, of course. Take 'nationism', as Jean-Louis Prat calls it — 'nationism' which expresses the request of stateless nations to receive recognition for their merits and their dignity[1] — take a telethon that

---

[1] As Jean-Louis Prat explains, 'nation' is to be understood in the way one talks about the tournament of the five nations. From this point of view the *amour propre* of Welshmen, Scotchmen, Basques, Catalans, Bretons, etc. — all of them making a precious contribution to the world, I would add — can be called 'nationist'.

mobilizes millions of donors in a kind of gigantic potlatch, take Lady Di's actions daring the British Crown — actions that fascinated the whole planet, by the way — and so on. All of them are related to and owe to the agonistic gift. I will not deal with street fights here, with what the media call 'urban violence', a problem which can doubtlessly be approached much better in the light of Marcel Mauss' *Essai sur le don*, than analyzed in the twilight of 'thinkers' such as Raoult, Gaudin or Chevènement.

## A little agonistic metaphysics

In my opinion, the agonistic gift refers to an agonistic world view, and even to an agonistic metaphysics, which finds itself supported by sportsmen, by most children, by certain artists, but also by many modern, 'unlabelled' men and women.

I know that today metaphysics is no longer part of the curriculum in the social sciences. That is a pity. Man is a metaphysical animal, and one cannot understand human beings unless one raises the veil that masks their fundamental choices.

Ardent followers of the *agon* never commit their world view in an explicit way to anyone. Besides, generally speaking, they are never asked anyway. It sometimes happens that they reveal things, of course, but even then they offer but small fragments of their mental landscapes. They never worry about the contradictions or incoherencies that might appear if, by mere coincidence, the odd listener would undertake to assemble the bits and pieces of the puzzle, or to look at the tangram in the light of the logos.

To talk about the *agon* is to talk about life, about relations, about the cosmos, that is to say about everything that emerges out of itself, with no other purpose than to appear, to exist and to disappear again, with no other finality than to make sure there is something rather than nothing. From this point of view, words themselves are their own end: words for words' sake — words because there would be words and not nothing. The words say this, very simply, and then they vanish into thin air. In *agon*, one resembles M.C. Solaar: one loves sharp answers, one loves to give tit for tat, and when one has been talking for quite some time, one tends to digress, and words become free. As Gaston Bachelard observed, "the syllables begin to shake, the words abandon their meaning as if it were too heavy a burden to bear; they jump to other significations as if they had the right to be young. And the words go away looking for fresh company, for bad company, in the stuffing of the vocabulary."

I think I am a follower of the *agon*, or at least I used to be one not so long ago. Lately I have betrayed it a bit, in trying to commit to my readers the outlines of the agonistic metaphysics. It is, of course, only a would-be, do-it-yourself picture, and not a rigorous discourse. How could it be otherwise? From the very beginning of my text I have been using the word 'be', for instance, and I have tried to respect the logic of the grammar. This logic refers to a principle of identity, even though being and the logic that ensues from it, mean nothing or close to nothing in *agon*.

Now that we have touched upon the subject anyway, let us begin by looking at the question of being.

**Being and appearing**

The adepts of the agonistic gift, particularly the sportsmen and the friends of sports, are subject to a 'fundamental' existential experience, an experience in which they profoundly undergo something; it is the experience of change, the experience of the absence of a stable identity, the experience of loss and ephemerality. Nothing lasts forever, victory nor defeat, youth nor old age for that matter, nor beauty, nor the 'perfect' gesture, nor the perfect time (the *kairos*), nor the invention, nor the reputation, nor the prestige, nor the 'possessions', nor the strength, nor the smiles, nor the sobs, nor the thoughts ... Sportsmen regard each other as 'energies', as 'wills'[2], as forces, as actions — and indeed all the things in the world appear to be forces that emerge and come across one another. It is a matter of standing up in front of nothing, of resisting nothing, knowing very well that one can never affirm oneself definitely, but also knowing that one is not alone, that one can count on the others, contemporaries or ensuing generations — like the ancients have counted on their 'descendants' — in order to continue the big combat against nothing.

Giving means, first of all, giving oneself as an appearance[3], which means — in the human world at least, that is — engaging in battle in order to make sure that what one brings in against nothing is acknowledged. In (human) *agon* one can only think one has given something new to the world, provided one has been acknowledged as being an unlimited source of novelty by other human beings who have been acknowledged themselves as doing their bit.

The man of the agonistic gift knows that no one can keep himself unchanged, that there is no being; not an immutable being, nor permanent matter. All things prove to be fleeting appearances. Extensive (tangible) appearances and non-extensive appearances ('thoughts'), these constitute the

---

[2] In *agon* it is incomprehensible how Arthur Schopenhauer, who wanted to fight his predecessor (Kant), his seniors (especially Hegel) and his contemporaries, could possibly think that the will was 'one'.

[3] Cfr. J. Dewitte, *Il ne fallait pas. Notes sur le don, la dette et la gratitude (You shouldn't have. Notes on Gifts, Debt and Gratitude)* Revue du Mauss semestrielle, n° 8, pp. 102-113.

world. The followers of *agon* are, in a way, familiar with Heraclitus, with Friedrich Nietzsche or with Marcel Conche, even if they have never read them.

Emphasizing the *agon* in one's dealings with others and with the world means stressing the certainty that everything is but an appearance that has to be brought about. In *agon*, what is usually called 'reality' exhausts itself in appearing. In *agon*, things — be they extended or not — have no essence or nature whatsoever. They are founded on nothing. They affirm themselves against nothing. This is what the experience of the friends of *agon*, what their intuition and their immediate, more or less conscious knowledge is all about. A being is not, beings are not. There are only quasi-beings, fake beings, so to speak; they are appearances that constitute themselves through consumption of energy, and then dissolve themselves in the same way. These would-be beings are and are not at the same time, and from the same point of view. But still they do not reveal themselves as nothing. The *agon* just emphasizes the lightness of all things, including the densest. And all those appearances mask nothing. There is nothing behind them, there is nothing to unveil but yet other appearances, as the Talmud says according to Manfred Flamenbaum.

Sportsmen, amongst others, live this experience of ephemerality and accept it, or rather choose it. They are more or less conscious of the fact that the appearances are nothing but refusals of nothing, are nothing but energies that momentarily oppose the empire of nothingness. No 'hidden world' behind the gratuitous action, the action, that is, for the sake of the beauty of the mere gesture against nothing. They know that their supreme efforts, like those of Achilles or Cantona, have already vanished into thin air. The follower of *agon* cherishes the memory of the heroes, but knows that memories occupy people's minds only very temporarily and provided people have the will to remember. Memories will erase themselves in all sorts of ways when the species of appearances called 'human beings' will have disappeared, and no doubt even much sooner than that. The invincible nothing renders every appearance ephemeral. The battle can never be won by the appearances. It can only be resumed by new combatants. Combatants failing, the combat would cease.

The friends of the *agon* think that time results from the struggle against nothing; they think that time only lasts for as long as the struggle is going on, and that it is a good thing that the combatants are succeeded by other combatants. As to space, the friends of the *agon* know that it is constituted by a multitude of tangible appearances, struggling simultaneously against nothing. Wanting to abolish time and space means wanting the big game, the big combat against nothingness, to cease; it means craving for the empire of nothing.

In *agon* life makes a long nose at death — a death no one wants to eliminate. Not even by an artefact. No artefact is immortal. It is only a matter of fighting nothingness, of resisting nothing. And in fighting that battle the follower of the *agon* finds joy because he sees that nothing does not reign.

**Language**

"Being is the most fundamental category of language" observes Marcel Conche, after so many others. In *agon*, no being, we have said. Thus, as far as the *agon* is concerned, coherent language which necessarily presupposes stability, says nothing. Coherent language is an illusion. In *agon* one distrusts language, especially conceptual language, which tends to posit a world of 'ideas' behind the world of appearances. Each being is but an illusion conveyed by language.

When a follower of the *agon* tries to express the *agon*, he is contradicted by the language he uses, and arduous specialists of the concept will not refrain from showing that he is mistaken. Does that mean that in *agon* one has to be silent? Not at all. Chatter pretending to say nothing but what it says, makes a mockery of being, of contradicting and of logic. Chattering, then, suits the friends of the *agon* perfectly because, even though the words do not express being, they are not nothing. To express something, and at the same time express its exact opposite, is not nothing. The words are not totally devoid of meaning because they occur, become and disappear like everything else. From this point of view, they express the appearances, and they express themselves, without expressing being. By themselves, they express the agonistic world.

Of course, the word 'being' should at least be eliminated in order to talk about the *agon*. But the followers of the *agon* do not bother in the least. They make fun of the verb *to be* and listen to the scattering words. The words, the phrases, are but games of sound and sense, games which, like everything else, lose their way in the slowly evaporating space that is constituted by the appearances. The words are acts in the same way the appearances are actions. One could perhaps hold back Cyrano de Bergerac as a symbol of the followers of the *agon*, who agonistically gives a nose, words, thrusts of his sword and love.

**Meteor actions and agonistic polytheism**

I mentioned before that the appearances prove to be acts. The agonistic actions constitute the world. The agonistic action is, first of all, an action ('energy', 'force', 'will') facing nothing. In *agon*, an action has no origin other than itself. It proves to be its own origin. It causes and is caused at the same time. It is a free 'fiat' as it were. Generally speaking, the one who is his own origin, is called 'god'. This leads me to say that in *agon* every action is divine. The vision of an agonistic world is polytheistic. The *agon* that radiates within the agonistic gift, is a multitude of divine actions. This way, all the appearances are, without any exception, divine. The world is full of gods who establish relations, give, receive and render. It is quite simple, there is nothing more to it than that. In *agon* the gods are not restricted to the olympic gods. It was Heraclitus who claimed that even his kitchen was crowded with them.

The world is constituted by the gods who emerge, sometimes grow, and die. The gods arrange the world of appearances, that is to say, they arrange the world pure and simple. But it has to be understood that the gods are mortal, that they have no being. These gods ignore the meaning of cult or sacrifice, and they can give no commands whatsoever.

Consequently, in *agon* the world seems to be nothing but permanent emergences, rivalries and vanishments of the gods. Hardly abusing Marcel Conche, I would say that the agonistic world view deserves to be referred to as a meteorism, if I were not so deeply suspicious of the suffix 'ism', and if one can see in the emerging of the meteors, in their being sudden, unregulated, changing and 'disappearing', an image of the living, and more generally speaking, of all the appearances that compose the cosmos itself.

The multitude of appearances that inflame, collide, reconcile and fade away, appearances that make place for new, resembling or dissimilar appearances, cannot be a multitude of identical appearances. Among themselves the appearances play some of the games they play with nothing. They oppose each other, they rivalize, they distinguish themselves, without ever excluding themselves. All these meteors contradict one another, be it without presenting themselves as mutually exclusive. In *agon* there is no exclusion because there is no 'truth'. Only nothing seems to be bluntly refused. The differences are differences in appearance that are underlined in the conflict between the appearances. The *agon* loathes uniformity which resembles nothing. Diversity is a stranger to nothing. *Agon* favours the most outspoken diversity, novelty, originality. This shows itself in challenge, animosity, quarrel, controversy. In *agon*, everything thrives only on contradiction. But *agon* abhors extermination and complete destruction, even though it is not troubled by disappearance and death. *Agon* also loathes domination, oppression and persecution, even though it is not embarrassed by the display of the powers of the appearances. On the contrary

**The agonistic quasi-ethics**

Evil is nothing. Good are the appearances, the diversity, the profusion, the invention, the excellence, the supreme efforts, the gift, etc. But in *agon*, it is convenient to look at things from more than one angle. Compared to nothing, every thing equals every other thing: $1 = 1$ as a matter of principle, because, compared to nothing, every appearance proves to be something already. From that angle, that is to say as compared to nothing, this electron is worth as much as this blade of grass or this horse or this human being, because, like all the rest, an electron is not nothing. *Agon* is first of all combatting nothing, it is somehow causing that 'there be'. From this point of view, one appearance of whatever kind suffices to make sure that 'there is'. One appearance, only one, and nothing cannot triumph. The battle is not lost. As Marcel Conche explains, or Parmenides according to Conche, 'there is' cannot be half there. If there is something, it is not just a bit there or half there. There is, that is all. From this angle, it does not matter one whit what it is. On its own, one electron makes that 'there is'. From the angle of 'there is' the profusion and the diversity can be ignored.

It is a matter of fundamental equality between the different things that appear. In this kind of chess game which the big game of the world against nothing can be seen as, one chessman, as a chessman, is worth as much as another, because a piece is a piece like any other piece. In so far as it is a chessman, a pawn is worth as much as a rook or a queen.

Nevertheless, behind this basic equality facing nothing — 'behind' meaning if and when one finds oneself in the middle of the world of appearances — things are no longer equivalent. In that case it is the violence or the quality of the attack against nothing that counts. In that case, a queen is a lot more valuable than a pawn, an elephant clearly 'outvolumes' an electron, and a peacock is worth more than its weight in cow dung.

Why? Simply because this is the way the appearances want it to be.

What is fundamentally at stake in *agon* is to make the difference between the world and nothing. In the big game against nothing, the equality of the appearances reveals itself as a basic principle. But on the level of the relations between appearances, differentiation and originality are sources of value, provided they do not play the game of nothing. *Agon*, then, is both on the side of recognizing everything that appears, and on the side of searching for the distinction between those appearances.

It may also be noted that, notwithstanding the cannibalistic behaviour of the appearances, *agon* presupposes a certain solidarity of the appearances facing nothingness. Pure violence and pure destruction are unacceptable in *agon* because they play the game of nothing. It is disgraceful to love nothing. Shame! (*aidos!* said Jean Alruc) on he who favours nothing. Beauty and goodness are tied to what clearly opposes nothing ... for nothing.

All this entails a number of consequences in the field of 'behaviour' — undoubtedly one cannot speak of ethics here. First of all, there is the imperative need for solidarity between all the appearances in their struggle against nothing. If, to facilitate one's task, one looks at things from the human point of view — that is to say from the point of view of a species of appearances that is more or less conscious — some spontaneous attitudes can be observed. For instance, whoever sees a child which is about to fall into a well, will rush to its rescue. Whoever witnesses a man being crushed by a rock or attacked by an animal, will make every effort to help him. Whoever meets a lost stranger, will try to show him the way, etc. Hardly abusing Stobee and François Jullien, one could say that in *agon* one notices within man a feeling of benevolence towards all human beings; a feeling that demonstrates the bond between human beings or the importance of human solidarity; finally, a feeling that affirms the preciousness of humanity. This bond is found between human appearances of the same generation, but also and especially between the appearances of different generations; the ancient ones seem to be eager to strain every nerve in order for the new ones to be able to blossom.

What about 'quasi-ethics' then? What is more or less spontaneously and often unconsciously experienced within the scope of the big game against nothing, becomes conscious and sought-after for the champions of the *agon*.

And solidarity does not stop there. On another level it applies to animal, vegetative and mineral appearances. In *agon*, whoever notices a fledgling that has fallen out of the nest will try to save it. Whoever sees a drowning fly will attempt to fish it out of the liquid. Whoever sees a cut-off tree or a lacerated mountain is subject to sadness — many are those who risk being overwhelmed by empathic feelings arising from their agonistic world view.

In *agon* there is a kind of sympathy for everything that fights nothing, and one likes the sight of new appearances emerging; one takes much trouble for new appearances to be able to emerge. In the big fight against nothing, abortion for instance can posit a problem, and so can the extermination of certain animals, even though they may have been judged to be pests. To moderate somehow what I suggested just now and to avoid misunderstandings, let us say that all the species that aim at confiscating everything and at wiping out everything but themselves, must be fought. Clouds of locusts or flocks of starlings, for instance, that overpower other appearances and try to destroy them, must be weakened without any doubt because they have a tendency to install a kind of domination and uniformity resembling those of nothing. The overabundance of one single species of appearances on the one hand, and the profusion of the appearances on the other, are not a good match at all.

**First conclusion: equality, solidarity, difference**

I think this little agonistic metaphisics allows one to grasp the bond between the three dimensions of the gift in the agonistic perspective. The fundamental combat is the battle against nothing. This entails the following consequences:

1. A certain equality between things. Facing nothing, from the 'point of view of nothing' if one may say so, it proves to be indifferent whether this or that thing appears; it is in fact quite the same. This possible thing has neither more nor less value than that possible thing. Six of one, half a dozen of the other. They are both equally ruinous to the empire of nothing.

2. A certain solidarity between things. Facing nothing, from the 'point of view of nothing' (once more, if one may say so) the multitude of things that appear constitutes an entity that is uniform, homogeneous, solidary, united, unique. Besides, from the point of view of the big combat, things have an effective interest in working together.

3. A certain difference between things. Facing nothing, from the 'point of view of the appearances and of each appearance separately' (if one may say so) all things are neither equal nor undifferentiated. Facing nothing, between appearances, there is the struggle to distinguish oneself, to make one's difference, to characterize oneself, to appear more, to enrich the world, to add to its value. There is also the struggle for recognition, that is to say, the battle to get one's contributions and one's merits acknowledged, together with the search for the gratitude of the other appearances because of what one gives to the world, because of what one lavishly scatters in the combat with nothing.

On the human level, this triple exigence carries along an 'insociable sociability' that has little to do with the ideal relationships that are envisaged by the paralysed being.

**Second conclusion: agonistic gifts and love**

I think this little agonistic metaphysics also allows one to establish a relationship between the agonistic gift and love. From the angle of *agon*, there are at least three conceivable and always intertwined dimensions of love.

1. First of all there is the plain esteem, the unsophisticated consideration one has for all the things one knows to share fundamentally the combat against nothing. Here we are dealing with the respect we have for everything we recognize as similar to ourselves. This entails near-contractual relationships in which quasi-contractants try to respect each other mutually and to commit themselves reciprocally. This mutual disposition especially entails exchanges on a basis of equality. Trading or so-called swapping could set the tone here — I use the term *so-called* because in *agon*, as we know, there is no such thing as pure swapping.

2. Next, there is *agapè* (if you wish), fraternity[4], attachment, devotion, altruism, benevolence, etc., which entail sharing and communalization. On the level of the appearances of our species, this can be called 'philanthropy'. But this love dimension can go beyond the frontiers that enclose humanity, and can reveal itself as sympathy for all appearances, or rather sympathy *with* all appearances, whatever they are. Here everything counts. It is a matter of holistic love; it is perhaps a matter of a kind of tenderness for everything that

---

[4] Or 'phraternity' if on wants to rub out all references to filiation.

appears, a tenderness that is indifferent to differences. In short, the tendency to 'fusing' in love is at stake here.

3. Finally, there is the elective inclination. Here a *certain* appearance counts, not *any*. This particular appearance — its attraction, its seduction — is important because one attributes value to it, because it is what it is. We recognize the splendour of this appearance which is different from the other appearances, which is unique and incomparable, and we seek its recognition. This cannot be achieved without struggling. But this struggle can develop into a harmony which fits together all the dimensions of love in a kind of tense equilibrium. The equality of lovers that reveals itself then, is no longer the basic equality I mentioned before; it is an equality which is conquered in the struggle for recognition. It is the equality of the different 'equals'[5]. To illustrate what is at stake here, one could talk about Achilles and Patrocles, about Montaigne and de La Boétie, or many other more. But I shall rather tell the story of Oshun and Shango. For this purpose I will summarize and hardly modify the beautiful Afro-Cuban tale Julien Rémy tells in his text *Dons jouant*, a text which, as a matter of fact, deals with love from the agonistic point of view.

Oshun was a splendid young girl and an unequalled dancer. She fascinated all the young men of her island but she ignored all their glances.

At a party she was fascinated by the handsome Shango, the best drummer of the isle. After listening to him, she went up to him, greeted him ceremoniously and said: "Shango, you are the greatest among the *tamboreros*. Honour me with a visit." But Shango responded: "No, Oshun, you do not deserve my attention."

From that moment on, Oshun never missed a party where the *tamborero* who had dared to humiliate her in front of all her admirers was playing. Sometimes she danced, her body covered with honey. The people surrounding her contemplated the best dancer in extasy. But Shango was obviously not interested in her. And one day, he even declared to her in front of everybody: "Young girl, I have no confidence in you."

Oshun fled, head bowed, but she did not give in. One night, she even went so far as to slip into Shango's hammock. He was not strong enough to resist her caresses.

Nevertheless, Shango continued to humiliate her unceasingly. Oshun swallowed all these humiliations without cursing.

And then, suddenly, Shango did not play that well any more. And, utterly unmoved, the lovely Oshun watched the downfall of the *tamborero*. Finally, the day arrived on which Shango's pride obliged him to stop beating his drum at parties. He retired in an isolated house, then, where he could not hear the sound of drumming.

---

[5] In *agon* one can join Alain Caillé who considers 'equality' to be a value.

Then Oshun went to see and comfort him. She offered him everything she possessed.

From that moment on, Shango, overcome with admiration, started to admit the love he had already been feeling for Oshun for a long time, and, in his turn, he offered her everything he possessed.

It goes without saying that they married and had a lot of children, all of them rebels. Their life was not a *sinecure*, but they enjoyed it anyway.

A beautiful tale. A tale that shows how mutual recognition builds up through struggle and denial; how harmony rhymes with conflict; how, next to the equality of principle, a second equality can be constituted, born out of difference; and, finally, how communalization and sharing can be transfigured by the *agon*, and can become harmony.

Love can never be only *agapè*, exchange, or the will to reproduce the world. It also turns out to be the election of whatever radiates here and now in the world, that is to say, choosing the other, free recognition.

In the gift one cannot separate rivalry, solidarity and exchange. I think the same thing holds for love. The 'savages' think or decide that love is, first of all, rivalry, seduction; the christians think or decide that love is, first of all, *agapè*; the 'modernists' want love to be, first of all, exchange. The postmodern 'meteors' think and decide that love is all these things at the same time, and thus tend towards the *agon*. They also estimate that the only unacceptable passion is the passion one can feel for nothing[6], because that kind of love goes against the interests of the world and the gift. Obviously, those interests simply turn out to be that there be *something* rather than *nothing*.

---

[6] The film *Funny Games* shows very clearly what this passion can be like. Other examples that spring to the mind: the Algerian massacres, the contempt for the unemployed, the 'megamachine' (Serge Latouche), and the industrial pollution. Cf. S. Latouche, *La mégamachine* (La Découverte, Paris, 1995).

# Gift-giving Practice and Noncontextual Habitus: How (not) to be Fooled by Mauss[1]

Christian ARNSPERGER[2] (Hoover Chair, Université Catholique de Louvain)

## 1. The 'paradigm of the gift' and Mauss' inconsistencies

The widespread interest aroused by Marcel Mauss' analysis of gift and countergift in his *Essai sur le don* is puzzling in more than one respect. One of the reasons is that, as is quite apparent at least among Mauss' admirers, the famous 'giving-receiving-giving back' triad has come to be considered as the avenue towards the foundation of a new 'paradigm' of the social link[3]. I will, for the moment, remain content with this rather hazy formulation because it seems to me that any serious reader of Mauss is confronted with the classical question which any sociological and/or philosophical (let alone economic) endeavour must address: does the Maussian 'model' — assuming this expression can be made sense of in this context — offer the ideal image of what our society *ought to be like* if its members were to convert, so to speak, to an ethics of the gift which has been lost and has receded into the misty past? Or does it merely provide a phenomenology of unveiling which describes the way our society *in fact operates* without our being aware of it?

One can hardly say that Mauss' own position is unambiguous on this point. His "conclusions de morale", which make up but a small ten pages at the end of the *Essai* but have attracted more philosophical commentary than the one hundred and forty others, betray a deep difficulty as to the status of his analysis of the gift. On the one hand, Mauss[4] writes that

> "It is possible to extend these *observations* to our own societies. A considerable part of our morals and our lives themselves *are still located* within this atmosphere of the gift, of obligation and freedom intertwined." [my emphasis]

This passage seems to point to an unambiguously phenomenological approach, an approach of unveiling so to speak, to the observation of gift and

---

[1] M. Mauss, 'Essai sur le don: Forme et raison de l'échange dans les sociétés archaïques' ('The Gift: Forms and Functions of Exchange in Archaic Societies'), published originally in *Annales de Sociologie* (1924), reprinted in M. Mauss, *Sociologie et anthropologie* (Paris: Presses Universitaires de France, 1950).

[2] Thanks are due to Toon Vandevelde for his friendly last-minute invitation to the Leuven conference and his very kind hospitality throughout the two days of work, and to Alain Caillé and Luc Bouckaert for their stimulating comments during the session.

[3] See for example J. Godbout, *'Notes pour défendre le futur paradigme du don'* ('Notes to Defend the Future Paradigm of the Gift') in *Transdisciplines*, 1 (1997) pp. 109-115.

[4] M. Mauss, *op. cit.*, p. 258.

countergift practices. And indeed, at the very beginning of the *Essai*,[5] Mauss says he believes he has "found here one of the human bedrocks on which *our societies are built*" [my emphasis], so that the message seems to be simply this: if you observe things closely, you will see that our social and economic practices, although they look like they are based exclusively on exchange and on anonymous contracting, are *in fact* based on something different altogether, which exists in all societies. However, Mauss constantly slips from this phenomenological-descriptive stance towards a much more strongly prescriptive one — as if, somewhat in the manner of the modern *Dasein* as analyzed by Heidegger, we were these days living with a 'forgetfulness of the gift', a kind of *Gabensvergessenheit* which we need to counteract by putting ourselves back into a position where we lend our ears to the 'call of the gift'. Indeed, Mauss[6] writes that "it is not enough to observe the fact: *we must* deduce from it a form of practice, a moral precept" [my emphasis]. The two pages that follow contain mostly practical prescriptions punctuated (as Derrida[7] has very perceptively indicated) by numerous instances of 'it is necessary that' and 'we must'. And the list of prescriptions ends with the following sentence[8] which illustrates perfectly the Maussian paradox: "By doing so, we shall be returning, or so I claim, to the perennial foundation of law, to the very source of normal social life."

So this is Mauss' position: our society — our contract law, our market exchanges, our customs of good manners and civility, and so on — already functions 'secretly' along the lines of a 'giving-receiving-giving back' scheme, but by (re)gaining awareness of this we can tap into a surplus of interpersonal generosity; and this surplus is the only way to 'rescue' the (supposedly unavoidable and immutable) bedrock on which social relations have been built over millennia ... There is, on the one hand, a kind of nostalgic hope of a more 'authentic' reciprocity between persons, and, on the other, the claim that this reciprocity has in fact never ceased to be active, possibly even within our seemingly least reciprocitary activities, and at any rate in their immediate vicinity ... In other words, we are summoned to convert to something which is already active within ourselves without our being aware of it. (This is indeed the reason why Mauss writes of an 'atmosphere of gift' and why, more recently, Jacques Godbout has entitled one of his books *L'esprit du don*.[9])

---

[5] M. Mauss, *op. cit.*, p. 148.

[6] M. Mauss, *op. cit.*, p. 262.

[7] J. Derrida, *Donner le temps: 1. La fausse monnaie* (*Giving Time: 1. False Money*) (Paris: Galilée, 1991) pp. 85-87.

[8] *Ibid.*, p. 263.

[9] J. Godbout (in collaboration with A. Caillé), *L'esprit du don* (*The Spirit of the Gift*) (Paris: La Découverte, 1992).

This position seems to me rather surprising — not so much because it roughly replicates the conventional conversional scheme of a religion (this in itself is not disturbing since, as I will show below, the very notion of 'conversion' is not exclusively reserved for religious discourse), but because it introduces a stark contrast with the *substance*of Mauss' own ethnographic data. As Karsenti[10] has well demonstrated,

> "The disinterestedness and generosity displayed by the donator (...) are mixed with an aspect of ordering, of defiance towards the receiver, who is compelled to acknowledge the social superiority of his rival. In this sense generosity, far from being free and undetermined, is clearly geared to *the desire to dominate the person to whom one gives and to impress on him a form of power*. (...) What gift exchange expresses is *a fight for prestige, an essentially symbolic combat* in which what is at stake is the social positioning of the subject, his 'rank,' as well as his recognition by those members of the group to whom this gesture is addressed. Thus, gift exchange appears as the cristallization of the agonistic relationships that link the individuals together; it is, to borrow Marshall Sahlins' expression, the 'substitute of the war of all against all which for Hobbes characterized the State of Nature, and in this quality it represents the very condition of sociality. (...) Gift exchange therefore is an exchange, and introduces reciprocity, only to the extent that *it is also and at the same time a form of combat*. It represents symbolically *the never-ending fight which perpetuates the social link in the very movement by which it endangers it*." [my emphasis]

Gift and countergift, indefinitely repeated, thus act as a kind of mechanism for the *sublimation* of intersubjective violence. Therefore, it appears that in the last part of his *Essai*, Mauss has moved from a largely Hobbesian view of the gift-countergift system, in which rival factions seem to be engaged in infinite circles of reciprocal gift-giving designed each time to humiliate or to defy the opposing party, towards recommendations expressed in the form of an *anti*-Hobbesian ethical call. Let us carefully heed his formulation[11]:

> "Fortunately, everything is not yet classified exclusively in terms of purchase and sale. Things still have *a sentimental value* in addition to their value as commodities — provided the latter form of value can even be thought to exist. We do not possess only a *merchant's morality*. We still have in our midst people and classes which uphold *yesterday's moral standards* and almost all of us heed these standards, be it only at certain times of the year or in certain occasions." [my emphasis]

It is difficult here to disentangle the nostalgia for what once was and the factual description of what exists. Whatever the case may be, it does seem that in this passage Mauss locates the gift-countergift scheme *outside* the market logic which is expressed in buying and selling. This is confirmed by the well-known

---

[10] B. Karsenti, *Marcel Mauss: Le fait social total (Marcel Mauss: the Total Social Fact)* (Paris: Presses Universitaires de France, 1994) pp. 31-32, p. 34.

[11] M. Mauss, *op. cit.*, p. 258.

sentences which underlie the work of those who want to transform Mauss' analysis into a new 'paradigm'[12]:

> "Thus, from one extremity of human evolution to the other, there are no two forms of wisdom. Let us therefore adopt as a principle in our lives what has always been a principle *and will always be one:* to go out of oneself, to give, freely and out of obligation; we do not run the risk of making a mistake."[13] [my emphasis]

> "These facts shed light not only on our morals and are helpful not only in *shaping our ideal;* rather, using these facts as vantage points, we are better able to analyze the most general economic facts, and such an analysis even helps to *design better management procedures applicable to our societies.* At various points, we saw *how far removed* this gift exchange economy was *from the framework of the so-called natural economy, of utilitarianism.*"[14] [my emphasis]

These nice sentences are indeed liable to make us forget — and show that Mauss himself is quick in forgetting — what, like it or not, continues to underlie the gift-countergift scheme: rivalry and the desire for power and humiliation. Mauss' blatant inconsistency comes out particularly clearly in the following passage[15] in which he discusses the notions of 'utility' and 'interest':

> "To be the first, the most beautiful, the luckiest, the strongest and the richest — this is what one is looking for and this is how one gets it [in the magical *kula* ritual]. (...) In this case wealth is, in all respects, as much a means to prestige as an object of utility. But are we so sure that things are different today, and that even amongst us wealth *is not primarily a means to gain command over people?* (...) [The notion of interest], too, does not present itself [in the archaic societies studied here] in the same way as it functions in our own minds. If there is any common motive which drives the Trobriand or American chiefs, the Adaman clans, and so on, or which used to drive generous Hindus, noble Germans or Celts, in their gifts and their expenses, it is not the cool reason of the merchant, the banker and the capitalist. In these civilizations, people act out of interest, but in a way that is different from our times. People save, *but with a view to making expenses in order to have 'faithful henchmen'.* People pay back with usurious interest, *but with a view to humiliating the initial donator or exchange partner, and not only to reward him for the loss his 'differred consumption' caused him.* There is interest, but this interest is only analogous to that which, supposedly, drives us." [my emphasis]

Let us be clear: in their quality of descriptive observations, these claims are entirely valid and cannot be put into question. However, from a *normative*

---

[12] See, in particular, J. Godbout (in collaboration with A. Caillé), *L'esprit du don (The Spirit of the Gift)* (Paris: La Découverte, 1992) and A. Caillé, *Don, intérêt et désintéressement (Gift, Interest and Disinterestedness)* (Paris: La Découverte, 1994).

[13] M. Mauss, *op. cit.*, p. 265.

[14] *Ibid.*, p. 266.

[15] *Ibid.*, pp. 270-271.

point of view, we cannot but conclude that Mauss does not know what he wants — worse still: with alarming lightheadedness, he amalgamates the idea of 'generosity' with practices which, personally, I would certainly never want to see generalized in society. Deep down, and despite some of his undeniable left-wing commitments, Mauss is probably still influenced by a kind of turn-of-the-century aristocratism which highly valued 'noble' acts of heroism and the paternalism of the 'chiefs'. True enough, he himself acknowledges that the social scheme he has in mind "is in the painful process of being born"[16], but this hardly suffices to erase the normative force of the prescriptions he has drawn from his empirical data: "These facts shed light (...) on our morals and are helpful (...) in shaping our ideal."[17]

Thus, the main blind spot in Mauss' theory is this rather magical 'transmutation' of a social practice embedded within a thick web of mutual rivalries into a call for the practice of generosity. It therefore seems to me that taking Mauss as a point of departure to directly extract from his *Essai* the roots of a new 'paradigm' is to fool oneself: Mauss was unable to transcend his own inconsistency and to suggest real philosophical foundations for the place to be occupied by gratuity in society. If, on the contrary, one does believe that he proposed an interesting avenue of reflexion by showing how the 'giving-receiving-giving back' triad could serve as the cement of society, one is then compelled to recognize that this view has hardly moved beyond a quasi-Hobbesian vision of society, a vision of generosity as the sublimation of violence. How, then, can we make sense of this 'transmutation' of gift-giving into generosity on which Mauss relies without ever offering a foundation for it? How can we think along the lines of Mauss, but better than Mauss and hence, necessarily, *against* him?

I will now try to show that in order to carry out this task we have to start from Bourdieu and go against Bourdieu — in the direction of Levinas ... And we have to do this without ever losing sight of the fact that what is at stake is not merely the crudite juxtaposition of authors, but an answer to the question of *the conditions under which the practice of gift-giving can be seen as foundational for the social link.*[18]

---

[16] *Ibid.*, p. 273

[17] Already quoted earlier.

[18] I will leave aside here the (in itself very important) question of what room there might be within the Maussian and the Levinasian perspectives for the kind of individual calculation and 'optimization' postulated by economists. I discuss this question in detail in Ch. Arnsperger, 'Action, responsabilité et justice: Pertinence et limites de la notion économique d'altruisme' ('Action, Responsibility and Justice. Scope and limits of the Economic Notion of Altruism'), in *Revue Philosophique de Louvain* 95 (1997) pp. 484-516, and Ch. Arnsperger, 'Gratuité, don et optimisation individuelle: Levinas, Derrida et l'approche économique' ('Gratuity, Gift and Individual Optimization: Levinas, Derrida and the Economic Approach), in *Transdisciplines,* 1 (1997) pp. 43-74. In both of these papers, I defend the position that the critique usually directed against economic theory about its alleged inability to account for altruism otherwise than by 'calculation'

## 2. A first step to avoid being fooled: Bourdieu, the 'work of time', and the social habitus

A hard-line sociologist can directly answer my objection that Mauss remained at a quasi-Hobbesian stage in his understanding of gift-giving by saying that the point is not to dream up the social link, but to describe it. If the 'giving-receiving-giving back' scheme does indeed act as the cement of society, there is no use in lamenting what is then a factual state of affairs; rather, one has to investigate the channels from which the practice of gift-giving derives this power. As we know, this is the position of Pierre Bourdieu, in particular, for whom philosophers are always much too preoccupied with ideal types and hence fall prey to a 'scholastic' mode of thought instead of trying to apprehend the social link as it is. Bourdieu's merit is that he points out the aspect of Mauss' analysis which, in my view, deserves the most attention, namely, what Bourdieu calls the 'double truth of the gift', its quality of being both free and obligatory.[19] As Mauss[20] observes very insightfully at the outset of his study,

> "Of all [the possible themes concerning exchanges and contracts in archaic societies], I want here to consider but one single trait, which is deep but isolated: the voluntary character, or one might say *the apparently free and gratuitous, yet constrained and interested* character of these provisions. They have almost always taken the shape of a present, of a gift generously offered — even when in this gesture which accompanies the transaction there is only fiction, formalism and social lie, and when in the end it is driven by obligation and economic interest." [my emphasis]

By now we know that the notion of economic interest which Mauss invokes here is not necessarily that of monetary gain or of 'utility', and that it includes

---

is misguided — or, more precisely, that the fact that altruism might involve a form of calculation (which may sometimes be the case) can in no way serve to *criticize* economic theory. The reason is that, first of all, the existence of calculation need not in any sense indicate an egoistic interest. Furthermore, to the objection of Bourdieu that economics is the science of conscious calculation (an objection not addressed explicitly in the two above-mentioned papers), I would reply that it does not seem to me that economic theory needs to necessarily postulate a literally *conscious* mode of calculation. It seems to me one ought rather to see optimization as a *phenomenological description* of individual choice — independently of whether or not the self who optimizes is really 'fully self-conscious'. More precisely: Friedman's 'as if' seems to me to describe economic methodology rather adequately — as long as one views it not as a 'scientific' method of prediction, nor (more crucially) as a 'normative' prescription of rationality, but indeed as an *'analytical' descriptive metaphor*. The agent may not act *consciously* by optimizing such and such an order relation on such and such a feasible set, but the economist's effort is to *deconstruct* action as finely as possible in order to display the various components which may play a role. But this debate cannot be further developed here. (I am grateful to François Maniquet for the opportunity he gave me to first expand on these ideas informally in his graduate seminar on economic methodology in Namur in May 1998.)

[19] This theme of the 'double truth' is crucial in Bourdieu. See, in particular, post-scriptum no. 1 to chapter 5 of P. Bourdieu, *Méditations pascaliennes* (*Pascalian Meditations*) (Paris: Seuil, 1997) pp. 229-240.

[20] M. Mauss, *op. cit.*, p 147.

symbolic and/or magical aspects which, as I explained above, are equally undesirable. Nevertheless, the Maussian view as expressed here could very simply be restituted within a theoretical framework where agents maximize their interest *over time* by implicitly 'rewarding' their own present generosity with a discounted gift to be received in a more or less distant future. This is the kind of *intertemporal optimization* problem which economists would favour were they to translate Mauss' idea. In fact, Mauss himself does little else when, at some point in the *Essai*[21], he foreshadows what was later to become George Akerlof's theory of efficiency wages as gift exchange[22]:

> "One senses that *it is possible to elicit work effort only from men who are certain to be paid loyally* over their whole lives for the labour they have loyally executed, for others as well as for themselves. Today the producer-trader feels — and he has always felt — but this time with great acuity, that he exchanges more than a product or a quantity of work, and that he gives something of himself: his time, his life. *He therefore wants to be rewarded*, be it with moderation, *for this gift*. And to frustrate him of this reward means *to create an incentive for shirking and reduced productivity*." [my emphasis]

More generally, Mauss' tripartite scheme can be rather well explained in terms of the strategies of agents playing a repeated, *tit-for-tat* type game: in equilibrium, (1) no agent has any interest in not giving (possibly more than he received in the previous stage of the game) because the future sanction in terms of social exclusion would outweigh the short-run gain; and (2) no agent has any interest in refusing a gift, for much the same reason. Therefore, rational calculation seems to fit rather well with the conclusions which Mauss draws from his data. The reason is that the game theorist can perfectly well postulate an intertemporal structure of payments that takes into account what Mauss calls the 'collective expectation' (*attente collective*).[23] Indeed, as Sen[24] has shown among many others, game theory and the often used concept of Nash equilibrium does not at all exclude the possibility that the strategic calculations of the agents be influenced by noneconomic norms.

---

[21] *Ibid.*, pp. 272-273.

[22] See G. Akerlof, 'Labor Contracts as Partial Gift Exchange', in *Quarterly Journal of Economics*, 97 (1982) pp. 543-569. In fact, Akerlof refers to Mauss in his bibliography and briefly discusses the now famous relationship between the English *gift* and the German *Gift* (i.e. poison) in his section III. Surprisingly, however, he does not refer to the passage which I quote here.

[23] Quoted by B. Karsenti, *Marcel Mauss: Le fait social total (Marcel Mauss: the Total Social Fact)* (Paris: Presses Universitaires de France, 1994). Here is the whole passage from Mauss: "The expressions 'constraint', 'force', 'authority', have been used in the past, and they have their value, but this notion of collective expectation is, in my view, one of the fundamental notions with which we need to work. I do not know of any other notion that would thus generate law and economy: 'I expect' is the very definition of any collective action."

[24] A. Sen, 'Choice, Orderings and Morality', in S. Körner (ed.), *Practical Reason* (Oxford: Basil Blackwell, 1974).

Bourdieu never objects to a fundamental interpretation of the gift-countergift scheme in terms of interest: in fact, to his mind, few spheres of existence — if any — are free from interest in the broad sense — and Mauss, despite his lyrical evocations of generosity, never really contests this, either. The issue on which Bourdieu[25], however, parts with the economic approach is the assumption that the agents *perform calculations*:

> "Agents who are well-adjusted to the game [thanks to the internalization of the complex set of rules of the game which make up the habitus] are possessed by the game, and probably all the more so the better they are able to master it. For example, one of the privileges of having been born into a game is that one can dispense with cynicism because one has a sense of play [le sens du jeu] (...). Against the reduction to conscious calculation I pin the relationship of ontological complicity between the habitus and the field. The agents and the social world entertain a relationship of infraconscious and infralinguistic complicity: the agents constantly engage in their practices theses which they have not posed as such. (...) The social agents who have a sense of play, who have incorporated a myriad of practical schemes of perception and evaluation which function as instruments in the construction of reality, as principles of vision and division of the universe in which they evolve, have no need to posit the objectives of their practice as ends. They are not like *subjects* facing an object (or, even less so, a problem) construed as such by an intellectual act of knowledge; they are, rather, as we say, *immersed in their business* [tout à leur affaire] (...): they are present in 'what is to come' [l'àvenir], in 'what is to be done' [l'à faire], in the business [l'affaire], which are an immediate correlate of a practice(...) not posited as an object of thought, as a possibility envisaged within a project, but rather inscribed within the present of the game."

Thus Mauss' collective expectation, which forms the habitus of a constraint which people do not directly perceive as a constraint, constitutes a 'law' which imposes itself on the agents behind their backs, so to speak: one gives because 'that is the way things are done', one gives with a view to unconsciously capturing a fraction of 'symbolic capital', and so on.[26] It is the social habitus inside of which decisions to give are carried out which makes for the fact that 'the agents constantly engage in their practices theses which they have not posed as such.'

Bourdieu[27] emphasizes that the practice of gift-giving appears to each agent as free to the extent that, due to the *time interval* which separates gift and countergift, the overall social constraint which articulates the various acts of

---

[25] P. Bourdieu, *Raisons pratiques (Practical Reasons)* (Paris: Seuil, 1994) pp. 153-155.

[26] I will not insist here on this well-known dimension of the notion of interest in Bourdieu, i.e. the idea that a substantial part of what 'interests' agents lies in the order of symbolic capital. See, in particular, chapter 7 of P. Bourdieu, *Le sens pratique (Practical Meaning)* (Paris: Minuit., 1980), as well as chapter 6 of P. Bourdieu, *Raisons pratiques (Practical Reasons)* (Paris: Seuil, 1994).

[27] P. Bourdieu, *Le sens pratique (Practical Meaning)* (Paris: Minuit., 1980) pp. 178-189.

gift-giving never becomes visible, so that each particular act of gift-giving appears in itself as a free one. However, at the same time, the whole thing rests on a society-wide make-believe, on a collective relegation of the constraint into the unconscious: the Maussian gift is "a social constraint whose falseness or denial in the form of a free and gratuitous act is also the only truth".[28,29] In the end, the practice of gift-giving is able to act as the cement of society if it ignores its own nature of being a constraint and *appears to itself* as the putting into practice of generosity. The formation of a Bourdieusian habitus would then lead to a sort of self-evidence of the gift — one which would disqualify any assumption that agents perform *conscious* calculation, contrary to what is assumed, according to Bourdieu, in game theory. Indeed,[30]

> "For someone endowed with the dispositions that are appropriate to the economy of symbolic goods, generous behaviour is not the product of a choice of freedom and of virtue, or the product of a free decision made after a deliberation in which other possibilities of action are envisaged: it presents itself as 'the only sensible thing to do'."

Here we are, therefore, both very close to and very far from Mauss. On the one hand, through the idea of play (or of 'field', as Bourdieu often says) and that of habitus with which it is combined, one acknowledges the fact that the gift *as a practice* is conditioned below the surface by something which lies beyond the freedom of the individual — something which, on the contrary, gives individual freedom its contextual form: to give to such and such, in such and such a situation of *implicit and hence unrecognized debt*. On the other hand, with Bourdieu we are compelled to give up the 'generic' dimension of the gift which had led Mauss to designate the practice of gift-giving as 'one of the bedrocks upon which our societies are built'. But let us recall that it is precisely this generic dimension which we are here trying to 'salvage', in order to think in Maussian fashion but better than Mauss himself, and better than many

---

[28] B. Karsenti, *Marcel Mauss: Le fait social total* (Marcel Mauss: the Total Social Fact) (Paris: Presses Universitaires de France, 1994)

[29] See also the idea of "common miscognition" expounded in P. Bourdieu, *Méditations pascaliennes (Pascalian Meditations)* (Paris: Seuil, 1997) p. 230. The mention of the 'social lie' can be found in M. Mauss, *op. cit.*, p. 147. This idea renders rather problematic, it seems to me, the 'modest' characterization of the gift suggested in A. Caillé, *Don, intérêt et désintéressement (Gift, Interest and Disinterestedness)* (Paris: La Découverte, 1994) p. 270): "A gift is any provision carried out without any expectation of a well-defined return, [and] with a view to nourishing the social link." This is problematic, first of all, because the expression *without any expectation of a well-defined return* does not exclude that what might be at work, 'underneath' or 'unconsciously' as it were, is still Mauss' collective expectation; second, because the expression *with a view to* appears to express a *telos* without explaining who edicts it. Is it the donator? If so, there is still an expectation of return in the sense of Bourdieu because the *habitus* is at work. Is it the sociologist? If so, again, a 'secret' mechanism is at work which inscribes the gift within a circle of exchange.

[30] P. Bourdieu, *Méditations pascaliennes (Pascalian Meditations)* (Paris: Seuil, 1997) p. 231.

Maussians. Bourdieu's vision, in the end, reduces any decision to give, and even the *intention* to give, to an internalization of the social habitus, i.e. of the rules of the game which unconsciously govern the decisions and even the values of the members of a society. By definition, this habitus itself is never deconstructible, unless one lapses into what Bourdieu[31] calls the 'scholastic' spirit which, according to him, rests upon a much too naive faith in the 'absolute power of thought':

> "We have to renounce the illusion of the transparency of consciousness to itself as well as the representation of reflexivity commonly accepted by the philosophers (...), and we have to accept — in line with the typically positivist tradition of the critique of introspection — that the most efficient reflection is the one which consists in objectivating the subject of objectivation; by that I mean the reflection which, by stripping the knowing subject of the privilege which it usually attributes itself, makes use of all available instruments of objectivation (statistical surveys, ethnographic observation, historical research, and so on) in order to bring to light the presuppositions which it owes to its own inclusion within its object of knowledge."

The critique of pure reflexivity, the insistence on the 'infraconscious' or on what one might also call the *nonintentional*, the idea of a freedom governed by something which lies beyond freedom: all this brings us directly into contact with what Emmanuel Levinas writes about the relation between the 'I' and the 'other.' In fact, Levinas[32] writes these striking sentences, which bring us right back to the very heart of the problem from which we started, namely the Maussian 'transmutation' of gift-giving into generosity:

> "To say: here I am. To do something for another. To give. This is what it means to be a human spirit. The incarnation of human subjectivity guarantees its spirituality (for I do not see what angels might give each other or how they could help one another). I analyze the interhuman relation as if, in the nearness of the other — beyond whatever image I might have of the other person — his face, i.e. what is expressive in the other person (and the whole human body is, in this sense, more or less a face), were that which *orders* me to serve him."

This crystallizes a question which seems to me absolutely crucial for a correct understanding of Mauss' work: the conception of the gift-countergift scheme as a habitus, which, as Bourdieu has demonstrated convincingly in my view, is undeconstructible because any form of transcendental thought (of the Husserlian type, for instance) wrongly believes that it can fully clarify itself.[33]

---

[31] P. Bourdieu, *Le sens pratique (Practical Meaning)* (Paris: Minuit, 1980) ch. 1.
P. Bourdieu, *Méditations pascaliennes (Pascalian Meditations)* (Paris: Seuil, 1997) p. 21.
[32] E. Levinas, *Ethique et infini (Ethics and Infinity)* (Paris: Fayard, 1982). Page references are from the pocket edition (Paris: Le Livre de Poche, 1982) pp. 93-94.
[33] Throughout the present article I will assume that this critique of transcendental reflexivity is justified. In fact, I doubt that it is completely so, but I shall not enter this debate here. For a more detailed analysis of the place of the transcendental subject in the notion of altruism (in

But where does this undeconstructibility come from? Is it because the *social context* is undeconstructible, as Bourdieu claims, or is it because the *relation to the Other* is undeconstructible, as Levinas claims? Levinas might well turn out to be the most Maussian of all philosophers — if one accepts to *decontextualize the notion of* habitus *in a very specific way (i.e. in a nontranscendental way)*. This is an operation which many will find utterly unacceptable because at first glance it seems to empty Bourdieu's thought of its very substance; but it is the only operation, or so I will claim, which can allow us to give a foundation to gift-giving as the 'bedrock' which Mauss was searching for — although, as we shall see, that will lead us to abandon a good part of the Maussian (and Bourdieusian) discourse on 'interest' and to really focus on disinterestedness.[34]

## 3. Beyond Mauss' inconsistencies: Levinas' noncontextual habitus

Before moving on, let me briefly summarize the foregoing discussion. As I indicated, in his *Essai sur le don* Mauss abusively used his data on archaic social systems to draw prescriptions on 'generosity' for our contemporary societies. One might have concluded from this that his ethical call was unwarranted, and gone back to the classical political analysis of a quasi-Hobbesian contract based on the balancing of individual agents' violence. My personal option here, is completely different: on the contrary, I intend to *rescue* the Maussian ethical call — but in order to do this I need to eschew the Hobbesian undertones which Mauss himself upholds in his analysis of gift and coun-

---

connection with Husserl, Levinas and Derrida), see Ch. Arnsperger, 'Action, responsabilité et justice: Pertinence et limites de la notion économique d'altruisme' (Action, Responsibility and Justice: Scope and Limits of the Economic Notion of Altruism), in *Revue Philosophique de Louvain*, 95 (1997) pp. 484-516.

[34] In this sense, the name of M.A.U.S.S. ('Mouvement Anti-Utilitariste en Sciences Sociales') given to the movement which, in French-speaking circles, seeks to base a 'paradigm of the gift' on Mauss' *Essai* is difficult to justify — not so much because this movement is too confident in the ability of the practice of gift-giving to become installed as a social practice (which I believe is the case, but this objection can be directed with at least as much force against the thought of Levinas), but rather because, on the contrary, this movement *does not go far enough* in the exploration of the *transcendental foundations* which have to be provided for Mauss' thought if one is to escape Mauss' own inconsistencies. In my view, one should not just walk in Mauss' footsteps (as Alain Caillé urged me to do during the Leuven conference, saying that rather than working on Levinas I ought to join the Movement "*dans la fidélité à la pensée de Mauss*") — or, if one does, then only with a sort of ironic distance. The reason is simple: as I showed in section 1 above, no one has thought through the foundations of gift-giving as the basis for acceptable social relations (i.e. social relations that are not based on rivalry, be they only in sublimated form) less convincingly than Mauss himself. The present article therefore expands in a somewhat different direction the analysis which I began in Ch. Arnsperger, 'Gratuité, don et optimisation individuelle: Levinas, Derrida et l'approche économique' ('Gratuity, Gift and Individual Optimization: Levinas, Derrida and the Economic Approach'), in *Transdisciplines*, 1 (1997) pp. 43-74.

tergift, and which prohibit his jump from humiliation-oriented reciprocity to donation-oriented generosity. The contribution of Bourdieu's theory to this issue is ambiguous. He insists on the fact that 'something' makes it possible for the sequential and time-delayed gifts to appear to themselves as sincerely gratuitous — and this 'something' is a social habitus of the gift, a set of internalized rules which govern the agents unbeknown to them. However, this 'something' appears in Bourdieu as radically contextual and linked to *social rules* which he calls 'implicit', and which have shaped people's subjectivity *over historical time*.[35] Therefore, discovering this 'human bedrock upon which our society is built', as Mauss says, this transhistorical foundation of which he speaks when he writes that 'from one extremity of human evolution to the other, there are no two forms of wisdom', requires a rather different sort of analysis — one which is neither purely sociological (so as to uphold the normative character inscribed in Mauss' discourse) nor purely transcendental in a Husserlian sense (so as to take stock of Bourdieu's critique of reflexivity).

In my view, it is Levinas' analysis of intersubjectivity which best meets this challenge. In his description of the intersubjective relationship he insists on the fact that the subject's self is, in a way, taken aback by the irruption of exteriority and otherness, but that the latter is then, in turn, taken aback by the intentionality through which the self, by reclosing itself on itself, apprehends otherness 'from its own viewpoint', as it were. The description of this twofold phenomenological movement pervades a lot of Levinas' work; here is a formulation of it which is particularly well-suited for our present purposes:

> "The properly interhuman is a nonindifference of one for another, within a responsibility of one for the other, but *before the reciprocity of this responsibility, which will become inscribed in the impersonal laws, is superimposed on the pure altruism of this responsibility when it is inscribed in the ethical position of the self as self*; before any contract which would mark the moment where, precisely, reciprocity comes in and where, of course, altruism and disinterestedness can continue, but where they can also dwindle or become extinct. The order of politics — which is post-ethical or pre-ethical — inaugurated by the 'social contract' is neither the insufficient condition nor the necessary point of arrival of ethics. In its ethical position, the self is distinct both from the citizen who arises in the City and from the individual who, in his natural egoism, precedes

---

[35] See, in particular, P. Bourdieu, *Méditations pascaliennes (Pascalian Meditations)* (Paris: Seuil, 1997) p. 21: "The reason why there is so much implicit in what we think and say about the world is that we are involved in the world. To free thought of the implicit, one cannot be content with this return of thinking thought [la pensée pensante] on itself which is commonly associated with the idea of reflexivity; and only the illusion of the absolute power of thought can make us believe that the most radical of doubts will be able to suspend our prejudices, which are linked to our diverse affiliations, belongings, involvements, all things which we engage in our thoughts. The unconscious is a result of history — the collective history which produced our categories of thought, and the individual history through which they were instilled into us."

any order, but on whom political philosophy since Hobbes tries to build — or succeeds in building — the social and political order of the City. The interhuman lies also in the recourse to one another's help, before the other's prestigious otherness is made humdrum or becomes tarnished by the mere exchange of friendly services that will become established as 'interpersonal dealings' in our customs." [my emphasis]

Levinas[36] insists on the fact that the self is — paradoxically — *situated, but situated within a nonplace*, if by 'place' we mean a particular socio-economic environment. 'The self as self' is in a *position* which is ontological (in a non-Heideggerian sense) rather than inculcated, but which has to be in some way 'unveiled' or impressed anew upon the subject because it is so easy to become oblivious of it in the tendency of subjecticity to identify with the movement of intentionality. There is thus both a *formal* kinship and a *substantial* incompatibility between Levinas and Bourdieu: they both reject the idea that intentional-reflexive consciousness is 'primary' within the movement of subjectivity, but Bourdieu locates this implicit factor in a social and historical habitus whereas Levinas locates it in what I would venture to call a noncontextual habitus, the habitus of 'the otherness of the Other'.

But going further, we can discover that even inside their common opposition to self-transparent consciousness there is a difference which turns out to be revealing. For Bourdieu, the main flaw of the Husserlian analysis of intentionality (just like the vision of calculation which he attributes to economists) is the assumption that intentional movement is *capable of grasping itself as such*. What Bourdieu rejects is in fact not so much the 'primacy' of intentional consciousness as its alleged ability to transparently reflect on itself[37]:

> "If we want to account for human behaviour, we have to accept — against the intellectualist tradition of the *cogito*, of knowledge viewed as a relationship between a subject and an object, and so on — that they constantly rest on non-thetical theses; that they posit futures which are not targeted as futures. (...) Another way to express Husserl's opposition between protension and project is the opposition between *préoccupation* (which could serve as a translation of Heidegger's *Fürsorge*, but stripped of its undesirable connotations) and *planning* as the targeting of a future in which the subject thinks of himself as positing a future and organizing all available means by reference to this future posited as such, i.e. as an end to be attained explicitly. [On the contrary,] the player's preoccupation or anticipation is immediately present in something which is not immediately perceived and immediately available, but which is nevertheless virtually already here. Someone who dribbles with a ball acts in the present in relation to *something to come* [à un *à venir*] (and I am saying here 'to come' rather than 'future') which is almost present, which is inscribed in the very physionomy of the present, of the opponent who is *in the process of* shift-

---

[36] E. Levinas, *Entre nous — Essais sur le penser-à-l'autre (Between Us — Essays on Thinking-Towards-The Other)* (Paris: Grasset, 1991) p. 119.

[37] P. Bourdieu, *Raisons pratiques (Practical Reasons)* (Paris: Seuil, 1994) pp. 156-157.

ing to the wrong side. He does not posit this future within a project (I could move to this side or that): he sends the ball in that particular direction because his opponent is going in the other direction, i.e. is in a way already there. He determines himself in relation to a quasi-present inscribed in the present."

Thus, for Bourdieu (who symptomatically refers to his reading of Heidegger) subjectivity, immerged in its habitus, acts without reflecting (on) itself, but the locus where the habitus is inscribed remains a consciousness which is not 'disturbed' by otherness — an intentionality which is inchoative (this is the difference compared to Husserl) but which is nevertheless primarily intentional. Levinas, on the contrary, rejects precisely this primacy of intentionality itself (in the name, precisely, of a rejection of the Heideggerian vision of subjectivity as a 'letting come' or as a 'letting be'[38]). Still, his point of departure[39] looks deceptively close to Bourdieu's:

> "Once *intentionality* is introduced, consciousness must be understood as a mode of the voluntary. This is suggested by the word 'intention', and it provides the justification of the denomination of 'acts' conferred to the units of intentional consciousness. Furthermore, the intentional structure of consciousness is characterized by representation. This allegedly lies at the root of all consciousness, whether theoretical or non-theoretical. (...) Consciousness implies presence, positing-before oneself, in other words 'worldliness', the fact-of-being-given. It means being exposed to grasping, to taking, to com-prehension, to appropriation."

> "Is not intentional consciousness, within being, an active grasping of the stage where the Being of being [l'être des étants] unfolds, gathers and manifests itself? Is not consciousness like the very scenario of the never-ending effort of the *esse* towards this *esse* itself, the almost tautological exercise of the *conatus*? (...) But a consciousness directed towards the world and towards objects, structured as intentionality, is also *indirectly* — almost 'in addition' — conscious of itself (conscious of the active self which represents world and objects), as well as conscious of its very acts of representation, and conscious of its mental activity. But it is, nevertheless, an indirect and immediate consciousness, without an intentional goal [visée], an implicit and purely accompanying consciousness. (...) One is then — perhaps too quickly — drawn to consider, in philosophy, that this life is a knowledge not yet made explicit, or something like a still hazy representation which reflexion will bring into light."

Up to this point, Levinas' judgement of the Husserlian vision of consciousness is very similar to Bourdieu's: a totally sovereign reflexivity thinks it can dispel the veils which keep practice implicit. However, in the lines just following these, Levinas[40] suddenly parts from the Bourdieusian position:

---

[38] E. Levinas, *Entre nous: Essais sur le penser-à-l'autre* (*Between Us: Essays on Thinking - Towards - The Other*) (Paris: Grasset, 1991) pp. 17-18.

[39] *Ibid.*, pp. 145-146.

[40] *Ibid*, p. 146.

"The traditional critique against introspection has always suspected a modification which a so-called spontaneous consciousness would undergo under the scrutinizing, thematizing, objectivating and indiscrete gaze of reflexion — something like a violation and a disfiguring of some kind of secret. *This is a critique which is always refuted, and always born again."*

"What happens within this non-reflexive consciousness which is taken only to be prereflexive and which, being implicit, accompanies intentional consciousness when in reflexion it targets, intentionally, the self, as if the thinking self appeared in the world and belonged to the world? What occurs within this originary veiling, in this inexpressible thing, in this closing-on-itself of *the inexplicit*? *What might this alleged confusion, this implication, mean in positive terms so to speak?*" [my emphasis]

It is thus necessary, from a Levinasian perspective, to go beyond Bourdieu's claim about the implicit and his critique of the absolute power of reflective thought by investigating the 'positive' content of this implicit. As we saw, Bourdieu in this respect defends the idea of an 'objectivation of the subject of objectivation' through sociological analysis (surveys, ethnography, history, and so on). Levinas[41], on the contrary, rather suggests that we stay within the phenomenology of consciousness but that we push it further in order to rid it of its scolastic orientation:

"Does the 'knowledge' of prereflexive self-consciousness *know* in the usual sense of the word? Being a hazy consciousness, an implicit consciousness which precedes all intentions — or has relinquished all intention — it is not an act, but a pure passivity. (...) The nonintentional is outright passivity, and the accusative is, so to speak, its first 'case.' As a matter of fact this passivity, which is correlated to no action whatsoever, is less a description of the 'bad conscience' of the nonintentional than it can be described through this 'bad conscience'. And this bad conscience is not the finitude of existence signified by anxiety. (...) Within the passivity of the nonintentional — in the very mode of 'spontaneity' and before any formulation of 'metaphysical' ideas on this subject — what puts itself into question is the very justness of the position within being which gets affirmed by intentional thought, knowledge and grasp of the 'now-in-hand' [le main-tenant]: being as bad conscience; being in question, but also being put to the question, having to answer — which is the birth of language; having to speak for oneself, having to say 'I', being in the first person, being myself precisely; but, because of this, and in the affirmation of this being an 'I', having to answer for one's right to be. (...) One has to answer for one's right to be, not in reference to the abstraction of some anonymous law or of some juridical entity, but out of fear for the other. (...) It is a fear of all the violence and murder which my existing, despite its intentional and conscious innocence, is liable to perpetrate."

So here we are: the noncontextual habitus which Levinas has in mind is the *nonjuridical, one might say 'nonconventional'* locus where the subject is

---

[41] *Ibid.*, pp. 147-149.

summoned to answer for his 'I' in the face of the other. It is a *noncontextual habitus* because it is both general (we are talking about *the* relationship with the other, and with all others) and indeterminate (no social or cultural identity is being postulated); and it is a *habitus* in the sense that it gives subjectivity itself its form, shapes it without it being able to rebel — in short, it shapes it *implicitly*, as both Bourdieu and Levinas claim. The force of this Levinasian idea of 'passivity' is that it stays clear both of socio-historical contextualism and of transcendentalism.

Levinas draws from this analysis rather strong consequences for the notion of *freedom*. By inverting the idealist phenomenological sequence which would see the apperception of the other as a free intentional gesture, Levinas presents individual freedom as being 'set into motion' by the face-to-face with the other:

> "The face, the visage, is the fact that a reality is put in front of me; it is 'opposed' to me not in its manifestations, but in its manner of being which is, so to speak, ontologically opposite. It is that which resists me through its opposition, not that which opposes me through its resistance. I mean that this opposition does not reveal itself by clashing with my freedom: it is an opposition *which is prior to my freedom and which sets it into motion*."[42]

> "The self does not begin in the self-affectation of a self-sufficient self, but through the beginningless trauma, one which precedes all self-affectivity, of the sudden appearance of the other." (...) Starting from the situation of a responsibility which is not utopian, we have described the notion of a *finite freedom*. There exists a compossibility of freedom and the other which makes it possible to make sense of this notion of finite freedom without jeopardizing freedom in its finitude. (...) Within 'finite freedom', there emerges a region of freedom which is unaffected in its will — though not in its power — by finitude or limitation. Finite freedom is not infinite freedom acting within a finite framework, and hence limited. But it is the freedom of a self whose unlimited responsibility (not measured in terms of freedom, and irreducible to nonfreedom) requires subjectivity as that which nothing and no one can replace, and which shows it to be passivity in its naked form (...). It is finite because it is a relationship with another; it remains freedom because this other is the other person [cet autre est autrui]. It consists in *doing what one has the vocation to do*, doing what no one else than myself can do. Thus, *while limited by the other, it remains freedom*, because it emanates from *a heteronomy which is inspiration — an inspiration which can be compared to the very* pneuma *of the psyche.*"[43]

The description which Levinas offers of the social link is therefore based on *a freedom which is constrained in advance* by the face-to-face with the other. Let us now note futher — and this is absolutely crucial — that the notions of 'face' and 'face-to-face' in Levinas are not confined only to the momentary

---

[42] E. Levinas, *Liberté et commandement (Freedom and Commandment)* (Montpellier: Fata-Morgana, 1994) p. 49.

[43] E. Levinas, *Dieu, la mort et le temps (God, Death and Time)* (Paris: Grasset, 1993) pp. 205-206.

physical meeting of two persons, but that they can serve as a metonymy to designate 'the Other' as a potentiality of meeting present in any 'other'. We then see that we have come somewhat close to the Maussian idea of a gift which would be "apparently free and gratuitous, yet constrained and interested".[44] However, we have eschewed at the same time the insistence on 'appearing' — since Levinas' finite freedom is a genuine freedom — and the reference to 'interest' — since Levinas' main objective is to show how the trauma of responsibility leads the self to exit the realm of inter-*esse*. Indeed, as we just saw, for Levinas the 'command' which comes to the I from the face of the other is not a constraint, but rather *the form which freedom takes when it is called upon to act*; and this structure is the same as the one Karsenti[45] observes in Mauss' debate with Durkheimian social determinism:

> "What is put completely into question here is the criterion of the constraint and its absolute reliability. The *Essai sur le don* in fact inaugurates the requirement of holding two things together, without ever sacrificing one for the other: the obligatory dimension of the fact considered and the voluntary aspect in whose guise it appears. From this point of view, the issue at stake in the text is the following: one needs to transcend the theme of the constraint, and to break down its exclusive claim to explicative power, in order to move into the problematic of a *determination which acts precisely as a form of freedom*."

Bourdieu's option — which consisted in viewing precisely the unconscious habitus as the seat *par excellence* of this conjunction of obligation and freedom — is in my view less adequate than Levinas's for the question of the Maussian 'transmutation'. The reason is that Levinas is able to do something which is impossible for Bourdieu: he is able to think of free generosity not as *socially* determined within the boundary of historically acquired habits, but rather — all to the contrary — as determined *ontologically*, so to speak (again, in a non-Heideggerian sense), by the very structure of subjectivity. True enough, neither in Bourdieu nor in Levinas can freedom any longer be understood in terms of transcendental consciousness; but Levinas is able to show how this nontranscendentality is rooted precisely in a 'human bedrock', in a non-contextual 'foundation'.[46] Thinking in Maussian fashion better than

---

[44] M. Mauss, *op. cit.*, pp. 124-147.

[45] B. Karsenti, *op. cit.*

[46] In this sense, I now believe that in Ch. Arnsperger, 'Gratuité, don et optimisation individuelle: Levinas, Derrida et l'approche économique', *op. cit.* pp. 43-74, I used the idea of *transcendental foundation* a bit too loosely when speaking of Levinas (and Derrida). What I had in mind is, in fact, what I have expressed here (and which becomes clearer, I think, through the debate with Bourdieu), but using the term 'transcendental' for Levinas puts us at risk of misreading his disagreement with Husserl. (For Derrida, the question seems to me less easy to solve because of the section in J. Derrida, 'Violence et métaphysique' ('Violence and Metaphysics'), in *L'écriture et la différence* (*Writing and the Difference*) (Paris: Seuil, 1967) pp. 173-196, where he confronts Husserl and Levinas by trying to reconcile a 'pacific' transcendentalism with the Levinasian idea of 'transcendental violence'.)

Mauss himself thus amounts, in my view, to seek the Maussian 'bedrock' of the gift elsewhere than in the numerous variants on social habitus and on historically acquired modes of action which Bourdieu's thought makes possible.

Just in the same way as Mauss is looking for this 'transmutation' of agonistic gift-giving into generosity, Levinas is on a quest for an inner *conversion* of the subject. So neither of these two authors is outright utopian in the sense that they might have viewed their ethical calls as *descriptions*; it is quite evident that an appropriate social context is necessary to effect Levinas' ethical call — in that sense, the Levinasian approach does not *deny* the relevance of Bourdieu's analysis. However, that appropriate social context can never be reduced to a kind of unconscious and implicit inheritance as in Bourdieu; the Levinasian habitus necessarily has to be reactualized inside each subjectivity on the basis of the passivity which inhabits it 'from one end of human evolution to the other', as Mauss would say. Subjectivity is affected in advance by a command which defines its freedom: this is why, by going from Bourdieu's contextual habitus to Levinas' noncontextual habitus, we can give new life (a life which was considerably damaged by Mauss' own reflections on the agonistic gift) to the Maussian ethical call: 'Let us (...) adopt as a principle in our lives what has always been a principle and will always be one: to go out of oneself, to give, *freely and out of obligation*.' The passage from Bourdieu to Levinas occurs through the disappearance of the *space* between gratuity and obligation in the sense that Levinasian subjectivity is rooted in an obligation that harbours no expectation of reciprocity, least of all an implicit and unrecognized one. On the contrary: the Levinasian subject lucidly eschews all claims to 'receiving back'; it is an *explicit* renunciation of reciprocity.

So there is, of course, a price to pay for the possibility we now finally have of understanding the 'transmutation' desired by Mauss: the idea of a 'social lie', which is present explicitly in Mauss and which Bourdieu espouses in order to formalize what he calls the 'double truth' of the gift, becomes obsolete. 'To go out of oneself, freely and out of obligation', as Mauss would have it — this is something which appears possible, in the end, only on the basis of genuine *dis*interest, and not on the basis of a Bourdieusian simulacrum that would conceal an internalized collective interest. In Bourdieu (and in the Mauss of the agonistic gift), it is sociality as an occult binding force which induces a form of gratuity which is *in fine* falsely disinterested; in Levinas, on the contrary, it is freedom-as-gratuity-towards-the-other which induces sociality. In other words, Levinasian disinterest does not aim at safeguarding the social link; only in the sense that this disinterest *primarily defines* subjectivity as that which is disturbed by otherness, does it *correlatively define* a social link, without being reducible to this link, however. And in that sense, it is true that Levinas and the whole philosophical tradition to which he is an heir is a criticism of sociology viewed as the pure science of the 'reproduction of social relations'. Which does not deny the fact that it is *via sociology* and its understanding of the 'double truth' of the gift that I was able to arrive at Levinas and to show how his noncontextual habitus makes it possible to understand better than Mauss himself the Maussian 'transmutation'.

In order to still better grasp Levinas' contribution to the notion of the gift, it is worthwhile to investigate the connections which might exist between the analyses we have been conducting up to now and the even more radically philosophical standpoint recently adopted by Jean-Luc Marion in his book *Étant donné*[47] in a close dialogue with Heidegger, Husserl and Derrida. In order to extract the essence of the gift phenomenon, Marion carries out a threefold *epochè* of the receiver, the donator and the gift itself: as long as the gift is not described in this very abstract way, Marion claims, it can only be understood *in fine* as an epiphenomenon of exchange, of the gift-exchange circle which we discussed above in relation to Mauss. In comparison with this radical operation of putting all elements between parentheses, my present analysis might still seem exceedingly 'sociological' in the sense that it does presuppose, even in the case of Levinas, a habitus within which the gift is apprehended.[48] It seems to me that the difference between Levinas and Marion here (a difference which necessarily carries over to Mauss and his ethical call for generosity) lies in the fact that for Levinas, the 'bedrock' or the undeconstructible foundation of the description of the gift is the interhuman relationship *in the flesh* (which does not preclude generality, as we indicated above), the irruption of the other's face at the heart of the self's consciousness. There is of course, in his work, a putting between parentheses of all social, cultural, and other determinations, but not (on pains of no longer being able at all to describe the gift as an *ethical* gesture which renews itself in every face-to-face) an *epochè* of the donator and the receiver. In Marion[49], on the contrary, it appears that this method of putting aside the receiver is central in the description of the gift as gift:

> "Gift-giving not only tolerates, but in fact requires, the putting between parentheses of the receiver; the gift would simply vanish if the receiver were to remain still visible, accessible, and present. The reason is that, if the receiver *preceded the gift* — for example because he expected to receive it, *or even because he asked for it* — and if he subsisted after it — by appropriating it and profiting from it — the gift would be disqualified [as gift]." [my emphasis]

---

[47] J.L. Marion, *Étant donné (Being Given)* (Paris: Presses Universitaires de France, 1997).

[48] It is rather amusing to note that while in the perspective of Bourdieu or Levinas, Derrida's critique (J. Derrida, *Donner le temps: 1. La fausse monnaie (Giving Time: 1. False Money)* (Paris: Galilée, 1991)) of the gift as exchange appears as excessive because it wants too dearly to evacuate the donator and the receiver (and here I agree with A. Caillé, *Don, intérêt et désintéressement (Gift, Interest and Disinterestedness)* (Paris: La Découverte, 1994) but for different reasons, which I make explicit in Ch. Arnsperger, 'Gratuité, don et optimisation individuelle: Levinas, Derrida et l'approche économique', *op. cit.* pp. 43-74, this same critique is, in the eyes of Marion, still too much influenced by the idea of exchange (J.L. Marion, *op. cit.*, pp. 108-114).

[49] J.L. Marion, *op. cit.*, p. 124.

True enough, Marion's objective is different from ours: he seeks to fulfil a properly phenomenological task, i.e. to grasp the gift as a pure act, to grasp its determinations through ever more demanding 'reductions'. Nevertheless, his verdict, especially when coupled with a similar assertion for the donator, is in flat contradiction with Mauss' insistence on the need to 'go out of oneself' by giving and, especially, with Levinas' demand that the gift be effectively *preceded* by the receiver. Putting the latter between parentheses makes it impossible to formulate any social thought and leads, as in Marion, into phenomenological considerations which, quite logically, end with the study of 'saturated phenomena' such as religious and mystical experiences. This is not objectionable *per se*; however, for the question at hand, going that far in the *epochè* would no longer permit us to make sense of the Maussian 'transmutation', which was our main objective.

So what does the recourse to Levinas bring us in the end? As I already indicated, it brings us mostly a complete *reversal* in the description of the social: the social link is, in a way, 'preceded' and 'inaugurated' by a trauma of individual subjectivity. Is this a good basis for thinking about gift-giving? Not if we were to persist in reading Mauss as the apostle of the purely agonistic gift (as he presents himself at various points in the *Essai*). Indeed, in that case, Levinasian ethics appears to be totally utopian and even counterproductive since it exposes the self to the gifts of others, and to a virtually infinite indebtedness, without any possibility of 'reciprocating.' However, at the risk of sounding repetitive, this does not seem to me to be at all the orientation of Mauss' ethical call: 'to go out of oneself, to give' means much more than giving in order to affirm one's superiority to others — and Mauss himself shows at various points that he intuits precisely this, but he fails to make it nearly explicit enough. The type of sociality which emerges from Levinas' analysis is therefore radically different from that evidenced by Mauss in archaic social structures: rather than recovering a shady desire to 'possess faithful henchmen'or to 'command to others', we need to recover what Levinas calls an 'immemorial past' which we have only forgotten because the very structure of human consciousness drives us to forgetfulness. The Maussian citizen would then be less close to the practicioner of the *kula ring* than, perhaps, to the Buddhist *bodhisattva* moved in all his or her actions by compassion for others.[50]

By thus subverting the ethnological and sociological approaches to the gift from a Levinasian perspective, we are *in fine* led to reject, *in the very name of*

---

[50] And in this sense, it is perhaps true that Levinas advocates what Rose calls with some irony 'Buddhist Judaism', although not at all in the pejorative sense implied by Rose (G. Rose, *Mourning Becomes the Law: Philosophy and Representation* (Cambridge: Cambridge University Press, 1996) p. 38.

*Mauss' own ethical call*, the idea of the gift as a 'total social fact'[51]: as long as the practice of gift-giving is interpreted as something which is set within a social habitus characterized by the hold of the social totality on the individual, this practice can only be, in the end, agonistic — be it in an indirect way by aiming at 'nourishing the social link'. As Karsenti[52] puts it cogently:

> "It is clear (...) that the social totality is in the end the sole beneficiary of the generalized exchange which is installed on the sumptuary mode of gifts indefinitely given and restituted. (...) In and through the gift, therefore, it is society itself, considered in its globality, which expends *itself*, in the simple sense that it lives, recomposes itself and reaps new resources according to a particular rhythm of its own."

In such a vision, which is the one most Maussians uphold even today, Mauss' whole theory would concur not to the ethics of generosity he himself called for, but ultimately to an observation of society as an overarching being which 'swallows' human singularities in its desire to persevere in being. And one can live with this, as do Bourdieu and others, by viewing all social relations ultimately as — at least symbolic — antagonisms which create social stability; but by doing this one stops short of the Maussian ethical call to a 'transmutation' of the gift. To go beyond this, it is necessary to find in Levinas' work the foundations of a generosity located *outside of the social totality*. His whole effort consists precisely in elaborating an ethics of the gift in which intersubjective relations are not subject to being, to totality and to blind reciprocity. Indeed, in this renewed perspective, the social link has no value in itself; it exists only to the extent that it offers room for the deployment of *dis*interested generosity, flowing from the primary trauma of subjectivity inherent in every human being.

Only this vision of sociality — rather than that of sublimated violence or of a self-feeding social entity — can, in my view, do justice to Mauss' own prophetism. This, at least, is the central issue I sought to raise and discuss here.

## References

G. AKERLOF, 'Labor Contracts as Partial Gift Exchange', in *Quarterly Journal of Economics*, 97 (1982) pp. 543-569.
Ch. ARNSPERGER, 'Action, responsabilité et justice: Pertinence et limites de la notion économique d'altruisme', in *Revue Philosophique de Louvain* 95 (1997a) pp. 484-516.
Ch. ARNSPERGER, 'Gratuité, don et optimisation individuelle: Levinas, Derrida et l'approche économique', in *Transdisciplines,* 1 (1997b) pp. 43-74.

---

[51] M. Mauss, *op. cit.*, p. 151.
[52] B. Karsenti, *op. cit.*, p. 47.

P. BOURDIEU, *Méditations pascaliennes* (Paris: Seuil, 1997)
A. CAILLÉ, *Don, intérêt et désintéressement* (Paris: La Découverte, 1994).
J. DERRIDA, 'Violence et métaphysique', in *L'écriture et la différence* (Paris: Seuil, 1967).
J. DERRIDA, *Donner le temps: 1. La fausse monnaie* (Paris: Galilée, 1991)
J. GODBOUT (in collaboration with A. Caillé), *L'esprit du don* (Paris: La Découverte, 1992).
J. GODBOUT, 'Notes pour défendre le futur paradigme du don', in *Transdisciplines,* 1 (1997) pp. 109-115.
B. KARSENTI, *Marcel Mauss: Le fait social total* (Paris: Presses Universitaires de France, 1994)
E. LEVINAS, *Ethique et infini* (Paris: Fayard, 1982) (Page references are from the pocket edition (Paris: Le Livre de Poche, 1982)).
E. LEVINAS, *Entre nous: Essais sur le penser-à-l'autre* (Paris: Grasset, 1991).
E. LEVINAS, *Dieu, la mort et le temps* (Paris: Grasset, 1993).
E. LEVINAS, *Liberté et commandement* (Montpellier: FataMorgana, 1994).
J.L. MARION, *Étant donné* (Paris: PressesUniversitaires de France, 1997)
M. MAUSS, 'Essai sur le don: Forme et raison de l'échange dans les sociétés archaïques', published originally in *Annales de Sociologie* (1924), reprinted in M. Mauss, *Sociologie et anthropologie* (Paris: Presses Universitaires de France, 1950).
G. ROSE, *Mourning Becomes the Law: Philosophy and Representation* (Cambridge: Cambridge University Press, 1996)
A. SEN, 'Choice, Orderings and Morality', in S. Körner (ed.), *Practical Reason* (Oxford: Basil Blackwell, 1974).

# COMPARATIVE AND HISTORICAL PERSPECTIVES

# Value Switching and the Commodity free zone

Chris A. GREGORY[1] (Department of Archaeology and Anthropology, Australian National University)

## 1. Introduction

The prime aim of this conference, I note, is to make some progress towards a mapping of models of the gift and to show the relevance of these models for understanding actual social practices; my particular brief is to examine how gift-relations differ from economic relations and to analyze the way in which neoclassical economic theory influences our perception of the practice of gift-giving.

These are issues I first addressed in my book *Gifts and Commodities*,[2] and I am delighted that the organizers have given me the chance to revisit these questions. That book was based on ethnographic reports from Papua New Guinea where I worked as a lecturer in economics for three years from 1973 to 1975. In 1982 the ethnographic focus of my research moved to central India where I carried out fieldwork. My most recent fieldtrip was for two months in December-January 1997-98 when I made special inquiries into the different modes of exchange for the purposes of this paper. I will present some of this evidence with the aim of developing some general answers to the questions I have been set.

I will argue that what is at stake here is a theory of value, that no one theory of value is adequate to the task of dealing with gifts and non-gifts, and that while value theorists — be they neoclassical, Marxist, or anthropologist — tend to see the world from the perspective of one value theory, those involved in the social practice of exchange are constantly switching value regimes and creating commodity free zones in a world dominated by the market. The implication is that value theorists of whatever persuasion need to see the limits of their particular perspective if our theoretical understanding of the practice of gift-giving is to advance.

My paper is divided into four sections. In the first I outline, very schematically, some of the various forms of exchanging done in Bastar District, central India. I will then try to develop the general conceptual framework implicit in

---

[1] This is a slightly amended version of a paper presented at the Gifts and Interest Conference held at the Catholic University, Leuven on 3-4 April 1998. I thank the participants for their comments; I would like especially to thank the organizer, Toon Vandevelde, for his assistance and encouragement.
[2] C.A. Gregory, *Gifts and Commodities* (London: Academic Press, 1982).

this material. Next I examine how neoclassical value theory influences our perceptions of these different forms by comparing different value perspectives, and, finally, I raise the problem of value switching and consider its theoretical implications.

## 2. Some ethnographic evidence from Bastar

The Bastar District of central India is, in the popular imagination of many Indian people, a 'backward' area inhabited by forest dwelling tribes. This image, like many popular urban images of rural dwellers, is wide of the mark. From an anthropological point of view, the villagers of Bastar are peasant proprietors whose main crop is rice. As such the socio-economic organization of agriculture in Bastar is a variation of that found in other rice-growing areas of Asia. On the other hand, it is different from that found in Papua New Guinea (Papua New Guinea) where the expression 'forest dwelling tribe' still has some meaning even though the country, like Bastar District, is now well integrated into the global market economy. Thus the spectacular competitive gift exchange systems for which Papua New Guinea is famous — *kula, moka* and the like — are nowhere to be found in Bastar; but, nevertheless, a similar variety in the forms of exchange exists.

Halbi is the local dialect in Bastar and people use it to distinguish many different types of exchange. I restrict myself to a discussion of just eight of these terms here. As I did not want to prejudge the question of what is a 'gift' and what is not, I asked my informant, Mr M.S. Mali, to explain to me the various ways in which labour could be mobilized. The labour involved in the procurement of food, clothing and shelter, I figured, can be considered 'useful' or 'economic' no matter what the value perspective.

Our conversations on this matter began as we were walking through his rice fields on Saturday 3 January 1998. Winter is the time of year when capital improvements are made in preparation for the growing season which begins around July-August and ends around October-November. We came across a husband and wife team who were engaged in leveling land to make a new rice field. The husband would dig the soil with his hoe and the women would remove it by means of a small dish which she carried on her head. The contract they were engaged under is called a *khundi godi*. Under this system the workers receive Rs100 for every cubic *hath* of soil removed, a *hath* being that distance from the elbow to the tip of one's fingers. They have the option of taking their pay in the paddy equivalent of one *khundi* which is approximately 40 kg. Beside them was a stick 5 *hath* long which was used to describe a rectangle of 20 x 5 *hath*. This would be excavated to the depth of one *hath* which gave the cubic unit by which they were paid. Another variation of this type of contract is called *phut godi* where the workers get Rs25 for every 49 cubic *phut* (from the English 'foot' = 12 inches). These systems are two ways of expressing the same rate of payment.

While the capitalist farmer in Australia or Europe would marvel at the labour intensity of such an operation and the cultural units by which it is expressed, the labour contract is, nevertheless, a very familiar piece rate system; the anthropologist is not faced with any difficult problems of cultural translation in trying to describe it.

When leveling work under the *godi* system is completed some finishing off work remains. This is done using the *mazduri* (daily wages) system. Workers are contracted at a daily wage rate of Rs25. This is about half the wages a diligent worker can earn under the *godi* system but the significant difference between the two systems is that *mazduri* workers must be supervised.

Again, this system of wage labour is very familiar but it is necessary to stress that the contract is daily not weekly and that the worker who secures a daily labour contract only expects to work for a day. It is important to note that while some tasks can be done by either piece rates or daily wages, many cannot. In other words, the worker's choice of which method to work under is limited: in many cases there is no choice.

A third form of labour arrangement, often used at planting or harvest time, is *bethiya*. Unlike the above two forms which are readily translatable into Hindi and English, this term has neither Hindi nor English translation. However, its meaning is not difficult to grasp. The proverb 'Tomorrow's work must be done today' (*kal ka kam aaj karna hai*) draws attention to the urgency of the work to be done. Another crucial factor is lack of ready cash to pay people to do the job. Such problems are overcome by calling upon neighbours to. Suppose the rains are about to come and, for whatever reason, you have not finished your preparatory ploughing. You call on your neighbours to help you. The many hands gets the job done quickly; your only obligation is to provide food and drink, of good quality and in generous measure, at the end of the day. Another example: the bank of a flooded rice field is cut by water and many hands are needed to fix it quickly to avert a potential disaster. Yet another example comes from Mr Mali who used the *bethiya* system when he needed to tile the roof of his new house. Twenty men helped him out and it took two days to complete the task. He hosted a party at the end of each day. This cost him quite a bit of money but it was far cheaper than the Rs1000 it would have cost him to hire 20 daily labourers for two days. Furthermore, the motivation of the *bethiya* worker is different: their concern is to help a neighbour in need and they work eagerly, quickly and long hours if necessary.

While the word *bethiya* has no ready translation into English, the concept is not entirely foreign. Work parties of this kind exist in all cultures but the particular form they take, and their relative importance in the economic scheme of things, varies greatly. Such systems have elements of a market morality in them in the sense that the employer of the labour is getting it on the cheap; but it also has elements of a gift morality in the sense that the worker does not consider the food and drink as wages but, rather, has an eye on the uncertain future and the potential benefits it may bring him when he finds himself in a similar situation. We must also recognise the fact that the supplier of labour may be acting out of a simple altruistic desire to help a neighbour. Systems like *bethiya*, then, are ambiguous in the sense that they mean different things to different people. However, the ethic of 'helping a neighbour in need' is the one that is required to dominate in Bastar. Thus even if one's private motives are tinged with greed one's public actions must convey the opposite impression.

The next category I want to consider is *dan*. This term describes the classic Hindu gift and its meanings are many. I restrict myself here to the explanations my informants gave me. "*Dan,*" insisted Mr Mali, "is not *bethiya;* there is no expectation of return. When my elder brother's son was building his house I helped him out by paying the workers who built it. I also helped out my daughter in a similar way." Mr Mali also said that many temples are built by *dan*. Another informant, Mr J. Baghel, gave similar examples and added another. During the final days of the mortuary ritual for his dead sister, her relatives were given *dan* twice when they paid him a ritual visit prescribed by custom. The first gift was given as they crossed the threshold into his yard; the second as they crossed the threshold into his house. *Kanyadan*, the gift of the virgin bride, is, perhaps, the supreme gift in the *dan* category.

These examples are sufficient to establish the point that *dan* circulates among close relations and that, on many occasions, its circulation is defined by Hindu religious belief. There is no direct material return for a gift of this kind but the possibility of spiritual return of some kind no doubt motivates the thoughts and actions of believers.

Another important form of giving is *bhent*. What distinguishes this form of giving, I was told, is that it is not informed by family or by Hindu religious custom as is the case with *dan*. "An example is the gifts you gave my family on Christmas day", said Mr Baghel, my host during my stay in India.

The next category is called *begari*. This refers to labour done without taking wages or food. The following examples reveal the community spirit behind this form of giving: community labour to repair the road to the temple; cleaning of the village 'tank' (a dam where daily bathing, clothes washing, and religious cleaning rituals are performed); repairs to community buildings. Mr Mali said that *begari* was rarely done in urban areas because of the absence of the communal spirit that one finds in villages and small towns. He contrasted this with *dan* which is very much an urban practice based, as it is, on family and religion rather than community.

## TABLE 1. SYNOPTIC TABLE OF HALBI EXCHANGE TERMS

| Name | Translation | Examples | Distinguishing features |
| --- | --- | --- | --- |
| *godi* | piece rates | leveling land | supplier of labour is self motivated to work. |
| *mazduri* | daily wages | finishing of leveling work; government work Rs30/day | supplier of labour needs supervision |
| *bethiya* | work party | 'tomorrows work must be done today'; tiling roof of house | giver of labour has expectation of food and drink; receiver has obligation to reciprocate sometime in the future |
| *dan* | gift giving | help brother/child build his house; gift of land to a temple, school; gifts given during certain stages of a mortuary ritual | giver has an obligation to assist a family member; no expectation of any return; regulated by religious and family custom |
| *bhent* | gift giving | the Christmas gifts I gave to my Hindu host | not governed by religious custom as with *dan*. |
| *begari* | community work | to repair road to a temple; to repair community building; to clean village tank | no return of food or money; giver has an obligation to work as a member of the community for the welfare of the community |
| *chanda* | contribution | the contribution (usually money) that a member of a religious community is asked to make when building a new temple; the contribution levied on all members of a village to meet the costs of a school tournament | amount of contribution set by community not left up to individual as in *dan* |
| *lamsena* | labour in exchange for a bride | when the son of a poor family works for his future father-in-law as a substitute for paying the expenses of a marriage | father obligated to give his daughter in marriage at the expiration of the agreed time |

Closely related to *begari* is *chanda*. This refers to a fixed contribution that is levied upon all community members to fund some communal activity such as a school tournament, an annual fair, or a temple. The contribution usually takes the form of money. The amount of money is fixed by the community leaders and not left up to the individual as in, for example, *dan*.

The last form of exchange that I will consider is *lamsena*. This is a culturally specific form of marriage arrangement that is entered into by a father, who has an unmarried son but no money to pay the expenses of his marriage, with another father, who has an unmarried daughter but no labour to help him run his farm. The unmarried son moves into the house of his future father-in-law and works for him for an agreed period of time and then marries his daughter. Such arrangements are called 'bride service' in the anthropological literature but as marriage customs vary greatly from one place to the next the term does not always refer to the same thing. In Bastar, for example, there is no dowry system nor is there a 'brideweath' system where a man is expected to 'pay' for his bride with money and other items of indigenous wealth. In Bastar the father of the groom is expected to pay 75 % of the costs of the wedding celebration and the father of the bride the remaining 25 %. In days gone by these expenses could be very high as the ceremony went for many days and hundreds of guests attended, all of whom had to be fed.

I append the following synoptic table of Halbi exchange terms to aid the exposition which follows.

## 3. A conceptual framework

The data presented above only consider a small number of the terms used to describe exchange in Bastar, but the examples are enough to illustrate the generality, the 'continuum' of exchange types first reported by Malinowski[3] in his classic ethnography on the *kula* system of the Trobriand Islands in Papua New Guinea. Many ethnographers have reported similar 'continuums'. Sahlins, in his classic article 'On the Sociology of Primitive Exchange',[4] reviews this literature and attempts to a theoretical generalization. This article has been the subject of much discussion. Vatuk and Vatuk[5] have advanced an important critique. They extended Sahlins' argument from tribal to peasant economies by, firstly, presenting original data from village India and, secondly, by questioning the theoretical basis of his 'continuum'.

---

[3] B. Malinowski, *Argonauts of the Western Pacific* (New York: Dutton, 1961) pp. 177 ff.

[4] M. Sahlins, *Stone Age Economics* (Chicago: Aldine, 1972) pp. 185 ff.

[5] V.P. Vatuk, S. Vatuk, 'The Social Context of Gift Exchange in North India', in G. Gupta (ed.), *Family and Social Change, Modern India* (Delhi: Vikas, 1975).

Vatuk and Vatuk argued that Sahlins' "argument is greatly flawed by its reliance upon the insubstantial variable of 'degree of self-interest'".[6] They note that evaluations of generosity or selfishness can only be based on the moral preconceptions of the analyst and that, where based on indigenous concepts of 'altruism', the problems of cross-cultural comparisons are so difficult that the translation is meaningless. They point out that the necessity of separating out the pretence and self-deception involved in the practice of gift giving creates insuperable problems of interpretation.

Their response was to tackle the problem from a *linguistic* point of view and to examine the semantic fields of 35 Hindi exchange terms. They found that these can be grouped into six general categories, each bearing an indigenous term. Such an exercise is a very useful one but the generality of Sahlins' model is lost in the cultural specificity of the Hindi dialect language terms they seek to interpret. My aim here is to grasp the socio-economic generality of actual exchange practices without doing violence to the cultural specificity of the example in question.

One way to do this is to approach the problem from the *logical* point of view by constructing a conceptual model based on logical principles of opposition. But where to start? Where is the common ground? History provides it with the market, an institution of great antiquity and global modernity. Everybody knows the language of the market today and everybody understands the implications of its buy-cheap-sell-dear logic even they may not be able to use it to their advantage. As such, Halbi terms such as *mazduri* and *godi* are readily comprehensible in English as 'daily wages' and 'piece rate'; there is no problem of cultural translation here. Even in the Trobriands, which unlike India had no indigenous marketing system, the term *gimwali* is readily translated as 'barter'. All these terms fall under the generic head of 'market' (or 'commodity') exchange. If to these exchanges we add their opposites, 'non-market' exchanges, we have, by the law of axiomatic contradiction, the universe of possibilities.

But is this conceptual language appropriate? Does it have sufficient generality? The terms 'commodity' and 'market' are questionable because they are not independent of an historically specific theory of value. The word 'commodity', for example, belongs to the classical political economy tradition of Smith, Ricardo and Marx and, as such, is historically linked to the labour theory of value. This much is clear from the history of the marginalist theory of value. When this rose to dominance in the 1870s the term 'goods' replaced 'commodity' in the theoretical language of the post-1870 economic treatises.[7] Thus the term 'commodities' is inappropriate in a general logical framework

---

[6] *Ibid.*, p. 212.
[7] C.A. Gregory, *op. cit.*, pp. 10 ff.

because of its historical specificity. The word 'market', a term common to both Marx and Friedman and therefore otherwise acceptable, also suffers from a lack of generality because barter is not, strictly speaking, a form of market exchange.

Wherein lies the general term? If we examine the social consequences of market and barter exchanges we find that, no matter how many actual examples we consider, the end result is the same, an *objective relationship of equivalence* between the things exchanged is always established: one gun equals 10 kgs of butter, or 40 Indian rupees, or two English pounds, or six bags of rice, etc. The fact that these objective relationships of equivalence vary from place to place and time to time in no way alters the form of the general relation.

What divides theorists is not the fact of this relationship but its essence. What is the homogenous essence that enables two heterogeneous objects to be equated? Is it equal units of abstract labour? Or is it equal units of marginal utility? In other words, the objective relations of equivalence provide a value problem that theory must answer. For many political economists and neoclassicals, this problem has its origins in a 'natural' propensity for human beings to 'truck, barter and exchange'; however, a century of ethnographic research and anthropological theorizing has revealed the cultural specificity of this 'natural' problem.

Logically speaking, the universe of possibilities includes the *objective relations of equivalence* and the *non-objective relations of non-equivalence*. The latter is a residual category that includes everything not contained in the former; the law of axiomatic contradiction tells us that nothing is excluded. But there is another kind of logic that is better suited to our purposes, that of *topical* or *commonplace* logic. Aristotle distinguished between these two forms of logic but the latter fell into disuse around the 17$^{th}$ century with the rise of science and mathematics. The difference between them lies in the notion of logical opposition. In the axiomatic tradition opposition is negative and universal and the middle is always excluded; in the topical tradition the opposition is affirmative and general and the middle can be included. Thus not-hot is the opposite of hot in axiomatic thought and cold the opposite of hot in topical logic with wet and dry the mediating terms.

My opposition between gifts and commodities is a *commonplace* opposition (I can now see) but, because of its partisan approach to classical political economy, the opposition lacks logical generality and cannot serve as a general conceptual framework that allows room for marginalist theory. What, then, is the commonplace opposite of *objective relationships of equivalence?* The expression *ordered human relationships* suggests itself as the problem for another theory of value under the general heading of 'value problems'.

What is at stake here is best illustrated by use of an actual example. When my daughter was five years old she cut off some of her blond hair and exchanged it for the black hair of her close friend. This case can be analyzed as a problem of objective relationships of equivalence — what is the basis of the exchange rate that equates x pieces of blond hair with y pieces of black hair? — or as a problem of ordered human relationships — what is the quality of the human relationship established between the transactors? It is clear from this example that, logically speaking, both questions can be posed but that, in this case, the latter is the more socially meaningful one. Other examples could be given where both questions are socially meaningful. The *bethiya* ('work party') example given in the previous section is one of these. To be able to handle cases like this the logic of commonplace opposition must be progressively applied to each category to yield a Porphyrian tree of the type shown in Figure 1.

This tree is constructed by considering each new species as the locus of a new generic commonplace contradiction of a lower order. Thus 'human relations' considered as a genus is the commonplace contradiction that mediates those human relationships based on kinship (consanguinity and affinity) and those based on neighborhood; these, in turn, divide onto those based on direct reciprocity and those based on generalised reciprocity and so on.

Logical division of this kind, as the historians of logic[8] have correctly pointed out, is not 'universal' and 'formal' in the sense that mathematical logicians use that term. Rather, it is 'general' and 'humanistic' in the sense that it is grounded in history, society and culture. For example the category 'non-market' exchange can be formed by the logical process of universal negation but the affirmative opposite, 'gift exchange', is suggested by the ethnographic record. Needless to say, commonplace logic is riddled with doubtable divisions of a kind that are totally expunged from axiomatic logic. This kind of doubt is not something to be avoided in the study of human beings; to the contrary, it is something that must be embraced and given primacy. Mathematical logic has a role to play in the human sciences but when it is used to eliminate the essence of humanity — our capacity to question — then this use is tantamount to an abuse.

I include in the figure the indigenous terms introduced in the previous section to draw attention to the lack of a one-to-one mapping between indigenous linguistic terms, logical categories and social practices. Indigenous terms in any language are general and are often used to describe both a genus and a subgenus. In my discussion above, for example, I only gave one example of a *bhent*, the presents I gave to my Hindu hosts on Christmas day. This term is applied to a wide variety of other types of exchanges in India and Vatuk and Vatuk[9]

---

[8] I.M. Bochenski, *A History of Formal Logic* (I. Thomas, transl.) (Notre Dame: University of Notre Dame Press, 1956).

[9] V.P. Vatuk, S. Vatuk, *op. cit.*

discuss many of these. For example, it may include kinship gifts of various types: from the mother's brother to the sister's son on the occasion of the latter's marriage, from brother to sister on the birth of the latter's child, from bride-givers to bride-takers at a wedding, and so on. The Vatuks show that the term has a general usage that is almost the same as *dan* which includes gifts given by the bride's family (including *kanyadan*, the gift of a virgin bride), gifts to a beggar, etc.

Wherein lies the difference? They argue that it lies in the finer points of Hindu religious doctrine, noting that *dan* is informed by scriptural doctrines of reincarnation and spiritual reciprocity whereas *bhent* is more concerned with the worship of deified human beings and the spiritual returns this brings. They also note that the latter tends to involve direct material gifts to the gods from which intermediaries may indirectly benefit. This argument is obviously culturally specific to India and then only to certain parts. It is also interesting to note that some of the terms and examples found in Bastar, such as *bethiya* ('work party') are not included in their list of 35 terms even though they have a socio-economic generality that extends beyond India.

The logical tree in Figure 1 makes no claim to completeness. The branches under the heading 'objective relationships', for example, is one area where many subdivisions can be defined. My main aim has been to outline the basis of a conceptual model of exchange forms that overcomes the problems of the 'continuum' model and the 'degrees of self interest' calculus it presupposes. This continuum model is a metaphorical borrowing from differential calculus. The Porphyrian tree model, by contrast, gives us fine distinctions between the various exchange forms by means of a logical genealogy that is grounded problematically in history and culture rather than unproblematically in axiomatic thought.

Of course, this tree is a mere tool and its use must be informed by a theory of value. How are we to perceive *bethiya* for example? Is it a form of cheap daily labour (the material relations perspective) or a form of neighbourly social relationship? Logically speaking it can fit into either category in the same way that the hair-exchange example mentioned above can. The task of theory is to make a persuasive case to view it this way or that or even as both.

### 4. Theories of value

The neoclassical perspective on exchange is one value perspective among many. What distinguishes this perspective is that the Friedmanite form of neoclassical theory is the dominant paradigm both in the academy and in the global polity. The market is the dominant institution in the world today and neoclassical value theory not only describes how this institution works but

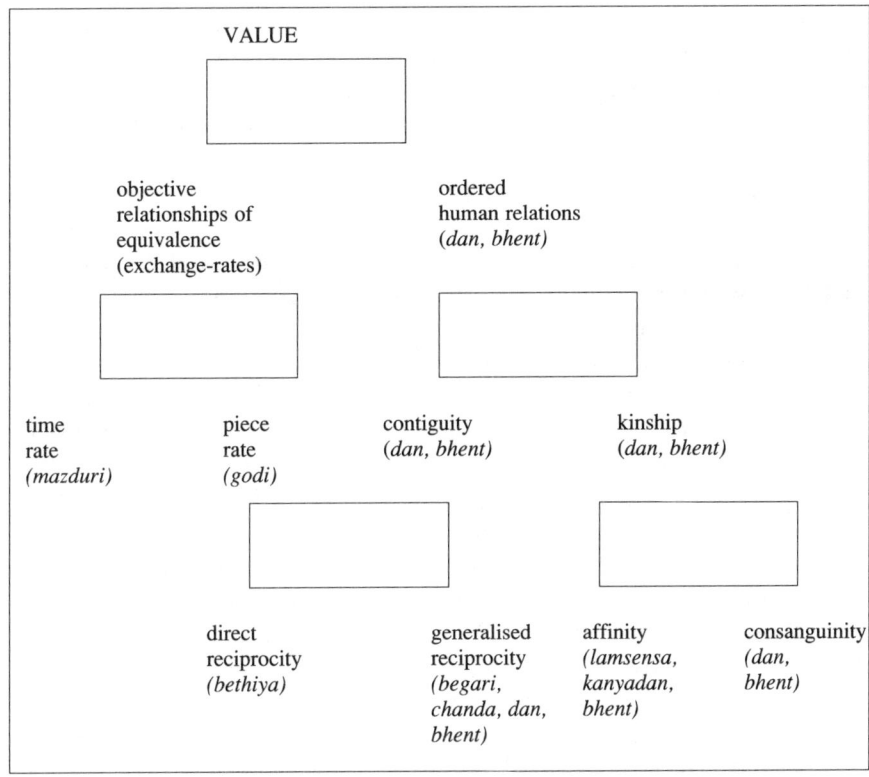

*Figure 1. A logical division of the value problem* (with some Halbi exchange terms superimposed)

how it should work. Neoclassical value theorists occupy positions of considerable power in the treasuries and central banks of governments, in international institutions such as the World Bank and the IMF, and in the private sector where their theoretically informed policy prescriptions are put into practice. Their ideas are enthusiastically adopted by today's free market revolutionaries as the Keynesian walls of government regulation tumble. Thus Melamed,[10] the entrepreneur behind the creation of the futures markets in Chicago in the 1980s and 1990s, celebrates Friedman as the saviour of freedom and democracy in the world today. Now that Marx, the Satan of the eastern bloc, is dead, Friedman's apotheosis seems nigh.

How does neoclassical theory influence our perception of gift giving? As a description it views all exchanges from the perspective of the market and distinguishes them in terms of the size of the marginal utility of consumption or

---

[10] L. Melamed, *Leo Melamed on The Markets: Twenty Years of Financial History as Seen by the Man Who Revolutionized the Markets* (New York: John Wiley, 1993).

the marginal product of labour; as a prescription, it judges non-market forms as barriers to development and argues for their removal in the name of community welfare by appealing to the Mandevillean morality that private greed leads to public good. In recent years neoclassical theory has expanded its reach to include all domains of human endeavour: law, politics, education, marriage, extra-marital affairs, and even babies whom, for most people excepting the Friedmanites, are the supreme gift. One neoclassical in the Chicago tradition argues for a free market in babies to overcome the problems of irregularity in adoption procedures, dismal foster care, scarcity of white babies and surplus of black babies, and excessive abortion.[11]

Arguments like this have led many people to view neoclassical economics as simply a theoretical apology for an extreme right wing political agenda. A persuasive case can be made for seeing neoclassical economics as the polar opposite of Marxian theory. Who can deny that the leading gurus of the two schools, Marx and Friedman, occupy extreme ends of the political spectrum? However, while it is correct to equate Marx with the labour theory of value and Friedman with the utility theory of value, it is an error to conclude that the labour theory of value is to the working class as the utility theory is to the capitalist. It is true that the two theories of value take up different perspectives that lead to different political consequences; it is true, too, that Marx's labour theory takes the perspective of the worker on the factory floor, but it is not true that utility theory takes the perspective of the boss who looks down upon the worker. The neoclassical viewer is located elsewhere but what this viewer shares with the Marxian viewer is that this perspective is *fixed* and this is the main point I want to establish here.

The idea that Marx views the world from the perspective of the worker on the factory floor is, of course, totally uncontroversial. This perspective was an almost inevitable consequence of the historical development of the labour theory of value. Smith opposed the Physiocratic doctrine that land was the source of wealth and proposed labour as the replacement; Ricardo developed the idea and Marx finished it off, as it were, by arguing that surplus-value was produced on the factory floor by the worker. The sphere of exchange for Marx was thus of secondary importance. He begins his analysis here only to note its 'fetishistic' character. For him exchange was a realm where relations between people took the 'fantastic' form of relations between things. The freedom and equality of the sphere of commodity exchange masks the unfreedom and inequality of the class relations of production. In terms of Figure I, Marx views all exchanges from the perspective of the worker on a daily wage. What interests him is the coercive nature of the relationship between the owner of the means of production (land in

---

[11] A. Wolfe, *Whose Keeper? Social Science and Moral Obligation* (Berkeley: University of, 1989) p. 37.

this case) and the worker. Piece rates are seen as a variation of this basic relation. All other relations shown in Figure I are outside the scope of inquiry for Marx as they are 'pre-capitalist'; like the evolutionary theorists of his time, any contemporary evidence that could not be fitted into the theory was seen as a 'survival', a relic from a former era in the prehistory of capitalism.

Neoclassical value theory does not take the perspective of the factory owner and in this sense it is not the opposite of Marx's theory. Neoclassical theory rose to dominance in the 1870s when shopping was going through a revolution. The periodic markets in rural Europe began to lose their importance with the rise of the department store and the supermarket. The neoclassical value theorist took the perspective of the pusher of a supermarket trolley and posed the new problem of choice.[12] Faced with unlimited things on the shelves, but constrained by a budget, what does one put into the trolley? This is a problem that an individual faces and they are free to make whatever choice they want. Subjective individual values are at stake here but, given the way the human being is, the logic is general: if we get more and more of x and less and less of y the marginal utility of x falls and that of y rises. The things x and y, *commodities* in the Marxian world, become *goods* to the neoclassical theorist, a linguistic shift that marks, very accurately, the underlying shift in value theory from a measure based on unfree productive labour to one based on free consumer choice.

The neoclassical theorist universalizes this perspective and finds the problem of choice everywhere. This theoretical imperialism, as it has been called,[13] was underwritten by economic imperialism: the global expansion of the market and the 'deindustrialisation' of Britain and other similar countries put an end to the old debate about the applicability of 'Western' theory to non-Western economies.

But the market was the only thing the neoclassical economists saw as they traveled abroad. To the extent that non-market exchanges of the type charted in Figure 1 were observed by the handful who have carried out fieldwork, they were perceived of as 'distortions', as variations from the Pareto optimum of balanced marginal utilities. In Papua New Guinea the marginal product of labour is seen as negative and the marginal utility of consumption as zero.[14] The Indian villager is seen as an 'individual decision-maker' who makes choices subject to universal constraints and under the universal sky of uncertainty. The theoreticians who pull the strings of this puppet[15] are deaf to the

---

[12] 'The image neoclassical economists have of the decision maker is one of a home-maker going down the aisle in the supermarket, or an investor calling a broker: both are isolated individuals acting on their own' (Etzioni 1991:6).

[13] G.C. Harcourt, *The Social Science Imperialists* (London: Routledge & Kegan Paul, 1982).

[14] C.A. Gregory, *op. cit.,* pp. 102 ff.

[15] C. J. Bliss, N.H. Stern, *Palanpur: The Economy of an Indian Village* (Oxford: Clarendon Press, 1982).

indigenous language of exchange and when they see a gift exchange in the field they reduce it to a market transaction by means of the magic of shadow prices. Thus they see the familiar system of daily wages and piece rates but when they see employers giving meals to *bethiya workers* they fail to understand the full social context. How could they? They went to the field with a questionnaire informed by marginalist theory and got the answers they were looking for. Where culture constrains economic activity, as in the case of the high caste person who will not work for one of a lower caste, the 'wage rate' is reckoned not to measure the opportunity cost of labour as required by the rationality of marginal theory.

Least I be accused of special pleading for an anthropological view of the world, let me assure readers that value theorists in this profession do the same thing but from a different perspective. Anthropologists view all exchanges from the perspective of the family or, to be more precise, from the perspective of the husband or brother who does the exchanging. The question of gift exchange was posed by Mauss who, building on the ethnographic work of Malinowski and others that demolished the prevailing notions of 'natural' economy, noted that people in certain social settings have obligations to give, receive and repay. Lévi-Strauss proposed the incest taboo as the supreme rule of the gift and distinguished between restricted and generalized reciprocity, the former being where fathers (brothers) exchanged daughters (sisters) and the latter where the return was delayed with the aid of a symbolic substitute (bridewealth). Sahlins generalized this model to included *all* exchanges. In terms of the categories in Figure I, market transactions became 'negative' reciprocity in opposition to the forms of 'positive' reciprocity on the right hand side of the diagram; the latter, in turn, were subdivided along the lines suggested by Lévi-Strauss. Thus everything was viewed from the perspective of the father or brother (as the feminist critique of this theory clarified).

Subsequent developments have resulted in a new perspective. The study of the social relations of kinship have given way to a perspective that privileges culture, consumption, and meaning. In a recent review of this literature by Miller,[16] himself an advocate of this approach, we find the triumphal claim that 'the study of consumption and commodities ... may come to replace kinship as the core of anthropology'.[17]

Thus this new theory of value, like all the others considered above, claims its own particular perspective as the superior one; only they have identified the core issue.

---

[16] D. Miller, Consumption and Commodities, in *Annual Review of Anthropology*, 24 (1995) pp. 141-61.

[17] *Ibid.*, p. 141.

## 5. Value switching

In *Gifts and Commodities* I developed a critique of the neoclassical approach to value from a position that combined elements of the Marxian and Maussian perspective. This contradictory value perspective, which locates the theorist both in the social relations of production and in those of kinship, reflects a contradiction I perceived in the socio-economic history of Papua New Guinea. On the one hand there was a tendency for gifts to be transformed into commodities as a result of colonization; on the other there was a tendency for commodities to be transformed into gifts as the village people of Papua New Guinea struggled to create a social world of their own choosing.

My critics have questioned my binary approach to the problem but I draw some comfort from the fact that villagers seem to see the world in the same way with the terminological distinctions they draw between *bisnis* (business) and *kastom* (custom). Nevertheless, my work was a synthetic overview and the idea that people only switch between two value realms is clearly a simplification. General theoretical arguments of this kind must, of necessity, abstract from the complications of daily life but the tension between simplifying theory and complicated social practice needs to be constantly aggravated.

In a recently published book, *Savage Money*,[18] I develop the argument *of Gifts and Commodities* in a ethnographically-grounded way that reports fieldwork data from India supplemented by comparative and historical observations from Africa and Papua New Guinea. I affirm my commitment to an approach to the value question that gives primacy to human relations against the reifications of the culturalists but repose the question of *goods* as a value category of importance. I refer here not so much to the neoclassical theory of goods but to those objects that people never, or very rarely, exchange. In India, land is the classic example of a *good* but there are also many other items, loosely called 'heirlooms' that fall under this category.

Things, as Appadurai[19] notes, have a 'social life' in the sense that they are now a gift, now a commodity, now a good, and now something else. The life of a piece of gold, for example, may begin as the result of some geological process in Africa, get dug up by a black miner and sold as a commodity by the owner of the mine for money, get transformed into a necklace and displayed in a shop, get purchased by a villager in India and given to his daughter as a wedding gift, handed down the female line for five generations, lost, found, sold to a gold dealer, melted down to form part of a gold bar, stored in Fort Knox for

---

[18] C.A. Gregory, *Savage Money* (London: Harwood, 1997).
[19] A. Appadurai (ed.), *The Social Life of Things: Commodities in Cultural Perspective* (Cambridge: Cambridge University Press, 1986).

50 years, sold as part of a scheme to demonetise gold, purchased by a dentist and used as a tooth filling.

History of this kind is tedious and difficult, if not impossible, to do. It is also unnecessary. This hypothetical history is sufficient to make the point that things are valued in many different ways over the course of their 'life'. This valuation is not intrinsic to the thing itself but created by the people who handle them. The example also shows that people can switch from one value regime to another as, for example, when gold is purchased as a commodity, given as a gift to a daughter and passed on to descendants as a family heirloom. These liminal states are marked by various ways in different cultures.

In Australia, for example, custom demands that one take a bottle of wine when one is invited to someone's place for dinner. Custom also demands that one remove the price tag even though the brand name immediately identifies the gift as a bottle of cheap red from Woolworths. Understanding value transitions of this kind poses problems related to, but distinct from, the logical (§3) and theoretical (§4) problems raised above. The transition phase is a moment of ambiguity between one set of socio-cultural relations to another. This is also a move from one code of morality to another.

Some of these transitions have a technological or economic basis as my discussion of the various forms of giving in Bastar above (§2) suggested. Piece rates, for example, are not a viable option when no unit of work can be defined. Bride service (*lamsnea*) is not an arrangement a family would like to see their son in but nor do they want to see him unmarried and will therefore resort to it as a matter of last resort. Work parties (*bethiya*) are partially motivated by lack of ready cash but, as mentioned above, the moral code that prevails here is that of helping someone in urgent need of large amounts of labour for circumstances beyond their control. If someone were to systematically abuse this morality they would suffer the fate of the person who 'cried wolf' and find themselves without the urgent labour when they really needed it. Communal forms of labour and/or cash contribution involve a switch to yet a different moral code. These presuppose the existence of community leaders whose decisions obligate its members. The giving of *dan* is motivated by religious and family obligations. These obligations can over-ride all others and even the very poor try to meet them by whatever means they can.

Anthropologists (see, e.g. Parry and Bloch)[20] have long drawn attention to facts of this kind noting, for example, that as money is often radically redefined as it enters the tribal world of people in Africa, Oceania, South America and elsewhere. They show that money does not necessarily depersonalise and corrode human relations as predicted by some value theorists. This argument

---

[20] J. Parry, M. Bloch (eds.), *Money and the Morality of Exchange* (Cambridge: Cambridge University Press, 1989).

is now being brought home, as it were, by the sociologists. Zelizer[21] in her study of 'domestic money' in the United States over the period 1870-1930. When money leaves the market place and enters the domestic sphere it is, she notes, 'earmarked' and its social meaning changes. Here it mediates the relation between husband and wife and is subject to new controls, restrictions, and modes of allocation and valuation. In terms of Figure 1, Zelizer is primarily concerned with the value switch from material (market) relations to that of family relations but notes that other switches are possible.

Clearly, an approach to the theory of value, such as that of neoclassical value theory, which sees the world from the perspect of the back of a shopping trolley, is unable to perceive different value regimes clearly let alone the value switching that goes on between them. This switching creates commodity free zones of various types. Switching between these value regimes is sometimes a matter of free choice but not always so. People everywhere are caught in complex social relationships — a factory worker, for example, does not stop being a father and husband when he leaves home each morning to go to work — and the cultural expression of these relations creates conflicting obligations.

## 6. Conclusions

In this paper I have argued that understanding the social practice of gift giving in comparative perspective raises philosophical questions of logical classification, conceptual issues in the history of value theory, and ethnographic and historical questions concerning the place of people in a changing economic and moral world. I have tried my best to give a sympathetic account of neoclassical theory by drawing attention to the theoretical and moral limits of any value theory. I showed, for example, that all value theorists have a tendency to claim superiority for their particular perspective be it from the factory floor (Marxian theory), behind the shopping trolley (neoclassical theory) or from that of the father (classical anthropology) and argued that the social practice of exchanging involves constant switching of value regimes. This does not mean that fixed-perspective value theory is wrong. To the contrary, a fixed perspective is needed for a coherent theory but the theorist needs to see the limits of their theory if it is to be useful. Neoclassical economists seem singularly incapable of doing this; indeed they seem to believe that its explanatory power has infinite horizons.

Despite my best attempts to do otherwise, I feel that I have not been able to conceal my overall lack of sympathy with neoclassical description and prescription. In this sense, I belong to a long tradition of critical anthropological thought. It could be argued, in fact, that economic anthropology began as a

---

[21] V. Zelizer, *The Social Meaning of Money* (New York: Basic Books, 1994).

negation of neoclassical economics. Malinowski's attacks on the 'economic man' of the neoclassical textbooks is well known; his classic work, *Argonauts of the Western Pacific*,[22] can be read as an attempt to develop a socially and culturally informed approach to economic analysis. It could be argued that Mauss's main concern in *The Gift*[23] was to develop a critique of the French economy and society of his time. The moral and theoretical conclusions he draws from his vast survey of the data suggest this. He argues, for example, that 'over-generosity, or communism, would be as harmful to himself and society as the egoism of our contemporaries and the individualism of our laws';[24] his assertion that the 'brutish pursuit of individual ends is harmful to the ends and the peace of all'[25] contradicts the Mandevillean morality upon which neoclassical economics is premised.

Neoclassical economics must be singled out for questioning if for no other reason than the fact that the free market anarchism it advocates is the dominant orthodoxy in the world today. Our obligation as intellectuals is to question; if we do not fulfil this obligation we run the risk of being converted into commodities by the global forces of commodification whose logic and morality we all struggle to comprehend.

## Bibliography

A. APPADURAI (ed.), *The Social Life of Things: Commodities in Cultural Perspective* (Cambridge: Cambridge University Press, 1986).

C. J. BLISS, N.H. STERN, *Palanpur: The Economy of an Indian Village* (Oxford: Clarendon Press, 1982).

I.M. BOCHENSKI, *A History of Formal Logic* (I. Thomas, transl.) (Notrue Dame: University of Notre Dame Press, 1956).

A. ETZIONI, Socio-Economics: A Budding Challenge, In *Socio-Economics: Towards a New Synthesis*, A. Etzioni, P.R. Lawrence (eds.), (New York: M.E. Sharpe, 1991) p. 3-7.

C.A. GREGORY, *Gifts and Commodities* (London: Academic Press, 1982).

C.A. GREGORY, *Savage Money* (London: Harwood, 1997).

G.C. HARCOURT, *The Social Science Imperialists* (London: Routledge & Kegan Paul, 1982).

B. MALINOWSKI, *Argonauts of the Western Pacific* (New York: Dutton, 1961).

M. MAUSS, *The Gift: The Form and Reason for Exchange in Archaic Societies* (New York: Norton, 1990).

L. MELAMED, *Leo Melamed on The Markets: Twenty Years of Financial History as Seen by the Man Who Revolutionaized the Markets* (New York: John Wiley, 1993).

---

[22] B. Malinowski, *Argonauts of the Western Pacific* (1921) (New York: Dutton, 1961).

[23] M. Mauss, *The Gift: The Form and Reason for Exchange in Archaic Societies* (New York: Norton, 1990).

[24] *Ibid*, p. 69.

[25] *Ibid*, p. 77.

D. MILLER, Consumption and Commodities, in *Annual Review of Anthropology*, 24 (1995) pp. 141-61.
J. PARRY, M. BLOCH (eds.), *Money and the Morality of Exchange* (Cambridge: Cambridge University Press, 1989).
M. SAHLins, *Stone Age Economics* (Chicago: Aldine, 1972).
V.P. VATUK, S. VATUK, 'The Social Context of Gift Exchange in North India', in G. Gupta (ed.), *Family and Social Change, Modern India* (Delhi: Vikas, 1975).
A. WOLFE, *Whose Keeper? Social Science and Moral Obligation* (Berkeley: University of, 1989)
V. ZELIZER, *The Social Meaning of Money* (New York: Basic Books, 1994)

# Beyond Purity and Danger:
# Gift-Giving in the Monotheistic Religions

Ilana F. SILBER* (The Hebrew University of Jerusalem)

## I Introduction

Ranging from charity to sacrifice, and entailing the cultivation of such related virtues as love, kindness, generosity or compassion, gift-giving is clearly a tenet of central importance in all the 'great', 'other-worldly' religions. Strangely enough, however, research on the complex range of ideals, institutions and practices of giving shaped by the impact of such religious traditions has remained rather limited, as well as heavily slanted towards the Buddhist and Hindu traditions of India and Southeast Asia.[1] Very little attention, in contrast, has been devoted to religious giving in the context of the three monotheistic traditions — Judaism, Christianity, Islam.[2] We are thus faced with a field of research that is still overwhelmingly the product of Western scholarship, and yet has hardly begun to address itself to those religious traditions (Judaism and Christianity primarily) which have been and still remain most deeply associated with the history of Western civilization.

It will be my aim in this text to raise a few comparative and conceptual issues emerging from that state of affairs. To begin with, I shall show that some of the issues at stake have been already intimated, if ever so sparsely, in the very brief section that Marcel Mauss devoted to religious giving in his classic and ever-seminal *Essai sur le Don*. Second, we shall see that while current treatments of religious giving have largely remained within the basic para-

---

\* I wish to thank David Shulman, and the participants of the colloquium "Gifts and Interests" at the Katholieke Universiteit Leuven for questions and comments which have contributed to improving the arguments of this paper.

[1] See most recently, also for a convenient access to a literature too extensive to be referred to in full, see G. Toffin, 'Hiérarchie et idéologie du don dans le monde indien' ('Hierarchy and Ideology of the Gift in the Indian World') in *L'Homme*, 114: 2 (1990) pp. 130-132; C. A. Gregory, 'The Poison in Raheja's Gift: A Review Article',in *Social Analysis*, 32 (1992). I.A. Silber, 'Gift-Giving in the Great Traditions: The Case of Donations to Monasteries in the Medieval West', in *Archives Européennes de Sociologie/European Journal of Sociology,* 36: 2 (1995) pp. 209-243.

[2] See however C. Tarot, 'Repères pour une histoire de la naissance de la grâce', ('Notes for a History of the Birth of Grace'), in *La Revue du Mauss semesterielle*, 1 (Paris: La Découverte, 1992) and C. Tarot, 'Christianisme et inconditionnalité' ('Christianity and Unconditionality'), in *La Revue du Mauss semesterielle*, 7: 1 (1996), pp. 338-366, in the field of Christianity; and for a survey of a remarkable surge of historical studies of gift-giving in the Christian Middle-Ages in particular; I.A. Silber, *art. cit.*

meters laid down by Mauss' original framework, some of them have also started showing signs of dissatisfaction with it.

Both Mauss and his critics, however, seem to me to impart an overly monolithic approach to religious giving in general and to ideas of reciprocity or interestedness in particular. I shall try here to suggest the need for a more differentiated and comparative approach, and will buttress my point through a brief consideration of religious giving in the context of traditional, rabbinical (i.e. Post-Exilic) Judaism — the very least examined, in this specific regard, of the three monotheistic religions.

## II Religious Giving in Mauss' *Essai sur le Don*

Marcel Mauss' central concern in the *Essai*, as well known, was to expose the generic features and principles of operation of the gift as a universal social phenomenon, displaying an impressive evolutionary continuity and an essentially similar nature across the most diverse historical periods and cultures. This heavy concern with continuity and similarity does not mean that Mauss never hinted at differences, or different forms and expressions of gift-giving. But even when he did, it is only in a marginal and subdued fashion, and never as to challenge the mainly essentializing and homogeneising thrust of his argument.[3,4]

This one-sided emphasis on the generic similarities of the gift in diverse contexts also explains the way in which the *Essai* addressed, or more precisely did not *really* address itself to the subject of *religious* giving more specifically.[5] In the very brief if separate section of the *Essai* devoted to that subject and entitled "gifts made to men and gifts made to gods",[6] it is again the basic similarity between these two types of gift that is emphasized: both aim to obtain peace with the gift's recipient, and both entail the same principle of expected return,

---

[3] I.F. Silber, 'Modern Philanthropy: Reassessing the Viability of a Maussian Perspective,' in Wendy James and Nick Allen (eds.), *Marcel Mauss: A Centenary Tribute* (Oxford: Berghahn, forthcoming); 'Le champ du don: pour une perspective historique comparée', in Marcel Fournier (ed.), *L'héritage de Marcel Mauss* (Montréal: Presses of the University of Montréal, forthcoming).

[4] Far from being representative of Mauss' work at large, such a thrust is in fact at variance with the rich sensitivity to cultural and empirical variability that is otherwise associated with Mauss' writings and is now better understood to have often led him astray from Durkheim.

[5] Mauss devoted surprisingly little attention to that subject, given the fact that he was deeply steeped in the history of religions and already the co-author in 1898 with H. Hubert of a study on sacrifice. Mauss himself is the first to recognize this insufficiency: "We have not undertaken the general study that would be necessary to bring out its importance (...) We shall therefore confine ourselves to a few remarks." (M. Mauss, *The Gift, The Form and Reason for Exchange in Archaic Societies* (Routledge, London, 1990 p. 14).

[6] M. Mauss, *op. cit.*, p. 14-18.

of *do ut des*. However, it is also here — or more precisely in a page-long subsection that deals with alms-giving ('l'aumône') and is simply entitled "a further note" ("autre remarque") — that Mauss hints for the first and only time, and by way of a few sentences merely, to the fact that the gift might also have undergone some major historical developments and transformations.

Two historical phases of transformations are thus briefly alluded to. A first phase, which Mauss sees evinced in the early stages of development of the Jewish notion of *zedakah* and the 'Arab' *sadaka*, saw the gift transformed into a principle of justice. Underpinning this transformation is a moral notion, or what we would rather term now a process of 'ethicization' of gift-giving and wealth on the one hand, and of sacrifice on the other: the affluent had to be willing to rid themselves of some of their excess of riches to compensate, through their gifts, for the inequality of wealth and fate among men; and the gods had to agree to this new usage of wealth that used to be previously offered to them in fruitless sacrifices. Following upon this first phase of transformation, Mauss alludes to a second phase, which engendered a further metamorphosis of the gift, this time from a principle of justice into one of charity and alms-giving. No further clue is given as to what was precisely meant by such distinctions and to what was entailed in that second transformation. Alluding to a change of rather momentous import, however, Mauss underscores the broad diffusion that awaited the new 'charitable' principle, fostered as it would be by the world expansion of Christianity and Islam.

For present purposes, it is of course striking that these brief and condensed allusions to important historical developments pertain only to what Mauss called the 'semitic' religions, or are now more commonly addressed as the three monotheistic religions, i.e. Judaism, Christianity and Islam. Moreover, later chapters of the *Essai* that deal with topics such as Roman and Hindu ancient systems of law, do not explore any further the theme of historical stages or transformations, nor provide us with any additional insights into the specific dynamics of religious giving proper.[7] As we shall see, however, it is precisely on the basis of research on religious giving in India that the first signs of dissatisfaction with Mauss' approach have begun to appear, together with a novel interest in historical processes and developments; while no effort was made to pursue the subject in the context of the monotheistic religions, where Mauss did explicitly start addressing the gift's distinctive processes of historical transformation.

---

[7] In fact, as already amply underscored by Trautmann and J. Parry, 'The Gift, the Indian Gift, and the Indian Gift', in *Man*, 21 (1986) pp. 453-473. Mauss appears to have somehow "blinded himself" to the significance of a major feature of the Brahminic ideology of giving — namely, the importance of non-reciprocity — of which he was evidently aware (see M. Mauss, *op. cit.*, p. 249), but which could not but collide with his own emphasis on the obligation to return as one of the universal principles of operation of the gift across historical periods and civilizations.

Let's now try to go beyond Mauss, and see the main terms of the debate as they currently present themselves in what is still a very small body of literature. As we shall see, much — and I dare already say *too* much — has revolved around the issue of reciprocity.

### III  Reciprocity Reconsidered: Beyond Mauss?

Far from contesting Mauss, most anthropologists or scholars of archaic religions have in fact largely accepted his general approach and even further built upon it. A most recent work in this vein, for example, is Walter Burckert's *The Creation of the Sacred*.[8] Religious giving, as Burckert sees it, is basically conform to a fundamental, biological principle of homeostatic balance and reciprocity, diffusely applied by human beings in their interaction with their human and physical environment, and naturally extended to their relation to the sacred. Admittedly, Burckert does take note of certain features that would seem difficult to reconcile with this general argument, such as the absence of evidence for returns from the gods, or the sharp opposition occasionally voiced by such major historical figures as Plato or Jesus. For example, against an overly 'commercial', reciprocal conception of religious offerings. But such oppositionary currents are only made to appear in his scheme as marginal, temporary deviations from the dominant and more pervasive trend, deeply rooted in reciprocity.

For Burckert as indeed for most of those who have treated that theme after Mauss, religious giving appears thus as just another variant of gift-exchange, basically in line (whatever the particulars) with the three-fold sequence of obligations (the obligation to give, to receive, to return) that was so fundamental to Mauss' approach to the gift.[9]

In contrast, a small minority of scholars have sensed some important divergences and discontinuities between religious giving and the basic features or principles of the gift more generally as outlined by Mauss.[10] And significantly,

---

[8] W. Burckert, *Creation of the Sacred: Tracks of Biology in Early Religions* (Cambridge, Mass.: Harvard University, 1996).

[9] In the sense of emphasizing a basic continuity and homology between patterns of social giving and religious giving, I would also include Alain Testard, *Des dons et des dieux, antropologie religieuse et sociologie comparative* (*About Gifts and Gods. Religious Anthropology and Comparative Sociology*) (Paris: Armand Colin, 1993) even if disclosing a diversity rather than unity of patterns among the three civilizational areas it explores.

[10] Although primarily concerned with a form of giving which he declares to be resolutely secular, another, much more extensive and yet insufficiently acknowledged challenge to the Maussian approach is to be found in P. Veyne, *Le pain et le cirque (Bread and Circuses)* (Paris: Presses Universitaires de France, 1976); a study also entailing number of interesting passages on the differences between Greek-evergetic and Jewish or Christian patterns of religious giving. See I. Silber, 'Le champ du don: pour une perspective historique comparée' ('The Field of the Gift:

it is again the principle of reciprocity, or more precisely of its opposite — i.e. the absence or negation of reciprocity — that has been at the center of attention. While hints of similar arguments may be found scattered in other works,[11] I shall only address here the fuller statement advanced by Jonathan Parry in an article published already more than a decade ago.[12]

Rather than reciprocity, it is the development of elaborate ideologies of non-reciprocity and disinterestedness indeed which strikes Parry as a characteristic feature of the gift in all the great 'world religions'.[13] Such a strong ideological stress on 'pure', disinterested giving, the argument follows, implies a radical rupture with the obligation to return (however stretched or delayed in time) that had so monopolized Mauss' attention, and seems to Parry to have been facilitated by the combination of two major conditions which could not be found in archaic settings and would only obtain in the 'great traditions': first, a high level of social (mainly economic and political) differentiation, that allowed the gift to be 'unburdened', as it were, of much of its previous economic, social and political functions; and second, a religious belief system with a strong emphasis on transcendental, other-worldly orientations.[14]

To that extent, in fact, the interest of Parry's thesis lies not only in the challenge it poses to the Maussian approach, but also in the attempt it entails (the only one to date to my knowledge) to approach religious giving from a comparative-historical and macrosociological perspective. As such, it also augurs the possibility of a new, non-monolithic approach, more intent to start mapping out a diverse range of gift-processes (e.g. ideologically reciprocal vs. non-reciprocal) than to keep searching for the latter's 'essential', or ubiquitous features. As we shall see, however, Parry's formulation still keeps approaching the issue of *religious* giving, specifically, from what remains an overly general and monolithic point of view.

## IV Religious Giving Diversified

Rather than opting wholesale for either Burkert or Parry, we may want to ask ourselves whether they have the same kind of religious giving in mind. It is

---

Towards a Comparative Historical Perspective'), in Marcel Fournier (ed.), *L'héritage de Marcel Mauss (The Heritage of Marcel Mauss)* (Montréal: Presses of the University of Montréal, forthcoming).

[11] P. Veyne, *op. cit.* M. Godelier, *L'énigme du don* (The Ethics of the Gift) (Paris: Gallimard, 1996).

[12] J.P. Parry, 'The Gift, the Indian Gift, and the Indian Gift', in *Man*, 21 (1986) pp. 453-473.

[13] For a closely related but less general argument, limiting itself to India, see Trautmann 1986. Both Parry and Trautmann have criticized Mauss (himself well-trained in Indology) for half-noticing, and yet understating this aspect of the gift to Brahmins in India.

[14] J.P. Parry, *op. cit.*, p.468.

perhaps not incidental that those few authors (including Mauss himself) who elaborated on the essential continuity or homology between religious and ordinary giving, have mostly focused on giving to the god(s).[15] We may also include in the same line of thought those treatments of sacrifice that have seen in it a strong component of gift-giving (not all do).[16] In contrast, it is worth noticing that Parry's argument had its starting point in the study of a different kind of religious giving, namely gifts to Brahmans, that is, to a kind of ritual specialists.

One reason thus for the divergence of approach to religious giving between scholars like Burkert and Parry may perhaps be that gifts to the gods and gifts to religious specialists are simply very different kinds of religious giving, and cannot possibly be expected to be accounted for by one simple and unified model or theory.

But even if we set aside gifts to the gods for the moment, we still need to take note of a number of problematic features in Parry's argument, which seem to me to undermine its validity as a general model of religious giving (even in the limited confines of other-worldly religious traditions).[17]

First, there is a tension between Parry's general comparative argument, which presents non-reciprocity as influenced and facilitated by ideals of other-worldliness and transcendence, and at least some of the reasons for the break in reciprocity that emerge from his own field research in India, and which have much more to do with a whole range of beliefs about pollution and sin.[18] From this latter angle, the gift is held to embody the sins of the donor, who so hopes to unburden himself of sinful substances by transferring them *via* the gift to a Brahman; the latter is in turn supposed to be able to cancel the entailed danger of contamination either by the proper enactment of related rituals, or by transferring it to other Brahmans. Both sets of beliefs — the other-worldly ideals of disinterested giving and the assumptions concerning the operation of the gift as vector of impurity and danger — are in fact shown to coexist in Parry's later and much fuller rendering of his study of gifts to Brahmans in the mortu-

---

[15] See however M. Godelier, *op. cit.*, for the sense of a sharp difference, even in so-called archaic context, between gifts to men and gifts to the gods — the latter entailing much more assymetry.

[16] There are different stances concerning the relation between gift-giving and sacrifice. See A. Caillé, 'Sacrifice, don et utilitarisme; notes sur la théorie du sacrifice' ('Sacrifice, Gift and Utilitarianism: Notes on the Theory of Sacrifice'), in *A quoi bon (se) sacrifier?: sacrifice, don et intérêt,* in *La revue du Mauss semestrielle,* 5: 1 (1995) pp. 248-293, and C. Rivière, 'Approches comparatives du sacrifice' ('Comparative Approaches to Sacrifice'), in F. Boespflug and F. Dunand (eds.), *Le comparatisme en histoire des religions* (Paris: Cerf, 1997) pp. 279-290. Much would seem to depend, moreover, on what conception of the gift is applied.

[17] I do believe though that Parry correctly points to a set of issues that are not easy to accommodate in the original Maussian perspective; the following points of critique are thus a tribute to his important empirical and theoretical pointers.

ary pilgrimage center of Banaras. It thus becomes difficult to attribute non-reciprocity to the sole and direct effect of other-worldly disinterestedness and purity, and even more so when the latter are anyway presented as hovering about in this context as real but largely ineffective ideals.[19]

Second, Parry repeatedly refers, in the general, comparative part of his argument, to what he calls the "charitable", pure gift. 'Charity', admittedly, may have a rather broad semantic application in the Christian tradition, where it may even come to overlap with a very general idea of pious, religious giving. More ordinarily, however, the term is primarily used to refer to giving to the poor or other needy, and are not so obviously applicable to the gifts to Brahmans which formed the starting point of Parry's discussion.[20]

Third, it seems to me that Parry posits too much of a self-evident overlap, even identity, between the break in reciprocity — what in contrast to Mauss' rule of the obligation to return the gift, may be called the law of *non-return* — and the more general notion of 'disinterestedness'. In fact, the version of the pure, disinterested gift which he advances is a rather moderate and non-absolute one, which fully admits the belief in eventual other-worldly, or even in some cases, worldly rewards to the donor.[21] The more important feature in his mind indeed is not the precise extent or absence of expected rewards, but rather the break in reciprocity, that is, the fact that such rewards as may obtain are not expected to come from the recipient, from the person to whom the gift is given in the first place.[22] This is of course a very specific conception, and it

---

[18] There are many intricate intersections which I cannot enter here with debates among Indologists and anthropologists of India, all still struggling in a way or another with Dumont's work, and its implications for the analysis of gift-processes. Differences of interpretation are thus themselves often rooted in broader differences of interpretation of the social and ideological features of Indian society at large. See especially G.G. Raheja, *The Poison in the Gift: Ritual, Prestation, and the Dominant Caste in a North Indian Village* (Chicago: University Press, 1988).

[19] The dynamics of giving are said to be rather shaped, in practice, through the ever-partial and inevitably imperfect efforts at management, by both donors and donees, of a volatile economy of impure and sinful substances. Moreover, the very motive of alleviating oneself of one's sins via the gift is said to contradict, at the limit, the ideal of an utterly pure and "disinterested" gift (J. Parry, *Death in Banaras* (Cambridge: Cambridge University Press, 1994) p. 128.

[20] It should be noted that this term is not usually associated with offerings to the gods (sacrificial or not) either; confirming our feeling that the kind of giving that Parry has in mind is different from that focused upon by Burckert.

[21] Again, however, there is some tension with the fuller discussion of the Indian case in J. Parry, *op. cit.*, where the ideal gift (*dan*) is sometimes said to be conditional upon the absence of any expectation of *worldly* rewards, sometimes said to even be devoid of desire for any other-worldly rewards at all.

[22] Parry does insist, however, that the belief in such rewards imply a leap of faith on his part, due to the abstract nature of the mechanisms involved (such as god's grace, the laws of karma) and their being basically incommensurable to what was given as a gift in the first place. This is still of course very different from the modern, paradoxically much more radical conception of the disinterested, true gift, automatically tainted by the suspicion of any material or ideal interests or so-called "ulterior motives".

is for example a far-cry from our own current, and in fact much more radical conception of disinterestedness: whether coming from the recipient or not, the tendency now is to posit true disinterestedness as incompatible with the expectation of any sort of reward at all. Confirming the need to distinguish between these very different uses of the notion of 'disinterestedness', moreover, this more radical conception is by now understood by many and by Parry himself, as a historical development dialectically related to modern notions of self-interest and of the market[23] — thus also implicitly dismissing any connection to 'other-worldly' religious orientations.[24]

What emerges thus, to my mind, from the juxtaposition and critical reading of both Burckert and Parry's arguments, are three major points: first, the need to distinguish between at least three broad types of religious giving: giving to the gods, giving to religious institutions or religious specialists (what may be called, in brief, 'cultic' giving), and giving to the poor and needy; second, the need to avoid presuming that these various types of religious giving display the same essential dynamics, and in particular, a same emphasis on either reciprocity or non-reciprocity; and third, to perhaps start developing a more diversified approach to the meaning and importance of 'disinterestedness' itself.

It would be misleading, however, to overly reify the differences between these various patterns of religious giving. I propose, rather, to see them as coexisting and competing, with varying importance and degrees of mutual differentiation or interpenetration, in the context of differential 'repertoires' or 'fields' of giving shaped by the impact of diverse and historically evolving institutional frameworks and religious traditions. Religious traditions may thus vary in the kind of religious giving which they tend to most encourage, or most elaborate in doctrine and ideology. This of course should not be taken to mean that other forms of religious giving are totally absent in either ideology or practice, but that they remain relatively more marginal and less explicitly articulated.

## V The 'Indian' vs. monotheistic repertoires of religious giving

In such terms, I perceive a major and intriguing contrast between the repertoire of giving shaped by the impact of the broadly designated 'Indian' religions and

---

[23] P. Bourdieu,"The Field of Cultural Production or the Economic World Reversed", in *Poetics* 12: 4-5 (1983) pp. 311-356; J. Carrier, *Gifts and Commodities: Exchange and Western Capitalism since 1700*. (London: Routledge, 1995); J. Parry, *op. cit.*, pp. 453-473.

[24] I tend to see Derrida's discussion of the gift in J. Derrida, *L'éthique du don (The Ethics of the Gift)* (Paris: Métailié, 1992) as a philosophical variant of this more radical and absolutizing contemporary approach.

that of the three monotheistic religions. Occupying the centerstage in the repertoire of religious giving in the Indian traditions is the gift by laymen (including kings) to religious specialists and religious institutions — 'cultic giving' — to the point of powerfully overshadowing and pushing to the margins (if certainly never cancelling) charitable giving to the poor. Perhaps the most clear-cut case of this kind is the repertoire of giving characteristic of societies where Theravada Buddhism has been prevalent, and where offerings (*dana*) to the order of monks (the *sangha*) overshadow all other forms of religious giving; central ideals of universal compassion and loving-kindness notwithstanding, charity to the poor remains much more marginal.[25]

By contrast, and as indeed already intuited by Mauss, charitable giving to the poor becomes a much more central motif in all monotheistic religions. Conversely, donations to religious specialists and institutions recede in relative soteriological importance; this does not mean that religious specialists and institutions are not provided for, but that they are provided for through other means than donations: in the case of Christianity for example, or of pre-exilic Judaism, compulsory tithing and taxes rather than gifts were destined to function as the primary means of material support.

Of course, these very rough contrasts are not absolute and there may be important fluctuations in time: I have myself produced a detailed analysis of the specific convergence of contextual forces which enabled donations to monasteries in the medieval West to thrive on an enormous scale for a number of centuries despite the absence of any early doctrinal groundings calling for it.[26] Sustaining this process, among other factors, was also the tendency to view monks as both the true Christian 'poor' or alternatively, as the appropriate dispensors of charitable giving, thus fusing the two types of giving distinguished above.[27] And while not as explicit, a similar ambiguity in the understanding of religious elites or specialists — as spiritually/ritually superior and yet also materially poor and in need of 'charitable' support — emerges in Indian contexts as well.[28]

---

[25] See also R.A. Lohmann, 'Buddhist Commons and the Question of a Third Sector in Asia', in *Voluntas*, 6: 2 (1995) pp. 140-158, for a similar observation. I shall not try here to explain such important variations, but just to record them. To begin with, one would have to closely examine the very notions of loving-kindness and compassion propounded in Theravada texts, as well as their nearest equivalents in other religious traditions, and in particular in each monotheistic tradition.

[26] I. Silber, 'Modern Philanthropy: Reassessing the Viability of a Maussian Perspective', in Wendy James and Nick Allen (eds.), *Marcel Mauss: A Centenary Tribute* (Oxford: Berghahn, forthcoming).

[27] Although this would need more detailed and careful substantiation, the golden age of donations to monasteries does not seem to have been very favourable to more clearly differentiated "charitable" endeavours; and the latter seem to have enjoyed significant expansion precisely at a time when donations to monasteries underwent a drastic decline.

[28] Largely latent in classical Brahminical ideology, it thus seems to flare up in the changing climate of the late-sixteenth century Nayaka period in south India, with a new, emphatic preoc-

Undoubtedly, these remain very rough distinctions, and would demand further conceptualization, as well as some attempt at sub-differentiation within each broad type (there may be more), and a more refined understanding of their mutual relations.[29] Both analytically and phenomenologically, however, there is need to draw a distinction between charitable giving, i.e. giving as a way to provide for the usually basic and largely material necessities of the poor and other needy on the one hand, and 'cultic giving' — giving as a way to promote, pay tribute to, or in any other way relate to, a religious institution or spiritual-cultural elite geared to some form of supra-material, transcendent reality on the other. Furthermore, both cultic and charitable giving need be distinguished from, and may differentially interrelate with, giving to the gods.

Introducing the relative weight, differentiation and interrelation of various patterns of religious giving as a significant and variable feature of repertoires of giving is thus advanced here as one possible way of developing a more diversified approach than hitherto extant in either the classical Maussian approach or its more recent elaborators and critiques. No less intriguing, I wish to submit, is what happens to notions of interestedness versus disinterestedness that have played a central role in current discussions of religious giving once viewed from the perspective of such a comparative approach to historical repertoires of giving.

It is with such a set of issues in mind that I shall turn now to briefly examine the repertoire of religious giving in the context of the Jewish rabbinical tradition.

## VI Religious Giving in the Jewish tradition

Stating the case a bit bluntly, religious giving in the Jewish tradition — largely if not entirely subsumed under the key motif of *Zedaka* — is primarily concerned with giving to the poor and needy. Moreover, it seems to be strangely

---

cupation of kings with the lavish offering of food — rather than the more traditional royal gift of land — to large numbers of deprived Brahmins (R. Narayana, Velcheru, D. Shulman and S. Subrahmanyam, *Symbols of Substance: Court and State in Nayaka Period Tamilnadu* (Delhi: Oxford University Press, 1992)).

[29] One may wish to distinguish for example between giving to the gods, giving to men or institutions in name of god(s), or for the sake of some ultimate "religious" principle. Within this last category in turn, one may want to further distinguish between giving for the funding of religious activity, personnel or institutions — what T. Brook for one chooses to call religious patronage (T. Brook, *Praying for Power: Buddhism and the Formation of Gentry Society in Late-Ming China* (Cambridge: Harvard University Press, 1993) — which seems to emphasize the latter's need for material support, thus to that extent partly converging with giving to poor and other needy) on the one hand, and giving as a distinctive form of spiritual relationship on the other. While these dimensions of religious patronage — the more instrumental and spiritual-expressive — are often intertwined, they need be kept analytically distinct.

oblivious to some of the central issues we have seen hitherto associated with religious giving: it is not very perturbed by issues of purity or danger, nor much concerned at all with non-reciprocity, and not even terribly preoccupied with disinterestedness.

I shall only deal here with so-called rabbinical Judaism which emerged some two thousand years ago and whose classic texts, the Mishna and Talmud were written down and canonized in late Antiquity. Over the centuries, a massive corpus of rabbinical literature evolved containing both halakhic and aggadic material, the former largely legal in nature, the latter, speculative, ethical and even fictional. This traditional Judaism held sway until the end of the eighteenth century; its authority has been steadily eroded since then and it is now accepted unquestioned only by the Orthodox minority. Nevertheless, much of the basic thrust of classical rabbinical Judaism with regard to Zedaka and related 'ethico-religious' matters has continued to exercise its hold even on the other two main branches of modern Judaism, the Conservative and Reform movements.

Sacrifices and offerings to God, as well as obligatory tithes to priests and levites — roughly corresponding to what I have called here "gifts to the gods" and "cultic giving" — had been an important feature of earlier, biblical phases of Judaism. The context of the centuries following the destruction of the Second Temple (70 C.E) and the exile from the Holy Land, however, was one where these various forms of giving could no longer be performed anymore, and were to be replaced by prayers — which even before had already been conceived of as the other main form of *avoda*, or worship of God.[30]

As for charitable giving to the poor, it also already appeared in the Bible, mainly in the form of various types of tithing meant to reserve a part of the agriculture produce for the poor.[31] Yet it is precisely and only in the later, rabbinical period that *Zedaka* as a supreme religious commandment incumbent upon all (even the recipients of charity themselves) came to occupy the centerstage of the Jewish repertoire or field of giving, and to acquire there a remarkable level of doctrinal and practical elaboration.[32]

As rightly noted by Mauss, the concept of *zedaka* is primarily derived from, and strongly connotes, notions of righteousness and justice *(zedek)*. This was

---

[30] See S. Trigano, 'La fonction lévitique: le système du don hébraique' ('The Levitic Function: the Hebraic System of the Gift'), in *La Revue du Mauss semestrielle*, 8 (1996) pp. 220-242 for some important vistas into the religious matrix of the gift at those times through a focus on Levites.

[31] *Deut.* 15.7b, 8a; *Lev.* 25.35b.

[32] There is no recent, updated, history of Jewish charity. See however B. D. Bogen, *Jewish Philanthropy* (New York: Macmillan, 1917) and Y. Bergman, *HaZedaka be-Israel: toldoteia ve-mosadoteia* (Jerusalem: Reuven Mass, 1940). I shall only deal here with normative conceptions prevalent in basic halakhic sources, leaving aside the development of historical practices and institutions.

understood to mean, above all, that *zedaka* is not an occasional favour done to the poor, but something that rightfully belongs to them, to which they are entitled. Rather than being left to the initiative of individuals, charitable giving was thus made into a matter of collective responsibility, supervised by communal leaders or other appointed officials; the latter were allowed to actively constrain community members to contribute to the collective charitable funds if need be, or even imposing negative sanctions of all sorts upon those who try to evade the obligation. In a more positive vein, acts of *zedaka* were believed to be religiously meritorious and rewarded both in this and the after-life; to such an extent in fact that no loss could ever be incurred by the donor, since the gift was believed to be amply compensated by a whole range of possible rewards. Moreover, *zedaka* was to be given preferably in well-balanced proportions, one-tenth of one's current property being the common norm, one-fifth the maximal ceiling enjoined, and any excessive, let alone self-sacrificial generosity explicitly discouraged.[33]

In terms of gift-theory, however, we may well wonder if we are still in the realm of giving: commandment, obligatory tithes, justice, supervision, sanctions and rewards are all terms which would seem to contradict the kind of free, voluntary and disinterested impulse commonly associated with giving, and especially essential to what I have called here the contemporary, 'radical' conception of disinterestedness.

Admittedly, Mauss' conception of the gift may seem to somewhat mitigate the importance of such voluntary and disinterested impulses, and to be thus more compatible with the mainstream, rabbinical approach to Zedaka. The gift, for him is rather an intrinsically paradoxical social phenomenon, combining both freedom and constraint, interestedness and disinterestedness, and giving much weight, in the context of archaic societies at least, to the impact of obligations and shared expectations. Moreover, the 'interestedness' of Zedaka is itself of an ambiguous kind: one does find repeated praise of *Zedaka,* as indeed of all commandments more generally, enacted not for the sake of the reward (or in fear of negative sanctions), but with only the intrinsic value of the commandment itself in mind. Yet the picture hitherto presented of *zedaka* makes it such a heavily obligatory, institutionalized and regimented affair, that it may seem to lose this vital element of paradoxical tension between contradictory poles — to me still one of the most pivotal (and too often forgotten) insights of the Maussian approach.[34]

---

[33] See for example Maimonides, *Hilekhot 'Arakin* VIII-13.

[34] The paradoxical approach to the gift so important to Mauss seems to me to reemerge in a new fashion in Gregory's idea of "coevalness" of seemingly contradictory orientations (C.A. Gregory, *Savage Money: The Anthropology and Politics of Commodity Exchange* (Amsterdam: Hardwood, 1997)).

Could we not perhaps still perceive in Zedaka, as just described, something more akin to Parry's *idée force* of the 'pure' gift? The decisive feature then, as explained above, becomes perhaps not so much the free and disinterested aspect of religious giving, but rather the emphatic ideological valorization of non-reciprocity. True enough, no return gift to the donor is actually expected from recipients of charitable giving.[35] And although the charitable donor is expected to incur both heavenly and worldly rewards, these are not given to him by the donee, but by divine mechanisms of soteriological retribution.

Yet if elements of disinterestedness and non-reciprocity do obtain, the more interesting point perhaps is that they also acquire ideational and emotional connotations that seem substantially different from those obtaining in India, or in the Christian West. One paramount concern in the Jewish tradition, extensively elaborated upon in all relevant treatises and codexes, is the importance of *zedaka* given in the proper manner, in the sense of avoiding shaming or humiliating the recipient. This is the primary reason in fact for the well-known valorization of the anonymous charitable gift (or more precisely the hidden, or secret gift, *matan beseter*), where varying ways are devised to prevent mutual encounter or even mutual knowledge of the donor and the donee, as to allow not only the donor but chiefly the recipient to preserve his anonymity. Such was the well-known chamber that was set aside in the Temple, which one entered alone, enabled to take or leave donations unobserved. All of Moses Maimonides' (1135-1204) influential list of eight degrees of benevolence may be shown to be thus graded by reference to their relative protection of the recipient's feelings.[36] It is this kind of concern for the recipient's dignity in fact, rather than the precise amount of disinterested intention on the donor's part, that forms the backbone of any attempt at establishing a hierarchy of giving in the Jewish tradition. And while there is awareness and even praise of the special virtue of disinterested intentions, ample room is reserved for all forms of 'legitimate' interests (including the explicit public praise of generous

---

[35] The terms and manner of acceptance of charitable giving, however, would need further research. Recipients of charity were not forbidden to reciprocate; moreover, conveying blessings and good wishes for the donor's benefit were at least a formulaic, customary way for the recipient to expressing some form of gratitude and mutuality vis-à-vis the donor (as we shall see below, often unknown, or not in proximity). Recipients of charity may also be deemed to "reciprocate" by the very fact of allowing the donor to fulfill his religious duties.

[36] Three of those grades (second, third, fourth) discriminate between various types of absence of acquaintance between donor and donee. Significantly, the highest degree is "a gift, loan, business partnership or job", that is charitable help disguising itself as something else and rendering acceptance of what would obviously be a charitable gift altogether unnecessary. Moses Maimonides (1135-1204) "code of benevolence", listing of eight degrees of charity (Mishne Torah VII: *Matnot 'Aniyim* X, 7-14). The same degrees reappear in roughly the same form in Joseph Caro's (1488-1575) Shulkhan Arukh. See A. Cronbach, 'The Maimonidean Code of Benevolence', in *HUCA* 20 (1947), pp. 471-540, for a thorough examination of the relationship of Maimonides to previous sources in the elaboration of this code.

donors in synagogue services) to facilitate and reward charitable giving, as long as, once again, the prime interest of the recipient is properly served and protected.[37]

These features of *zedaka*, therefore, make it difficult to align with a straightforward, monolithic understanding of the gift in either its classicly 'Maussian' reciprocal, or 'disinterested' and non-reciprocal, versions. Rather than focusing on issues of either disinterestedness or reciprocity, it seems to me that we may well have to look somewhere else in order to retrieve some of the more elusive but vital forces of the gift in what otherwise seems to become a highly moralized, collectively enforced mechanism for the redistribution of wealth and social justice. While not able to enter those into any detail, it may suffice here to hint at three features mainly:

1. Repeated attempts at codification and hierarchization of various forms of Zedaka notwithstanding, uncertainty abounds in the Jewish tradition as to the hierarchy and priorities of giving. Much thought is given to the many possible dilemmas entailed in giving and some dilemmas seem to have received rather clear-cut answers. For example, one is supposed to give to one's own family first; within the family, to one's father and mother first; to one's poor neighbours before other poor of one's city; to the poor of one's own city before the poor of another city.[38] Issues such as giving to one poor or to many; giving always to the same person, or varying the choice of beneficiary; giving to the poor of one's city first or to the Jewish communities in Israel;[39] giving to the poor or giving for the material maintainance of the synagogue; giving or accepting charity from non-Jews etc… are also given rather explicit, albeit often debated answers. Yet uncertainty and contradictions also abound, opening a whole range of alternative options and giving room for free choice. And it is far from uncommon to find the text first opting for a specific stance and then seemingly subverting it a few lines later.

2. The distinction obtaining in the Jewish tradition, albeit far from absolute and ever systematically pursued, between *zedaka* and *hesed*. (The latter is also often called *gmilut-hassadim*, acts of loving-kindness). Unlike *zedaka*, *hesed* is seen by some as corresponding to a realm of voluntary supererogatory giving, and connotes a freer, as well as more personalized (rather than impersonal) form of help, one also less necessarily or exclusively geared to urgent material

---

[37] Secret giving has also been valorized in other religious traditions, but only as a way of maximizing disinterestedness on the part of the donor, and without acquiring that same additional emphasis on the need to protect the recipient's feelings.

[38] At the same time, there are repeated assertions of the overriding priority of giving to the poor and scholars in the land of Israel, although here again, there are divergences of opinion. See M. M. Rotschild, *The Haluka; A Facet of the Relationship of Diaspora Jews to the Jews of Eretz Israel from 1810 to 1860* (Hebrew) (Jerusalem: Rubin Mass, 1986).

[39] See fn. 29.

or immediate needs. Independently of the above-mentioned distrust of excessive generosity, moreover, there is also replete textual evidence of telling and retelling of vivid heroic personal examples to the contrary.

3. The existence of a partly overlapping, partly distinct realm of voluntary support of Torah scholars and learning, that eventually will develop an entire range of independent themes.[40] Somewhat close to what we addressed above as 'cultic' giving, and yet perhaps a distinct subvariant of it, giving for the support of Torah scholarship is often found to closely compete in *halakhic* texts and *responsa* (questions-and-answers) for priority over charity to the poor, and to connote a much greater degree of freedom than implied within the confines of the general parameters of *zedaka* as outlined above. And yet again, interestingly, textual treatments of this distinct set of themes do not seem to convey any more emphatic concern with disinterestedness — be it in its moderate or radical versions. To the contrary, there even evolved (at least in theory) a peculiar brand of fully explicit, contractual models of gift-relationship between sponsor and recipient — as manifested in the development of multiple variants of the motif of Zevulon and Issachar in particular — whereby the sponsor may in fact explicitly and in full legitimacy try to regulate such matters as the amount of spiritual merit which a scholar may agree to 'share' with him.

The importance of the above 'secondary' features of Jewish religious giving, I submit, is precisely that they tend to present zedaka as not only one but a range of possible orientations and practices, and to comprehend it, furthermore, within the context of a wider field, or repertoire of religious giving. Only then does a vital element of uncertainty and voluntary option, one also requiring on-going individual as well as communal selective practices, re-emerge as still very much alive and part and parcel of Jewish charitable giving — even after its transformation (as Mauss had originally formulated it) into a "principle of justice".

## Conclusion

I hope to have thus suggested the need to distinguish between at least three broad types of religious giving: giving to the gods, giving to religious institutions or religious specialists (what may be called, in brief, 'cultic' giving), and

---

[40] Although I shall not have the place to enter this issue into any detail, we need to note that there is no clear-cut institutional differentiation of scholars from others. Moreover there are divergent stances on whether scholars should be allowed to devote themselves totally to study or also work for their material support. Support to scholars was partly taken care of through marriage and kinship, mainly by the mariage of a promising scholar to a wealthy man's daughter; or by the scholar's wife's income, usually from some small commerce.

charitable giving to the poor and needy. (there may be more).[41] Moreover, I have argued that we should avoid presuming that these various types of religious giving display the same emphasis on either reciprocity or non-reciprocity; and that we should perhaps start developing a more diversified approach to the meaning and importance of 'disinterestedness' itself as it has been shaped in the context of diverse religious traditions.

This may well mean the need to depart (if perhaps only as a temporary heuristic step) from Mauss' relentless quest for continuities and similarities between varying expressions of the gift phenomenon across historical periods and civilizations, and rather follow those like Parry and many others who have now started to give a new importance to discontinuities and differences.[42]

The point, though, is not simply the need for more refined typologies. Here I am more than satisfied to conclude with borrowing the felicitous statement by Nicholas Thomas, nurtured by his own search for a more diversified conceptualization of the gift: "...once the distinctiveness of a particular entity or process has been established, the general concept needs to be fractured; not split up, as a partitioned essence in a formalistic typology, but instead scattered through the nuances of practice and history".[43] A delicate task indeed, but one which I believe will have to become part and parcel of a truly comparative sociological understanding of repertoires of giving.

**Bibliography**

T. BROOK, *Praying for Power: Buddhism and the Formation of Gentry Society in Late-Ming China* (Cambridge: Harvard University Press, 1993).
Y. BERGMAN, *HaZedaka be-Israel: toldoteia ve-mosadoteia* (Jerusalem: Reuven Mass, 1940).
B.D. BOGEN, *Jewish Philanthropy* (New York: Macmillan, 1917).
P. BOURDIEU, "The Field of Cultural Production or the Economic World Reversed", in *Poetics* 12: 4-5 (1983) pp. 311-356.
W. BURCKERT, *Creation of the Sacred: Tracks of Biology in Early Religions* (Cambridge, Mass.: Harvard University, 1996).

---

[41] Another kind is perhaps giving to the dead. There may be a distinction to be made between gifts aimed at helping the dead to achieve salvation or peace in the hereafter vs. just at appeasing their anger and preempting their punishing, retaliatory actions. This whole issue, however, would demand a thorough assessment.

[42] Such a trend, finding its early (and extreme) starting point in Paul Veyne's *Bread and Circuses, op. cit.*, is now acquiring new importance — albeit in very different terms — in such works as Alain Caillé, *Ni holisme, ni individualisme méthodologiques. Marcel Mauss et le paradigme du don (Neither Holism nor methodological Individualism. Marcel Mauss and the Paradigm of the Gift),* in *L'obligation de donner. La découverte sociologique capitale de Marcel Mauss (The Obligation to Give. Marcel Mauss' Captial Sociological Discovery).*

[43] N. Thomas, *Entangled Objects: Exchange, Material Culture and Colonialism in the Pacific* (Cambridge, Mass.: Harvard University Press, 1991).

A. CAILLÉ, 'Sacrifice, don et utilitarisme; notes sur la théorie du sacrifice' (Sacrifice, Gift and Utilitarianism, Notes on the Theory of Sacrifice), in *A quoi bon (se) sacrifier?: sacrifice, don et intérêt,* in *La revue du M.A.U.S.S.* 5: 1 (1995) pp. 248-293

J. CARRIER, *Gifts and Commodities: Exchange and Western Capitalism since 1700.* (London: Routledge, 1995).

J.B. CARMAN, F.A. Marglin (eds.), *Purity and Auspiciousness in Indian Society* (Leiden: E.J. Brill, 1985).

A. CRONBACH, 'The Maimonidean Code of Benevolence', in *HUCA* 20 (1947), pp. 471-540.

J. DERRIDA, *L'éthique du don* (The Ethics of the Gift) (Paris: Métailié, 1992).

F. EPHRAIM, *A Historical Survey of Jewish Philanthropy* (New York: Macmillan, 1924).

M. GODELIER, *L'énigme du don* (The Ethics of the Gift) (Paris: Gallimard, 1996).

C.A. GREGORY, 'The Poison in Raheja's Gift: A Review Article', in *Social Analysis,* 32 (1992).

— *Savage Money: The Anthropology and Politics of Commodity Exchange.* (Amsterdam: Hardwood, 1997).

T. LINDERS, G. NORDQUIST (eds.), *Gifts for the Gods* (Upssala, 1987).

R.A. LOHMANN, 'Buddhist commons and the question of a third sector in Asia', in *Voluntas,* 6: 2 (1995) pp. 140-158.

M. MARRIOTT, 'Hindu Transactions: Diversity Without Dualism', in B. Kapferer (ed.), *Transaction and Meaning* (Philadelphia: ISHI, 1976).

M. MAUSS, *The Gift, The Form and the Reason for Exchange in Archaic Societies* (Routledge, London, 1990).

R. NARAYANA, Velcheru, D. Shulman and S. Subrahmanyam, *Symbols of Substance: Court and State in Nayaka Period Tamilnadu* (Delhi: Oxford University Press,1992).

J. PARRY, 'The Hind Lexicographer: A Note on Auspiciousness and Purity', in *Contributions to Indian Sciology* 25 (1991), pp. 267-85.

— *Death in Banaras* (Cambridge: Cambridge University Press, 1994).

— 'The Gift, the Indian Gift, and the Indian Gift', in *Man,* 21 (1986) pp. 453-473.

— 'Sacrificial Death and the Necrophageous Ascetic', in M. Bloch and J. Parry (eds.), *Death and Regeneration of Life* (Cambridge: Cambridge University Press, 1982).

G.G. RAHEJA, *The Poison in the Gift: Ritual, Prestation, and the Dominant Caste in a North Indian Village* (Chicago, University Press, 1988).

C. RIVIÈRE, 'Approches comparatives du sacrifice', in F. Boespflug and F. Dunand (eds.), *Le comparatisme en histoire des religions* (Paris: Cerf, 1997) pp. 279-290.

M.M. ROTSCHILD, *The Haluka; A Facet of the Relationship of Diaspora Jews to the Jews of Eretz Israel from 1810 to 1860* (Hebrew) (Jerusalem: Rubin Mass, 1986).

D.W. RUDNER, 'Religious Gifting and Inland Commerce in Seventeenth Century South India', in *Journal of Asian Studies,* 46: 2 (1987).

I.F. SILBER, 'Gift-Giving in the Great Traditions: The Case of Donations to Monasteries in the Medieval West', in *Archives Européennes de Sociologie/European Journal of Sociology,* 36: 2 (1995) pp. 209-243. Abridged French translation in *Revue du M.A.U.S.S.* 8 (1996), pp. 243-266.

— 'Modern Philanthropy: Reassessing the Viability of a Maussian Perspective,' in Wendy James and Nick Allen (eds.), *Marcel Mauss: A Centenary Tribute* (Oxford: Berghahn, forthcoming).

— 'Le champ du don: pour une perspective historique comparée', in Marcel Fournier (ed.), *L'héritage de Marcel Mauss* (Montréal: Presses of the University of Montréal, forthcoming).

C. TAROT, 'Repères pour une histoire de la naissance de la grâce' (Notes for a History of the Birth of Grace), in *La Revue du Mauss* (semestrielle), 1 (Paris: La Découverte, 1992).

— 'Christianisme et inconditionnalité' (Christianism and Unconditionability), in *Revue du Mauss* 7, 1 (1996), pp. 338-366.

A. TESTART, *Des dons et des dieux: anthropologie religieuse et sociologie comparative* (About Gifts and Gods: Religious Anthropology and Comparative Sociology (Paris: Armand Colin, 1993).

N. THOMAS, *Entangled Objects: Exchange, Material Culture and Colonialism in the Pacific* (Cambridge, Mass.: Harvard University Press, 1991).

G. TOFFIN, 'Hiérarchie et idéologie du don dans le monde indien' (Hierarchy and Ideology of the Gift in the Indian World), in *L'Homme* 114: 2 (1990) pp. 130-132.

S. TRIGANO, 'La fonction lévitique: le système du don hébraique' (The Levitic Function: the Hebraic System of the Gift), in *Revue du M.A.U.S.S*, 8 (1996) pp. 220-242.

P. VEYNE, *Le pain et le cirque* (Bread and Circuses) (Paris: Presses Universitaires de France, 1976).

# Gift and Grace: A family to be recomposed?

Camille TAROT (Université de Caen)

This text is a modest contribution to the construction of a theory of grace from the point of view of the anthropology of the gift. I will argue that such a theory is both necessary and extremely promising. However, very little has been done until now on this subject. In general, sociologists and anthropologists have neglected the theme of grace (notwithstanding Pitt-Rivers).[1] Theologians on the contrary seem to ignore sociological work on the gift, for instance the theory of M. Mauss. As the research to be undertaken is too comprehensive for one person and for a short textlike theory on the other hand, I will offer no more than an exploration of the theme. My text will be divided in two parts: I first offer a quick audit of the current state of the anthropology of grace and in a second part, some propositions about how such a research should be undertaken.

## A Quick Audit

*Mauss' discovery, its significance, its implications*

Mauss has made a discovery. One can treat it in three different ways, if one conveniently takes over Dan Sperber's categories.[2] One can treat it as if it were an *interpretative generalisation* of the genre: everything is gift, the gift is everything. The saying is famous and has already been expressed by a novelist: *"everything is grace"*. But it is always better to avoid generalisations and their ideological effects. A *structural* reading would be more rigorous. This has already been done by Mauss himself, because, in disclosing the triple obligation for the gift to become fully articulate, he has discovered a structure. This does not mean that Mauss is a structuralist.[3] He always had a keen eye for the fact that the form of the gift collides and combines with dissymmetry, with excess, with violence and with debt. In order to be, the gift simply comes into play; it does not come into play in advance. Finally, one can, according to

---

[1] J. Pitt-Rivers, *The Place of Grace in Anthropology*, postface à J. G. Perpistiony, J. Pitt-Rivers (eds.), *Honor and Grace in Anthropology*, 1992.
[2] D. Sperber, *La contagion des idées. Théorie naturaliste de la culture (The Contagion of Ideas. A Naturalistic Theory of Culture)* (Paris: Odile Jacob, 1996).
[3] C. Tarot, *De Durkheim à Mauss, l'anthropologie du symbolique. Sociologie et sciences des religions (From Durkheim to Mauss, the Anthropology of Symbols. Sociology and Sciences of Religions)* (January 1999).

Sperber, read it *epidemiologically*: combined with the structural permanence of the gift, one has to take notice of the enormous variations in the social and historical setting of the gift. There is as much variability as far as grace is concerned, for that matter, and it is, of course, these variations one has to consider first of all. They already reveal themselves in the various ways in which Mauss' discovery has been received.

Indeed, the destiny of Mauss' discovery of the gift was and remains paradoxical. It has been unequally received, as if it were judged to be unequally credible or important. Ethnologists have taken it into account most of all, because in it they recognized one of the goods that they recurrently encounter on home ground. At the outset of the *Essay sur le don* there is Boas and his potlatch, and in the end there is Malinowski and his kula. Even if they claim Mauss to be definitely one of theirs, sociologists[4] have doubtlessly not conceived all the consequences of the Maussian gift for the reflection on the nature of 'the social', of the social facts and the social bond,[5] for sociology in general[6] or its repercussions on the relation of the social with the psychological and even the somatic, in short with the complete human being.[7]

Mauss' method and discovery shocked and still disturbs all the thoughts dominated by evolutionism. In a more marxist or a more liberal disguise these thoughts have never ceased to dominate the public opinion and even the specialists themselves, as evolutionism is the religion of modernity. Hence the temptation to relegate — with a clear conscience of occidental, modern or developed superiority — the gift to the exterior obscurity of an alterity, be it that of a wild exoticism, be it that of a remote past, generally qualified as medieval by the stupid counter-identity the Age of Enlightenment has bequeathed to us, be it in the more or less tolerated margins of a surviving folklore without significance. This is the first front where the decision is not yet clear to everyone: must one see in the gift a residue or, on the contrary, as

---

[4] J. Cazeneuve, *La sociologie de Marcel Mauss (The Sociology of Marcel Mauss)* (Paris: PUF, 1968).

[5] C. Tarot, *Symbolisme et tradition. Pour renouer avec une sociologie générale de la religion. Tome 1, Durkheim et Mauss (Symbolism and Tradition. Linking up with a General Sociology of Religion. Volume 1, Durkheim and Mauss)* (Caen, 1994) (University thesis, promotor: Alain Caillé). C. Tarot, 'Du fait social de Durkheim au fait social total de Mauss' ('From Durkheim's Social Fact to Mauss' Total Social Fact'), in *The Obligation to Give. Marcel Mauss' Capital Sociological Discovery (L'obligation de donner. La découverte sociologique capitale de Marcel Mauss)* (1996).

[6] A. Caillé, 'Ni holisme ni individualisme méthodologiques. Marcel Mauss et le paradigme du don' ('No Methodological Holism, No Methodological Individualism. Marcel Mauss and the Paradigm of the Gift'), in *The Obligation to Give. Marcel Mauss' Capital Sociological Discovery* (1996).

[7] B. Karsenti, *Marcel Mauss. Le fait social total (Marcel Mauss. The Total Social Fact)* (Paris: PUF, 1994); B. Karsenti, *L'homme total. Sociologie, anthropologie et philosophie chez Marcel Mauss (The Total Man. Marcel Mauss' Sociology, his Anthropology, his Philosophy)* (Paris: PUF, 1997).

Mauss claims, the permanent bedrock; must one see in it a sign of primitivism, or *a*, or even *the first* social fact?

Though it may represent a big step, the acknowledgement of a structural permanence does not make the whole discussion unnecessary. Thanks to its positively synchronic approach, structural anthropology has attributed to the Maussian gift the status of an essential pillar in a permanent synchronism that no diachronism is able to pass by;[8] nevertheless it has simplified and reduced the gift in order to integrate it with the theories of exchange and of communication. It has reduced the gift to be a special case of a more extensive genre, the exchange. Lévi-Straussian structuralism separates the Maussian gift from affectivity and violence, from bonds and debts. In doing so it has expurgated the donator and the sacrifice from the gift, when according to Mauss, giving at the same time and inevitably means giving oneself. He has reduced the difference between the gift and the market exchange which can be settled without debts, whereas the gift recreates debts and in so doing recreates social bonds which the economic exchange has a tendency to weaken or even to destroy.[9]

The Maussian discovery, thus, has but scarcely succeeded in reimposing the gift as *a*, or even *the central* fact of the social life, as irreducible, not only for the societies of the past, in which they are more readily acknowledged, but also for the modern contemporary and future societies. In fact, Mauss' *Essay sur le don* was made possible by the author's capacity to cross disciplinary barriers, and by his virtuosity to implement the idea of the total social fact, an idea more quoted than grasped, as a matter of fact. The *Essay* used a method of decompartmentalization without putting it into a theory; Mauss demonstrated the heuristic fruitfulness of this method, but not its principles. The usual view of philosophers as well as sociologists has continued to be that Mauss is but an appendix to the Durkheimian sociology, and that to fully understand it, it suffices to read only bits and pieces of it.[10]

The implications of Mauss' discovery for religious studies has been only barely hinted at, let alone fully exploited.[11] One might have thought that after the *Essay* one would have been eager to study the gift in the great historic societies and religions. The oriental ethnology studied a substantial part of the

---

[8] C. Lévi-Strauss, *Introduction à l'oeuvre de Marcel Mauss (Introduction to the Work of Marcel Mauss)* (1950/1968).

[9] As Marcel Drach — whom I voluntarily acknowledge being in*debt*ed to — shows in his monthly seminar of 1997-1998 at the Collège international de philosophie, Maison des sciences de l'homme (International College of Philosophy, Centre for Social Sciences), Paris.

[10] C. Tarot, *De Durkheim à Mauss, l'anthropologie du symbolique. Sociologie et sciences des religions (From Durkheim to Mauss, the Anthropology of Symbols. Sociology and Sciences of Religions)* (January 1999).

[11] C. Tarot, 'Repères pour une histoire de la naissance de la grâce' ('Landmarks for a History of the Birth of Grace'), in *Ce que donner veut dire, don et intéret (What Giving Means, Gift and Interest)* (Paris: La Découverte, 1993) p. 93.

great 'oriental' traditions, particularly Hinduism and Buddhism,[12] but not the monotheisms. To study the Christian grace as a variety of the gift, thus, largely remains a task to be accomplished. It has to be said that Mauss himself placed things in an impasse because in his *Essay* he jumps from the archaic societies to the modern ones with an enormous enjambment. Of course he mentioned the 'classic' societies, but he bluntly ignored the Christian facts.

*Difficulties for theologists*

In their sources[13] as well as in the elaborations of an academic theology,[14] in the definitions pretending to be 'scientific' as well as in those of the neo-scholasticism that will serve as a reference,[15] theologians have always affirmed, without ambiguity, that grace is a gift. So special a gift that in the end they rushed to isolate it completely. Because they worried less about elaborating on how and why grace is a gift, than on why that gift is a grace. This reveals difficulties — maybe even close to impossibilities — connected with an approach of grace that would rely on the anthropology of the gift, especially if the latter is elaborated starting from the archaic societies. Because once one has acknowledged that grace is a gift, it not only seems to distinguish itself from the gift in the archaic societies, but even to oppose it item per item.

The gift takes place between human beings, even if it often concerns chiefs who have a more than human status. Grace is a divine gift. If the archaic gift is inscribed in the chain of the triple obligation to give, receive and return, grace is but grace because it is absolutely free. This is the heart of the matter: God, the giver of grace, is not submitted to the obligation to give, and this absolute freedom is the first, definitional condition for grace to be grace. It is

---

[12] I. F. Silber, 'Gift-giving in the Great Traditions: the Case of Donation to Monasteries in the Medieval West', in *Archives européennes de sociologie*, 36:2 (1995) pp. 209-243.

[13] For instance Saint Paul: "But not as the offence, so also *is* the free gift. For if through the offence of one many be dead, much more the grace of God, and the gift by grace, *which* is by one man, Jesus Christ, hath abounded unto many. And not as *it was* by one that sinned, so *is* the gift" (Romans 5, 15-16).

[14] "A supernatural gift (or the totality of supernatural gifts) that is conceded by God to a creature endowed with intelligence in view of his eternal bliss" (J. Van der Mersch, 1925, col 1557). "Every supernatural gift God has granted an intellectual creature in view of his eternal bliss" (*ibid*. col 1558). Or even more generally, "every internal and supernatural gift that enables man to perform salutary deeds and to put into practice the divine precepts, the observation of which is required in order to obtain eternal beatitude" (*ibid*. col 1636).

[15] Having considered the limits of this work, we shall discuss things starting only from the catholic theology and the more classical — neo-scholastic — theology without trying to integrate here what the revival of the biblical studies, the influence of the non-aristotelian philosophical currents (personalism, philosophy of being, etc.), the conciliar climate and the debates after Vatican II, the ecumenism, and even — or especially — the inciting of an interreligious dialogue, particularly with Judaism, have been able to introduce — or will not fail to introduce — to new formulations.

absolutely free *ex parte Dei*, not only because God does not need the human beings or whatever they can give him, but because grace is never meritorious from the point of view of man who has no claim upon God.

Even if he is quite submitted to the obligation to accept this gift, and to return it at least by faith and conversion — both of them "good works" that are at the least signs of grace, as even the most strict Calvinist would admit —, man, that small and feeble being, is radically impotent to honour those two requirements. Because it takes grace to accept grace, and man will never return to God what he owes him. Even if he is blessed, he remains a debtor for life, and this not only to a Lutheran with his particularly mercantile views. On pain of destroying the whole idea of religion, of monotheism and of transcendence, "God owes us nothing", is what the Jansenists remind us of with headstrong nerve. It is obvious that the "virtue of religion" causes the circular aspect of the gift between human beings to explode.

Moreover, in the archaic gift, everything and anything can and will be given; grace, on the other hand, is essentially oriented towards spiritual gifts, the most spiritual of these spiritual gifts being God himself. Even if theology distinguishes between created and uncreated grace, it has no intention of reducing the transcendance of grace. *"Uncreated grace is God himself, in that, through his love, he gives himself to man in a supernatural way"*.[16] As Mauss points out, the gift serves very well indeed to determine one's social status, one's rank, one's prestige; grace only effectuates bliss, and only determines the 'meta-terrestrial' status of the elected ones in heaven. The gift often takes place in a strongly agonistic context; grace, *'sanans et elevans'*, creates saints which are indifferent to rivalry and mundane prestige, and which are even capable of preferring martyrdom to violence. The gift makes rich or enriched people, masters or friends, whereas only grace is capable of making righteous persons out of sinners.

It is, once more, the very operating procedure that changes. Even if the one who gives sometimes as it were has to tear away the gift from himself, this gift still remains more or less exterior to the one who receives it. Grace, on the contrary, intends to transform the receiver within his most inner self. If Jesus would be nothing more to Christianity than a wise man, like any philosopher, his doctrine would be a gift of wisdom, which is quite something indeed, but it is believed to be much more than that. Jesus realizes more, his grace metamorphoses human beings, it installs a new creation and new human beings. The difference between gift and grace translates itself into the difference between, on the one hand, human wisdom and its ensuing moral qualities, and, on the other hand, Christian sanctity offering the premisses of a new heaven

---

[16] J. Van Der Mersch, 'Grâce' ('Grace'), in *Dictionnaire de Théologie catholique (Dictionary of Catholic Theology)* (Paris: Letouzey et Ané, 1925) col. 1557.

and earth: *"The specific Christian sanctity is not a simple new orientation of the moral life determined by faith and revelation; it is not distinctly a moral perfection acquired by human activity that is sustained by God's help as well as Christ's example, and is characterized by the imitation of the virtues of the Saviour, but it distinctly consists of a spiritual and supernatural renaissance, realized in the soul through the infusion of a physical entity which transforms the soul and causes man to be a son of God, a member of Christ, a temple of the Holy Ghost. From this transcendental principle the moral activity of justice and its progress in sanctity derives."* [17]

In short, there is a large gap between the gift, and especially the 'archaic' gift, and grace. This gap can be ultimately summarized in the fact that the gift is a natural phenomenon, whereas, for the theologian, grace is a supernatural fact, meaning *"gifts positively induced in human nature"*.[18] *"Grace can by no virtue whatsoever belong to the natural order."* [19] *"The invigorating influence we are talking about is still supernatural in itself, in its physical reality: it is indeed participating in a life that is distinctly the life of God himself. The natural communication between creator and creation consists of God producing the finished substances with the accidents they claim, of God conserving their being that is their own, of God inciting them to actions that suit them, of God directing them or governing them, everything according to the divine plan. This way God remains infinitely superior to every creature, and has no personal communication at all with it. If it is blessed with intelligence, a creature is able to know its creator through its fellow creatures, and to discover the moral obligations that result from this as well as from the dependence of the created beings with respect to their creator, and from the relationships they have amongst one another. But no creature can realize or demand an immediate communication with God just as he is. All communication with God just as he is, is supernatural ..."* [20]

Every endeavour to inscribe grace too unilaterally in the gift cannot but destroy 'the object' the moment it pretends to understand it. The most suspicious theologians would certainly fear that such an approach resembles a new form of modernist offensive, which is supposed to utterly deny the supernatural.[21] The identifying mark of the Christian grace is precisely its pure gratuity which introduces in the gift a kind of *metabasis heis allon genos*. Besides, it is this gratuity of grace Luther has rediscovered. He understood that it had its fundamental formulation in Saint Paul, and that it stood for the originality and the strength of Christianism. The posttridental Catholic theology too, has

---

[17] *Ibid.*, col. 1563-1564.
[18] *Ibid.*, col. 1558.
[19] *Ibid.*, col. 1591.
[20] *Ibid.*, col. 1562.
[21] *Ibid.*, col. 1570-1571.

insisted on this absolute gratuity, and has claimed Paulinism. It is from this gratuity Christianity has derived the consciousness of its being different from paganism and its *do ut des* that has been judged to be primitive, calculating and magic. *"Saint Paul teaches us about the existence of a sanctifying gift and its complete gratuity ... pointing out that good works as such, or natural good works, do not make a sound or righteous human being; even more, that before God these good works are not a title calling for this sanctifying gift, that they are in no way meritorious. This is the first reason why the sanctifying gift is definitely not merited by the human being. But this already implicates that the sanctifying gift is not a purely natural entity: because if it were, it would be the necessary result of a human being's natural good works. The essence of such a gift is subsequently explained by its effects, more particularly by the fact that in possessing it, man becomes the adoptive son of God, the temple of the Holy Ghost. This dignity is absolutely supernatural: hence it follows that the entity which assigns this dignity, is itself supernatural and definitely not merited by every creature."*

Without any doubt the anthropologist cannot claim nor refute the ontology of the Christian discourse. But, whereas he might be indifferent to the objections of the theologist, he could not ignore those of the historian who reminds him that the difference claim which imposes itself there, is part of what has to be studied. That in Christianity a discourse on gratuity has been brought to the surface, is the fact one has to start from, without prejudging its truth or its illusory character. Moreover, the Christian dominance was and remains so overwhelming that gratuity remained the mark of the gift, at least up to Mauss.

Christian grace contradicts the very foundations of the Maussian gift, and vice versa, even more by the fact that the obligation to give does not apply to God, than by the impossibility of reciprocity and reversibility, which obviously do not apply to the relation between God and man, nor define the gift for that matter. There, apparently, lies the major difficulty when considering grace from the point of view of an anthropology of the gift.

*Difficulties for sociologists and anthropologists*

That sociologists and anthropologists have neglected the study of grace as a gift is not an effect of intimidation coming from theologists. Sociologists tend to be secular, and grace belongs to the arcana of clerical debates. Sociologists are modern human beings, and, as a whole, partisans of modernity; grace belongs to the antique and medieval history of Christianity, and if it touches on the prehistory of modernity with its great debates concerning Protestant and Catholic Reforms, one is accustomed to consider it to be the end of an era rather than the beginning of ours. Moreover, the few remembered aspects of the theology of grace in its Protestant and Catholic form of the classical era, would convince us that, though grace may be a gift, it is totally impregnated with and structured by a religious absolutism of which one ignores whether it is — on the level of imagination — the reflection or the continuation of a political absolutism of which the ensuing political history has tried to rid itself thanks to democracy and equality.

Finally, grace is not an object of study because it can hardly be grasped by traditional sociological means. No one has ever tried to conduct an inquiry asking every passerby the question of Joan of Arc's judges: "Are you in a state of grace?" But even if one would have done so, how was one to interpret such an ungraspable matter? Grace could not enter into the classical sociology but by means of analysing ideologies, that is to say analysing pure words and representations. So the extension and the heterogeneousness of the phenomena that are covered by the word grace do not facilitate the work, which, moreover, does not impose itself either by practical utility or by immediate actuality. Thus sociologists have left the study of grace to historians who go into the epochs dealing with the old theological debates.

If sociologists nonetheless want to deal with the subject, they have no other means but to treat it as if it were an ideology. To understand the discrepancy between theory and practice is and remains the very task of sociology. The fear, then, that nothing can be further away from practice and from genuine social reality than this kind of discourse on grace and gift is not unfounded. But will one ever be able to make any progress in this task if one immediately resorts to the classical doctrine of sociologists that an ideology masks the social reality, which is a superficial and deceitful discourse that maintains itself only through its function of hiding an exploitation? Even a sociologist like E. Todd, stimulating and, above all, scarcely suspected of marxist influences as he may be, seconds this seriously narrow-minded discourse which comes from a certain bygone philosophy of the Enlightenment in the shape of a rather unsophisticated anticlericalism — unless it would be quite simply a fragmentary reprise of an old Protestant discourse? Todd quotes a nobiliary charter of the XIth century which bestows various gifts to the Abbey of Cluny, and in which the language of gift and grace occur: *"The divine mercy which always brings back the errants on the path of salvation, and untiringly snatches man away from the domination of the antique exterminator in order to lead him to supreme and eternal joy, has graciously inspired me deep down in my heart, to offer God part of what he gave me, to obtain redemption for my sins. That is why, for the salvation of my soul, I, knight William, donate to God, to Saint Peter and Saint Paul, and to Cluny, where Abbot Hugh serves more than he lords, a part of what I have acquired from my ancestors by hereditary right, that is to say half of the revenues of a church ... I also donate the adjacent house ... half of a meadow ... a very fertile métayage and all that depends from it, cultivated and uncultivated land, meadows, fishponds, forests and running waters ..."* [22] It would not be too naive or unsuspectingly literal an interpretation of such a text to read it as Mauss would have invited us, and as its content requires: as a testimony concerning a total social fact. In fact, this text "mingles", as Mauss would call it, the great functions society is made of. It weaves in one single network of meaning of which gift and grace are the vector and the motor, the social (the statutes and the relations of the knight and the monk), the economic (the goods), the psychological (the inspiration, the heart), the ideological (theology, God, the hierarchic view of the world), and even the political (papacy, Cluny), real estate (houses and land) and the symbolical goods (salvation, sin, mercy). However, in the writings of our sociologist, this text, becomes a testimony of a system of exploitation which the Reformation has — blissfully, one believes to read — destroyed: *"The Reformation is a settlement of the old score between the two first estates that issued from the middle ages, between those who pray and those who fight. The secularization of the ecclesiastical lands inverts and then nullifies a very old mechanism of exploitation of the nobility by the Church. Terrified by the prospect of the Last Judgement and of hell, the medieval aristocracy or illiterate knights bought their place in paradise from the clergy. A XIth century testament can illustrate the domination of the aristocracy by the clergy* (follows the quoted text). *The nobleman as well as the citizen, the artisan or the peasant were exploited by the priest ..."* [23] To establish the fact that the Cluny monks were and remained noblemen themselves, even if they had switched suzerains or had chosen the greatest according to their contemporaries, would suffice to show the weakness of Todd's thesis, and, above all, its anachronism. Todd has read Duby and perhaps Dumézil, but like most sociologists he has either not read or not integrated Mauss. The point is not to defend a model of society that was already largely outdated two centuries before the Reformation anyway, but to know whether one takes into account the fact and the whole fact when translating the gift to the monasteries immediately into the market language of interest and investment, or in the more progressive language of exploitation. Because from the moment on every gift is supposed to hide a purchase in disguise or a swindle, the part of the gift is played and lost in advance as the gift is decreted to have no place in human reality.

Anthropologists, who are more familiar with gifts which — for want of a more appropriate adjective — one would call 'archaic', carefully keep their distance from such dangerous simplifications. But they too have difficulties in tackling grace from the point of view of the gift. Christian discourse and prac-

---

[22] A. Bernard and A. Bruel, Recueil des chartres de l'abbaye de Cluny (Compilation of Charters of the Abbey of Cluny), Nr. 3000, p. 196-197, as cited in E. Todd, *L'invention de l'Europe (The Invention of Europe)* (Paris: Seuil, 1990-1996) pp. 151-152.

[23] *Ibid.*, p. 151-152.

tice related to grace are European, and even Occidental phenomena, reactivated at the dawn of modern times, but too close anyway, and without an apparent link with the gift in primitive societies. Grace keeps itself too far from the visible, concrete, palpable "ring dance of exchanges" those societies are in the habit of performing. On the contrary, grace is a belief, and an intellectual belief on top of it, accessible through the speculations of scholars. Has it ever profoundly affected popular religion?

*Some attempts in another direction*

From a perspective of historical anthropology Ilana F. Silber[24] noticed there is a kind of black hole with regard to the gift in the great religious traditions, and especially in those of the Western world, because ethnologists were not interested in it. She has delimited her subject historically and placed some chronological beacons in her approach of the gifts in the Western Christian monasteries of the IX-XIIth century. With the appearance of the mendicant orders in the XIIth century things changed drastically already. The old configuration of the gift in the monasteries is shaken. Silber's work, moreover, testifies a profound comprehension of Maussian thought. Silber rightly noticed that the gift can not be separated from the problems of the total social fact, that it is a multifarious phenomenon, that one must not concentrate on *what* is given, since the gift inscribes itself in the social network, and this, in its turn, inscribes itself in the network of meaning and value.

This type of study provides one of the privileged sociohistorical frameworks for exploring the gift in Christianity. Nevertheless, it does not tackle our problem — grace — directly, because it concentrates on the other forms of gift. The era most certainly had its theoreticians of gift and grace, but their treatises do not represent the totality of the practices related to gift and grace, nor are they their immediate and sufficient norm. Part of the network of sense and representations remains to be linked to the whole. Whereas one disposes of a large enough number of testimonies on monastic theology and religion and on the vision of the world in which these practices inscribed themselves, the testimonies of the secular thought of donators that would be the most precious, are rare and, above all, less direct and to a large extent covered by the phraseology of the clerks.

In a former,[25] particularly restricted work, I have tried to provide landmarks for an outline of a history to be rewritten. The limitations of that work have to

---

[24] I. F. Silber, 'Gift-giving in the Great Traditions: the Case of Donation to Monasteries in the Medieval West', in *Archives européennes de sociologie*, 36:2 (1995) pp. 209-243.

[25] C. Tarot, 'Repères pour une histoire de la naissance de la grâce' ('Landmarks for a History of the Birth of Grace'), in *Ce que donner veut dire, don et intérêt (What Giving Means, Gift and Interest)* (Paris: La Découverte, 1993).

be underlined, but apparently it proved necessary to take into consideration the practices and the ideology of both gift and grace, in order to try and understand the birth of the Christian grace. However, notwithstanding its title, the article talked a lot more about the gift than about grace! These simple prolegomena partly dodged the fundamental critical difficulty of trying to refer each idea, each theme to the current of the primitive Christianism that is its bearer. Thus, one has not confronted the necessity of making a 'microsociology' of the beliefs of the New Testament, an endless and almost desperate task if one bears in mind the exegetic meticulousness it requires, since it passes through the preliminaries of a critical history of the writings and the traditions. This might lead to think that one has underestimated the major fact of the Christian origins: the sometimes conflictual plurality of the currents that traverse it. And gift and grace are in the middle of these conflicts between the first Christians.

This essay avoided to examine the subject of grace down to the last detail, because it did not deal systematically with the conception of grace that dominates all others: Paulinism. Not that one underestimates its powerful originality. But the sociologist may be afraid to fall prey to Luther's ingenious mistake. In rediscovering the essence of Paulinism in the theology of grace, as it is constituted starting from the Epistle to the Romans, Luther believed he rediscovered the whole of Christianism and the whole of primitive Christianism, in short: pure faith. What he rediscovered was obviously not the essence of Christianism — otherwise sooner or later a certain union might have been restored between the Churches and the currents of Christianism. However, without wanting or knowing it he did leave the door ajar for exegetes, sociologists and historians to discover, centuries later, a much more embarrassing fact that makes the discovery of the essence of Christianism much more problematic: the plurality of theologies in the New Testament (Christologies, ecclesiologies, and why not — even if the word does not exist ... yet — charitologies), and, consequently, the plurality of the sociocultural currents and environments in primitive Christianism, Judeo- as well as pagano-Christian. The investigations and the discoveries of this century (Qumran) confirm that this plurality was already extensively preformed in the ideological disintegration of the contemporary Jewish world at that juncture. It was an actually pluralistic Judaism that provided the habitat of Christianism. Thus, to tackle the problem of grace in the New Testament, it is necessary to reestablish the plurality of points of view, of options and positions. For that purpose it seems prudent to partly circumvent the preponderance of Paulinism, even if it were only to relocate it more appropriately in its context of controversy, of novelty, and eventually of partly eliminating its adversaries, as in the West it is Paulinism which reveals itself as *the* dominating force at least since Saint Augustine.

The issue now is to resume and continue the task. Taking the Christian origins to tackle the problems of grace entails dangerous fascinations and extreme complexities that originate from the nature of these texts. Other, equally complex posterior periods offer the incomparable advantage of being much better documented, and with writings the reading of which requires less preliminary preparation.

**Propositions**

As badly constructed as the *Essai sur le don* which culminates in long and incomplete conclusions, our argument would also like to conclude with a series of problems, recalling promising propositions.

*Methodological propositions*

To see the gift and to understand the discourse of grace, one had better not begin by denying them straight away! If one starts from the idea of the impossibility of the gift, because it is never really free, or of the impossibility of grace, because nothing is free, one does not run the risk of seeing the gift even though it leaps to the eye, nor to hear grace where it wants itself to be heard. The anthropologist must never forget that it is not his to pass either value judgements or judgements of existence that have an ontological bearing beyond the observable and audible phenomena. Not that he has no judgements of his own, but precisely because his own judgements would prevent him from perceiving, and hence, in the first place, from welcoming those of others. Whether grace and gift exist or not, human beings have believed in them, and talk about it or have talked about it. This suffices to pose a serious problem.

What I elsewhere have called Mauss' "microholism with variable geometry" has allowed him to invent the idea of the total social fact, and to perceive the existence of the gift and the implications of its reality. Here, more than anywhere else, object and method are inseparable. It is Mauss' methodological eclecticism, moderate and pragmatic, capable of suppling Durkheims method without renouncing its advantages, that permitted him to distrust the definitions of the gift that came his way, and to propose a definition far more comprehensive, profound and functional. To review and to transgress the blinkers the habitual definitions impose on a culture, is most often the condition to reassemble those realities that were previously perceived as distinct or as contradictory, whereas to others they are profoundly connected. Mauss' method in the *Essai sur le don* is closely related to an archeology or to a paleontology that reconstitutes systems with pieces of fossils. But something can be learned from it. The researcher will always have to reassemble all the aspects of the gift: discourse, practices, systems, institutions, traces, alleged survivals, gifts of things that can be evaluated and of invaluable things. He has to systematically break down all the barriers and put side by side gifts to the dead and gifts to the living, material goods and spiritual goods, without ever erecting *a priori* impervious partitions that are submitted to our categories — the natural or supernatural categories, or those of the spiritual and the material goods. All these aspects of the Maussian method impose themselves and will impose themselves still for a long time to come to those who will want to work on the gift, and on grace as a gift.

Furthermore, Mauss has never ceased to proclaim that after having analysed, one needs to reconstruct in order to get closer to the concrete; in the concrete everything has to do with everything. Culture is already an abstraction, because it is a system of distinctions, of separations, whereas the concrete is life, is the social practice in which everything is always mingled, in which all things give themselves together. After the analysis, thus, there is synthesis, after the decomposition into separate elements there is the recomposition into a functioning situation. Because the true is the whole, even if it were only intended. This is where one grasps the necessity of a historical sociology of grace joined to anything an anthropology of the gift contributes, particularly thanks to the comparative sciences.

This leaves one doubtlessly with the most difficult task: how to combine a synchronic and systematic reading of facts with an evolutionist interpretation, because in these gift stories as in other human affairs, there is at the same time permanence — be it through the absence of a structure that has been abolished, rejected or denied — and evolution, continuity and change. One simultaneously encounters history and metahistory, so to speak. It is on the occasion of the delicate appreciation of the respective parts of the one and the other, that the ideology of the researcher threatens to return most resolutely or sneakily.

But a lesson learned in the ethnological detour Mauss made so well, be it partially, must still be valued highly. To assess phenomena like the gift to the monasteries or the beliefs in grace and even more the bond established by the agents between gifts of concrete goods and gifts of invisible goods, it is necessary to break away the barriers between our disciplines, to relativize our conceptual fragmentations and get out of the habitual problems in order to find those of the agents, and not decode their conduct starting from a problem we declare real, realistic or last resort, be it a religious problem or an economic one. In short, the ethnocentrism underlying our idea of real religion, of pure faith or of the laws of the market, must be dismissed.

*Anthropological propositions*

The Christian grace emanates only from a transcendant and absolutely good God. Hence it presents itself as absolutely pure and good. It situates itself straight away beyond the oppositions between pure and impure, between beneficent and maleficent; it even escapes the antinomy of the sacred which attracts and repels, fascinates and frightens. It presents itself beyond every ambivalence as a gift without ambiguity. This is one of the reasons why theologians insist on the supernatural dimension beyond the gifts that are usually ambiguous and even dangerous.[26]

This suggests that there are good reasons to replace grace in the historical and logical evolution of the fundamental categories of the religious, more specifically of the mana and the sacred. In fact, this history doubtlessly does not present the natural display of a law of evolution, but in all probability it presents a history shaken with conflicts, repressions and imperfect sublimations. The Christian grace is, on the one hand, like the last avatar of the mana, and, on the other hand, one of the most surprizing efforts to surpass it or to invert it. If one defines the mana by the power obtained through the magic of transgression and the ultimate desire for immortality and omnipotence, and if one looks at impurity — the pure and the impure being connected with blood, with life and death and with the relations between the sexes — as a form of overdetermination of the magical power, the sacred appears as a transitional figure, an effort to surpass the impurity of the mana towards a less magic, more religious, more divine power. *"The people that created the manna, and then, 'enriching' it with the element of purity, made it into the sacred, did not and do not yet have religions. Their magical beliefs must be understood rationally. Nevertheless, they are the involuntary founders of the religions, because without the specific contribution they have made, religions would not be what they are."*[27] Hence one could say that the era of religions started with the sacred, of which the divine marks the unequal purifications, and with the monotheistic divine to which grace corresponds. With grace a figure of the gift appears that wants to reduce the ambivalence of the sacred and the gift. The crucial question, then, is to know where the disturbing negativity of the preceding figures ends up, if not in the devil, the witch, the savage and the heretic. From a historical perspective, the parallelism between, on the one hand, the passage of the discourse of the primitive, agonistic or dangerous gift to the discourse of the supernatural grace, and, on the other, the passage of the manna to the sacred and the divine imposes itself.

*Ethnological propositions*

In order to talk about grace, theologians frequently use classical terms in the School's strange "physical metaphysics", like, for instance, *"infused virtue"*,

---

[26] C. Tarot, 'Danger, don' ('Danger, Gift'), in *L'obligation de donner. La découverte sociologique capitale de Marcel Mauss (The Obligation to Give. Marcel Mauss' Capital Sociological Discovery)* (1996).

[27] L. Lévi-Makarius, *Le sacré et la violation des interdits (The Sacred and the Violation of the Forbidden)* (Payot, 1997) p. 335.

*"infusion of the supernatural gift, which penetrates the souls and becomes inherent to them"*, *"internal enchainment between vital activity and justification"*.[28] This metaphorical language — although a certain (realistic) scholastic conceptualization induces to take it literally — should doubtlessly, like any 'scientific' discourse, be analysed side by side with other metaphors well known to ethnologists[29] who buckle down to track down the immediately discernible fluxes and fluids (blood, sperm, water, liquids, humours) and the already more ethereal influxes, without which, doubtlessly and ever since the most traditional societies, there would be no representation of the social and of its contradictory characteristic of attachment and exchange, of loss and gain, of danger and life. One anticipates, thus, the archaic rootedness of this vocabulary of fluxes and influxes of grace, a vocabulary that, no doubt, bulges with information on the psychical conditions of socialisation and its effects.

Such an approach would pose reclassification problems. Must one consider the Christian grace, when it reveals itself in terms of "physical" influx and of "incorporation", to be a reaction or an attempt to surpass a dualism of body and mind that is far too irreconcilable in modernity? To be a way of giving a status to the imaginary, as a plenitude lost and regained, and as beyond the traumatism of the access to the symbolic? To be a cultural archaism, a nostalgic discourse deprived of sense in modern society and sociology? Or, on the contrary, influenced by anthropomorphism, to be a useful expression of unconscious overdeterminations that have the right to be voiced. Moreover, is the anthropomorphism in the anthropogenesis and in the sociogenesis stultifying or humanizing? If a purely objective world would be possible, would it be more human?

*Propositions from the sociology of religion*

Without prejudging what the traditional or the so-called primitive religions do and tell about the gift and about their fluids, and without projecting possible truths in Christianism on other monotheisms, limiting oneself to the Christian system only, it seems necessary to insist on the importance of the gift in the religious. Something must circulate in a religion, if there is to be any religion at all. That is, if it is not only a collective but also a social affair, a reality no individual can make for or give to himself alone, because it joins human beings closely together, and because this liaison cannot be realized unless it is mediated by gifts, grace or benefactions, by virtues and strength, by words or celestial messages, by sacred objects.

---

[28] See our citations from J. Van Der Mersch, 'Grâce' ('Grace'), *op. cit.*
[29] F. Héritier, *Masculin et féminin, la pensée de la différence* (*Male and Female, Thinking the Difference*) (Paris: Odile Jacob, 1996); P. Rospabé, *La dette de vie. Aux origines de la monnaie* (*The Debt of Life. On the Origins of Money*) (Paris: La Découverte, 1995).

All the great religious systems seem to articulate more or less straightly three systems of the gift. A system of the *vertical* gift and circulation, between the *world beyond* (or the *beyond world*) and this one, that goes from the disturbing strangeness of alterities immanent to the *Sapiens*, to the pursuit of pure transcendance. A system of the *horizontal* gift, between peers, brothers, 'co-tribals' or 'co-religionnaires', oscillating between the clan and humanity, because the religious plays a role in the creation of group identity. Finally — or first of all — a system of the *longitudinal* gift, according to the principle of transmission to the descendants, or of debts owed to group ancestors, or of faith, in short, of exchange between living and dead. It is by the way in which each religious system unfolds or limits a certain axis, and, above all, interweaves axes, it is in the dimensions and in the relative importance that is attributed to each of them, that religious systems distinguish themselves probably most of all from one another. But with the gift we can at last grasp some of the dynamics, of the movement, of the action of religious systems, action that so often is kept out of range from the historical studies or of sociology of religions.

To merely consider religions from the point of view of the sacred, is to take a much too unilateral view. Even if one tries to deduct the dynamics of the religious from the ambivalence of the sacred, by connecting it with the effect of attraction and fear it inspires, the sacred which would not give nor permit gifts could not move people for a long time in both literal and figurative sense. Without the gift, which it permits, whilst limiting and fixing it, the sacred alone would engender a paralysing inertia. Like other systems, religions doubtlessly need a motor as well as a brake: the gift and the sacred.

With respect to this, a partly contingent historical happening seems to keep putting undue weight on the sociology of religion, particularly on the one inspired by Durkheim. This sociology is in the first place centered on the sacred. Together with Weber's, it continues to occupy a prominent place in the sociology of religion, and as Mauss has contributed to it, he is seen as an appendix to Durkheim. Moreover, when Mauss starts to theorize the gift, he does not return to the problems of the sociology of religion and the sacred. If Mauss would already have had his views on the gift when he tackled the problem of the definition of the religious, or if he could have resumed the problems of religion that have dominated the beginning of his carreer after having discovered the place of the gift, he undoubtably would have been able to elaborate another sociology of religion.[30] But no one has ever resumed the matter on those grounds, because no one seems to have realized that, there too, the

---

[30] C. Tarot, *Symbolisme et tradition. Pour renouer avec une sociologie générale de la religion. Tome 1, Durkheim et Mauss (Symbolism and Tradition. Linking up with a General Sociology of Religion. Volume 1, Durkheim and Mauss)* (Caen, 1994) (University thesis, promotor: Alain Caillé); C. Tarot, *From Durkheim to Mauss, the Anthropology of Symbols. Sociology and Sciences of Religions* (January 1999).

chronology and the order of investigations can continue to put excessive weight on research.

*Propositions of the historical sociology of the Christian origins*

If religions are also systems of gift on the one hand, and systems of prohibition/sacred on the other, one can understand that there is tension between both and that the foundation of religious systems inevitably passes through some transgression of the sacred of the day, which fixes the due of the debt.

In my first essay on grace I may have given the impression that, on the one hand, I underestimated the conflicts in primitive Christianism, and that, on the other hand, I underestimated the importance of gift and grace in Judaism. With hindsight, these two problems now prove to be more closely connected than they would seem to be after the rupture between Judaism and Christianism, and after most trends of primitive Christianism have disappeared without posterity to reclaim them at present. Gift and grace are obviously not a prerogative of Christianity, even if it contributes to their inflexions and specific insistences. A substantial part of the conflicts, on the one hand, between Christians among themselves — to run ahead of things: between Paulinians and Judeo-Christians — and, on the other, between Christians and observant Jews, was about what is giveable and what is not. So the nongiveable as well as the compulsorily giveable is sanctioned by the sacred, which makes it inviolable or taboo. Hence, the gift of the nongiveable or the refusal to give what must be given, adopts the figure of transgression.

One is tempted, then, to hypothesize that one of the reasons of the predominance of grace in Christianism is to absolve, through God and in Gods name, the transgression of certain barriers that forbid gift and exchange with pagans. Is it a coincidence that the most enforced, the most powerful, the most sophisticated "theology" of grace is to be found in Paulinism which militates most actively for the lowering of the barriers between Jews and pagans, between Judeo-Christians and pagano-Christians, thus risking to be looked upon as "bargaining" the Law?

No doubt one also has to introduce the dialectics of the giveable and the nongiveable. This opposition is not a privilege of the Christian origins; it could indicate an essential dialectics of the systems of gifts in general, and especially of the religious systems of gifts. In doing so one should take note of the well-founded insistence of Maurice Godelier,[31] on the fact that totally different societies distinguish very carefully the objects that can be sold, those that must be given, and those that should not circulate outside the group, particularly because they must exclusively and unfailingly pass on from ancestors to descendants

---

[31] M. Godelier, *L'enigme du don (The Enigma of the Gift)* (Fayard, 1996) p. 234.

— what I have called the longitudinal gift. One should equally look at Ilana Silber's remarks which, following Annette Weiner, underline the necessity to pay as much attention to what one does not circulate as to what one circulates. There is 'no giving without retention'. *Sacra* and *dona*: is one allowed to give sacred things, and if so to whom can one give them, on what conditions, in what proportions? This debate has largely divided the Christians among themselves, and it has separated the Christians from the Jews. Is the appeal to the divine gift, to grace not a way of ridding oneself of these difficulties, of authorising the gift of whatever was forbidden to be given by means of a gift from above?

In this context, the appeal of Paulinism to predestination, hence to the absolute gratuity of the divine grace in particular towards pagans, clearly seems to result from the necessity to legitimate theologically these 'transgressing gifts' to the pagans, their participation in the heritage and in the promise made to the Fathers (longitudinal gift). Under these conditions, predestination, which plays a part in the dialectics between *sacra* and *dona* on the one hand, and between Israel and the pagans on the other, immediately offers a significance and an implication in the direction of universalism, elements that have found themselves largely inverted in the shape of an exclusion from or a restriction of grace, at first moderately in the context of Augustinianism, later on more radically, for instance in Calvinism.

It is regrettable that recent research on Christian origins[32] keeps depriving itself of the resources of this anthropological approach of the gift, which seems one of the most apt to account for the undeniable dynamics of the beginnings of Christianism.

*Propositions of the historical sociology of modernity*

Since Weber the role of Protestantism in the genesis of modernity, and above all, of capitalism, has become a *topos*, which sometimes passes on from sociology to apologetics[33]. Nevertheless, it is a debatable question whether Weber has posited the problem well in all its aspects. Are the determining factors the Lutheran *Beruf,* or in the Calvinist context, predestination and the anxiety for salvation as a motivation? Or do these elements also owe their subjective importance to the fact that they are extracted, disencumbered or liberated from the Catholic system of grace that 'contained' or 'neutralized' them by institutionalizing them? Is it not a mutation of the *whole* system of gifts, and, above all, of grace, the Protestant novelty results in?

---

[32] E. Trocmé, *L'enfance du christianisme (The Childhood of Christianism)* (Noêsis, 1997). E. Nodet, J. Taylor, *Essai sur les origines du christianisme (Essay on the Origins of Christianism)* (1998).

[33] A. Bieler, *La force cachée des protestants (The Hidden Strength of Protestants)* (Genève: Labor et Fides, 1995).

To answer this question in all serenity, one needs to dispose of a preliminary historical problem. Catholic authors often deny the presence of grace in Protestantism, a statement that can be understood in two ways, depending on which point of view, human or ideological, one takes — only the latter being of interest here. This aspect of the controversy has not been sufficiently taken into account by the historical sociology. One single Catholic argumentation should suffice as an example: *"Luther and Calvin are opposed to Pelagius. They teach that human nature is essentially perverted since Adam's sin; human nature is now inevitably subject to the confusion of concupiscence, the will is radically incapable of performing a morally good act, free will no longer exists. Man, thus, cannot by himself be or become righteous before God. His justification cannot originate but from an extrinsic principle, although this justification does not consist in the infusion of a supernatural gift that penetrates the souls and becomes inherent to them ... It is a simple imputation of Christ's justice; the necessary condition for this imputation is faith (fides fiducialis): faith alone is necessary, faith alone is sufficient. This faith is not an infused virtue, a supernatural quality; one never manages to determine what its essence may be according to Luther. Luther frequently spoke about grace and borrowed his expressions from the Holy Scripture and Catholic preaching; nevertheless, he does not acknowledge the existence of internal grace as such, customary or current. Besides, grace is logically excluded from his doctrinal system, and irreconcilable with it: in fact Luther only recognizes an extrinsic justification which is simply imputated in man; there is no real dependence, no internal coherence between the vital activity and the justification: from the moral point of view, man is radically perverted; all his doings are wicked, whether he is righteous or not; hence, grace has no reason for existence at all, it has no role to play whatsoever; it is not required as an internal aid that is superadded to the natural abilities, and strengthens man in his observation of precepts and his exercise of virtue; because Luther does not acknowledge liberty, and denies that moral perfection is connected with justification; nor is grace required as a principle of supernaturalization because Luther denies that, in its present state, human nature can be intrinsically supernaturalized, i.e. positively dedicated to God. The negation of grace in Luther's doctrine is confirmed by his teaching on the state of the first man: a natural state of righteousness in front of God, due to man's simply natural abilities, like light is compelled by the eye, and due to knowledge and love that are both characteristic of human nature."* [34] Of course sociology does not have to take this interpretation for granted, on the contrary. It has to confront these

---

[34] J. Van Der Mersch, 'Grâce' ('Grace'), *op. cit.* (Calvins use of a Catholic plea on the negation of grace can be found in the *Dictionnaire de théologie catholique (Dictionary of Catholic Theology)*, vol. II, col. 1400).

discourses on grace with the totality of problems concerning the gift, scrutinizing the interactions between discourses on grace and practices, to see if there has been a desire to abolish the gift, be it in the name of grace, and a desire to abolish grace itself, if it is already no longer a gift. Mauss has suggested it: there is a history of the gift, and in the Christian context it can be added that there is a history of grace. The Catholic Church and its church-state system has functioned and still functions to a large extent through the systems of the gift that are inextricably entangled with discourses and beliefs concerning grace, creating systems of 'conversion' and coherence between gifts and grace. It is this coherence and these systems of 'conversion' that have been refused by the Reformation.

*Propositions of the historical sociology of secularization*

These facts uncover a hypothesis on secularization and dechristianization.[35] Is the disenchantment of the world not strongly tied to the retreat of the magic world in which, by means of the transmutation that is brought about by the gift, everything could transform itself aleatorily in symbols, in bonds and debts, in protecting social capital? The 'enchanted' world is the human world in which the social is/seems omnipotent. The disenchanted world is the dismissal of the social that is made by gifts. Hence the hypothesis: is the decline of Catholicism (and in the first place of its holism of which its name bears the marks), and of all forms of Christianism, not *also* linked to the retreat of all the economic forms of gift and grace, in the religious domain (following the crisis of the Reformation), in the economic (market economy), the social (retreat of the primary sociality along the communal lines in front of the secundary sociality along the individualistic, mercantile, anonymous lines) and the political?

The decomposition of the relations between gift and gift/grace would certainly furnish the most economical hypothesis to explain the converging effects of all the secularization phenomena that culminate in the empire of an entirely mercantile economic system. This process is also linked with the hope to pay off the debt, the foundation of the religious dimension of the gift. Whence the undeniable effects of individual liberation, of equalizing and of personal 'autonomization', brought about by modernity,[36] whence also the

---

[35] The data on dechristianization have been adequately synthesized by Tod, albeit too exclusively interpreted in a restricted familial setting. The relation between model and structure of the family, on the one hand, and of religions, on the other, is much more dialectical than one is led to expect by the simplification of the Freudian hypothesis on the figure of God being an extension of that of the father, a generalization which, according to the author, substitutes the general theory of religion. E. Todd, *L'invention de l'Europe* (The Invention of Europe) pp. 189-227.

[36] As Jacques Godbout rightly observes in his paper *Homo donator versus Homo Oeconomicus* (see this bundle), the passage from gift to rights constitutes an essential amelioration, every

ambiguities of that process for the social bond, and, partially, the difficulties of the reproduction/transmission of socialization itself in postmodernity or ultramodernity; whence the mingling of undeniable and beneficial rationality on the one hand, and loss of meaning and of value, on the other, of individual liberation and solitude, of conquest and deprivation, which seem to be more and more experienced as the contradictory essence of modernity and its progress.

*Conclusion*

Many more hypotheses are left to be formulated, even though this essay already set up so many, that a lifetime would barely suffice to verify all of them.

But to introduce the problems of gift and grace in the sociology of religion, of secularization and of modernity, and to confront these with an anthropology of gift and grace which remains to be set up, confirms that sociology will never be able to answer its own questions on religion and secularization, without ethnographical and ethnological detours that are somewhat accentuated in order that the study of proximate data would gain anthropological depth.

Mauss has laid the foundations for such an anthropology that no one is in a hurry to acknowledge, maybe because it is so rich it would upset too many rich. Nonetheless, one would hope it is with this anthropology that all the human sciences will engage in dialogue; and if they want to, the same goes for theologists, who certainly talk about grace, but who take refuge behind their categorizations and avoid delicate confrontations and the problems of historicity and of bolstering the religious discourse, problems that are posed by the social sciences. And economists too, because in evacuating gift and grace, they create an imaginary space of pure rationality, in which the impossible *homo oeconomicus*, human being without body, without desire, without ancestors, without heritage, without imagination and without language, and, nevertheless, (thanks to which miracle?) not deprived of reason, will have all the liberty to die of boredom and solitude, possibly after having caused his planet to die.

---

time the receiver is incapable of returning. This is, indeed, what can be observed in the field of, for instance, volunteer work: in a poll questioning receivers, one observes that if and when they cannot or do not want to return, they adopt the model of the constitutional government, and they consider the organisation of volunteers as an extension of the government. But why is the passage to rights no longer a menace to one's identity? Because rights establish a debt of society towards the 'party entitled'. The donator no longer gives, he renders; to render is not a menace to one's identity. But surely the right must be acknowledged by the members of society". If one remembers that in the context of politico-religious absolutism, grace installs a perpetual debt to the donator, one can imagine the feeling of 'liberation' from this debt that is effectuated in the passage to a welfare state which renders to parties entitled.

## Bibliography

A Bieler, *La force cachée des protestants (The Hidden Strength of Protestants)* (Genève: Labor et Fides, 1995).

A. Caillé, 'Ni holisme ni individualisme méthodologiques. Marcel Mauss et le paradigme du don' ('No Methodological Holism, No Methodological Individualism. Marcel Mauss and the Paradigm of the Gift'), in *The Obligation to Give. Marcel Mauss' Capital Sociological Discovery* (1996).

J. Cazeneuve, *La sociologie de Marcel Mauss (The Sociology of Marcel Mauss)* (Paris: PUF, 1968).

M. Godelier, *L'enigme du don (The Enigma of the Gift)* (Fayard, 1996) p. 234.

F. Héritier, *Masculin et féminin, la pensée de la différence (Male and Female, Thinking the Difference)* (Paris: Odile Jacob, 1996).

B. Karsenti, *Marcel Mauss. Le fait social total (Marcel Mauss. The Total Social Fact)* (Paris: PUF, 1994)

B. Karsenti, *L'homme total. Sociologie, anthropologie et philosophie chez Marcel Mauss (The Total Man. Marcel Mauss' Sociology, his Anthropology, his Philosophy)* (Paris: PUF, 1997).

S. Latouche, Les dangers du marchè planètaire (The Dangers of the Planetary Market).

L. Lévi-Makarius, *Le sacré et la violation des interdits (The Sacred and the Violation of the Forbidden)* (Payot, 1997) p. 335.

C. Lévi-Strauss, *Introduction à l'oeuvre de Marcel Mauss (Introduction to the Work of Marcel Mauss)* (1950/1968).

E. Nodet, J. Taylor, *Essai sur les origines du christianisme (Essay on the Origins of Christianism)* (1998).

J. Pitt-Rivers, *The Place of Grace in Anthropology*, postface à J. G. Perpistiony, J. Pitt-Rivers (eds.), *Honor and Grace in Anthropology*, 1992.

P. Rospabé, *La dette de vie. Aux origines de la monnaie (The Debt of Life. On the Origins of Money)* (Paris: La Découverte, 1995).

I. F. Silber, 'Gift-giving in the Great Traditions: the Case of Donation to Monasteries in the Medieval West', in *Archives européennes de sociologie*, 36:2 (1995) pp. 209-243.

D. Sperber, *La contagion des idées. Théorie naturaliste de la culture (The Contagion of Ideas. A Naturalistic Theory of Culture)* (Paris: Odile Jacob, 1996).

C. Tarot, 'Danger, don' ('Danger, Gift'), in *L'obligation de donner. La découverte sociologique capitale de Marcel Mauss (The Obligation to Give. Marcel Mauss' Capital Sociological Discovery)* (1996).

C. Tarot, 'Du fait social de Durkheim au fait social total de Mauss' ('From Durkheim's Social Fact to Mauss' Total Social Fact'), in *L'obligation de donner. La découverte sociologique capitale de Marcel Mauss(The Obligation to Give. Marcel Mauss' Capital Sociological Discovery)* (1996).

C. Tarot, 'Repères pour une histoire de la naissance de la grâce' ('Landmarks for a History of the Birth of Grace'), in *Ce que donner veut dire, don et intéret (What Giving Means, Gift and Interest)* (Paris: La Découverte, 1993).

C. Tarot, *De Durkheim à Mauss, l'anthropologie du symbolique. Sociologie et sciences des religions (From Durkheim to Mauss, the Anthropology of Symbols. Sociology and Sciences of Religions)* (1999).

C. Tarot, *Symbolisme et tradition. Pour renouer avec une sociologie générale de la religion. Tome 1, Durkheim et Mauss (Symbolism and Tradition. Linking up with a General Sociology of Religion. Volume 1, Durkheim and Mauss)* (Caen, 1994) (University thesis, promotor: Alain Caillé).

E. TODD, *L'invention de l'Europe (The Invention of Europe)* (Paris: Seuil, 1990-1996) pp.151-152.

E. TROCMÉ, *L'enfance du christianisme (The Childhood of Christianism)* (Noêsis, 1997).

J. VAN DER MERSCH, 'Grâce' ('Grace'), in *Dictionnaire de Théologie catholique (Dictionary of Catholic Theology)* (Paris: Letouzey et Ané, 1925) col. 1557.

# On becoming human:
# Mauss, the gift, and social origins

Raymond CORBEY* (University of Tilburg and Leiden)

> "[but] then he gave us shell valuables in return for pigs, and we decided he was human."
> *new guinea highlander on first seeing a european, intially taken to be a pale-skinned cannibal spirit.*[1]

## 1. Mauss' 'archaeological' intentions

After the refutation of nineteenth-century evolutionist anthropology by early twentieth-century approaches, the evolution of society was until quite recently unpopular in anthropology and other human sciences. Those early twentieth-century approaches favoured fieldwork over speculation, the study of individual extant societies over their evolutionary origins, and interpretation in terms of cultural meanings over explanation in the style of the natural and life sciences. Evolutionary approaches from that era, for example Sigmund Freud's theorizing on the phylogeny of guilt and neurosis[2] or, indeed, part of Marcel Mauss' work on the 'archaeology' of the gift[3] and personal identity,[4] were generally viewed with suspicion. Part of the problem was, and still is, the disciplinary identity of approaches which, in the wake of Wilhelm Dilthey and Franz Boas, explicitly conceive of themselves as interpretive *human* sciences. Such new developments since the 1960's as sociobiology, behavioural ecology, 'gene-culture co-evolutionism,' evolutionary psychology, and Robin Fox' attempts to introduce biology into ethnological human kinship studies,[5]

---

\* For their stimulating comments, I would like to thank the members of the Tilburg University research programme Ethics-Politics-Economics II, as well as David van Reybrouck and Jos Bazelmans at Leiden University.

[1] A. Strathern, *The People of Moha: Big-Men and Ceremonial Exchange in Nount Hagen, New Guinea* (Cambridge, Cambridge University Press, 1971) p. XII.

[2] R. Corbey, 'Freud et le sauvage' ('Freud and the Savage'), in C. Blanckaert (ed.), *Des sciences contre l'homme II: Au nom du Bien (The Sciences against Man II: In the Name of the Good)* (Paris: Editions Autrement, 1993) pp. 83-103.

[3] M. Mauss, *The Gift: The Form and Reason for Exchange in Archaic Societies* (London: Routledge, 1990).

[4] See his 'Une catégorie de l'esprit humain: La notion de personne' ('A Category of the Human Mind: the Notion of the Person'), in M. Mauss, *Sociologie et anthropologie (Sociology and Anthropology)* (Paris: PUF, 1995) pp. 331-362.

[5] R. Fox, *The Search for Society: Quest for a Biosocial Science and Morality* (New Brunswick and London: Rutgers University Press, 1989).

influential as they were in other academic circles, have not yet taken hold of cultural anthropology because of that discipline's commitment to cultural meaning, especially in the United States.

Times are changing, however, and issues of social origins are back on the agenda in several disciplines.[6] There is a growing awareness of the desirability of bringing perspectives from the natural sciences and human sciences closer together, however difficult, impossible, or undesirable that may seem to many. The work of Marcel Mauss, as well as that of his teacher, uncle, and close associate, Emile Durkheim, is promising in this respect — ironically so, because much of the resistance against issues of social origins was, that of social anthropologists who 'largely stuck to their Durkheimian guns as has commented and were not interested.'[7] Mauss' approach to exchange and identity was an evolutionist one, although he did not go back in time beyond Celtic societies or 'archaic' Australian Aborigines except for frequent references to a 'primordial', natural state of mankind. He was well aware of the research on human origins by physical anthropologist Marcellin Boule and palaeolithic archaeologists Teilhard de Chardin and Henri Breuil, all three of whom he knew personally, and once enthusiastically reviewed Boule's handbook *Les hommes fossiles: Éléments de paléontologie humaine*.[8]

In the multifarious reception of Mauss' work, ranging from Claude Lévi-Strauss, Claude Lefort and Georges Bataille[9] via Louis Dumont and his school[10] to Mary Douglas and Jacques Derrida, an evolutionary approach is, typically, largely neglected. His ideas on the differences between 'archaic,' non-state, non-modern societies and modern ones have been taken up by, among others, Louis Dumont and his followers, but the relevance of the *Essai sur le don* for a better understanding of the earliest origins of human society, culture, agency, and identity has scarcely been explored. That relevance, I will argue, is considerable; assessing it is the purpose of the present contribution to this volume on Mauss and the gift.

On an empirical level, Mauss formulates fascinating hypotheses on the how and why of the evolution of exchange, social order, and personal identity, aim-

---

[6] M. Carrithers, 'Nature and Culture', in A. Barnard and J. Spencer (eds.), *Encyclopedia of Social and Cultural Anthropology* (London and New York: Routledge, 1996) pp. 393-396.

[7] R. Fox, 'Comment' (on Rodseth et al. 1991), in *Current Anthropology,* 32:3 (1991) p. 242.

[8] M. Mauss, 'L'Homme fossile' ('The Fossil Man'), in *Le Populaire*, 11 April (1921).
Boule, *Les hommes fossiles: Éléments de paléontologie humaine* (*The Fossil Men: Elements of Human Paleontology*) (Paris: Masson et Cie., 1920).

[9] R. Corbey, 'Gift en transgressie: Kanttekeningen bij Bataille' ('Gift and Transgression: Notes on Bataille'), in *Tijdschrift voor Filosofie,* 56 (1994) pp. 272-312.

[10] J. Bazelmans, *Een voor allen, allen voor een: Tacitus' Germania, de oud-Engelse Beowulf en het ritueel-kosmologische karakter van de relatie tussen heer en krijger-volgeling in Germaanse samenlevingen (One for All, All for one: Tacitus' Garmania, the Old-English Beowulf and the Ritual-Cosmological Character of the Relationship between Lords and Warrior-Servants in Germanic Societies)*, Doctoral Dissertation (Leiden, 1996) pp. 79-108.

ing at a set of more or less archaelogical conclusions ('conclusions de quelque sorte archéologiques').[11] On a philosophical level, a notion of the 'natural' or 'original' state of mankind, and at the same time of human nature, is continually present in his thought, guiding his empirically directed work as a conceptual or ontological presupposition, and linking his thought to that of the great social theorists of the Enlightenment. *État naturel* refers to *both* humankind before history and civilisation — its natural history — *and* a state of 'raw nature' that is partly constitutive for human society, as a condition that must continually be transcended to make humanness possible. "Becoming human", as Mauss analyzes it, "happens in time, in the course of the evolutionary development of certain primates, but it is also, on an ontological level, a permanent, structural feature of humans who, in this perspective, continually transcend the state of nature ... by giving." The 'natural state' is seen as primordial, both ontologically and phylogenetically, and social order as discontinuous with nature in both respects.

In the following, I shall analyze Mauss' ideas on how giving relates to social order and personal identity on both levels and evaluate their possible bearing upon issues of social origins as they are addressed nowadays, especially in two academic milieus: that of archaeologists and exponents of related disciplines (such as ethnology, paleoanthropology and primatology) working on early hominids, and that of philosophers pondering how and why human agency and identity evolved. Members of the first category are primarily interested in empirical questions, such as when do we see the first signs of cognitively and behaviourally modern behaviour in the archaeological record, but views of what culture and nature basically are are as important for them, for they guide their work as conceptual foundations.[12] Members of the second group, on the other hand, will probably be more interested in how society and identity are constituted ontologically, but for them what is known empirically on how we became human is as important.

On the first level, Mauss' work on exchange has a bearing on the periodization of the evolution of society. There is a certain consensus that our earliest ancestors, those living about five to ten million years ago and immediately preceding the bipedal Australopithecines, very generally speaking at least, were within the range of extant nonhuman primates behaviourally and cogni-

---

[11] M. Mauss, *The Gift*, p. 4.
[12] G. Clark and C. Willermet, *Conceptual Issues in Modern Human Origins Research* (New York: Aldine de Gruyter, 1997); R. Corbey, 'De l'histoire naturelle à l'histoire humaine: Comment conceptualiser les origines de la culture? ('From Natural History to Human History: How to Conceptualize the Origins of Culture?') in A. Ducros, J. Ducros and F. Joulian, *La nature est-elle naturelle? Histoire, épistémologie et applications récentes du concept de culture (Is Nature Natural? History, Epistemology and Recent Applications of the Concept of Culture)* (Paris: Éditions Errance, 1998) pp. 223-238; M. Sahlins, 'The Sadness of Sweetness: The Native Anthropology of Western Cosmology', in *Current Anthropology*, 37(1996) pp. 395-428.

tively, while Upper Palaeolithic humans — living about twelve to thirty-five thousand years ago — already were 'people like us' not only anatomically, but also behaviourally and cognitively. The latter buried their dead ceremonially and created the beautiful, intriguing cave paintings found in Western Europe. In between is a large grey area, the era in which we became human, on which opinions diverge sharply. Some authors see a quite continuous development from animal to human; others see a sudden shift when language comes into play; still others postulate an intermediate phase of functioning which differs from that of modern humans and from the generalized nonhuman primate mode of behaviour.

On the second, philosophical level, the following analysis is more widely relevant with respect to the fragmented, multiparadigmatic condition that holds much of the human sciences as well as philosophy captive. The most prominent divergence here is that between interpretive approaches, on the one hand, and natural science style explanatory ones, on the other hand, or, in philosophy, that between hermeneutical approaches and naturalist, utilitarianist ones. In anthropology, a similar divergence can be seen between perspectives which study cultural phenomena like kinship and ritual in terms of the reasons persons have for acting and the meanings they bestow upon reality and those, on the other hand, for whom what happens primarily has to do with the biology, ecology, economy, and technology of humans as organisms. Representatives of the first type of approach are Louis Dumont and his disciples with their — neo-Durkheimian — notion of culture as a system of ideas/values, British neo-Durkheimians such as Mary Douglas and Victor Turner, and American interpretive ethnologists such as Clifford Geertz. Outspoken representatives of the latter type of approach are ecological determinists in anthropology and the so-called Processual or New Archaeology.

The purpose of the following analysis is not so much to resolve the problems of an adequate reconstruction of how we became human as to articulate them clearly. I shall proceed as follows. A convenient starting-point for an analysis of the bearing of Mauss' essay on the gift upon the coming into being and constitution of human societies and persons is his notion of 'natural state' (Par. 2). In his view, it is not only social order which comes about by breaking with nature through exchange; the same goes for the human person who, in the Maussian view, is also constituted by giving. Many archaeologists tend to see the 'release from proximity' which is made possible by symbols and, subsequently, syntax, as the pivotal point when animals became human (Par. 3). Given the current deadlock between human sciences and natural sciences perspectives on issues of human origins, a heuristically or methodologically naturalist, 'bottom up' approach is required, in the line of Mauss' own methodological principle of 'total' explanation (Par. 4). There are indications of an intermediate stage or mode of functioning which was more complex than that of our remote apelike ancestors but less complex than, and different from, modern human behaviour and cognition. The ever-present danger when trying to make sense of the evolution of social order and personal identity is a reductionism that loses sight of the main concerns of the European philosophical tradition — rationality, normativity, subjectivity — which is precisely what Jürgen Habermas tries to avoid in his reconstruction of the evolution of human agency and society, partly inspired by the Durkheimian approach (Par. 5).

## 2. Human through giving

For Mauss, exchange is constitutive of social life and social order, for it is the earliest solution, both genetically and ontologically, to the Hobbesian *warre* of all against all that, in his view, ensues from man's selfish nature. "Societies have progressed", he writes in the conclusion to his *Essai sur le don*, "in so far as they themselves, their subgroups, and, lastly, the individuals in them, have succeeded in *stabilizing* relationships, giving, receiving, and finally, giving in return. To trade, the first condition was to be able *to lay aside the spear*. From then onwards, they succeeded in exchanging goods and persons, no longer only between clans, but between tribes and nations, and, above all, between individuals. *Only then* did people learn how to create mutual interests, giving mutual satisfaction, and, in the end, to defend them *without having to resort to arms*."[13] Two lines up he had characterized the natural state which is overcome — again: both phylogenetically and ontologically — through alliances and gifts as one of 'war, isolation and stagnation.' In that state, the 'fundamental motives for human action: emulation between individuals of the same sex, that basic imperialism of human beings'[14] still had free reign.

In a Durkheimian vein, anthropologists like Louis Dumont, Daniel de Coppet, and Cécile Barraud, to name but a few, take exchange to be constitutive of social order in their recent research on a number of tribal societies. Time and again they show by detailed ethnographic analysis how 'in every society, certain 'ideas/values' perpetuate themselves beyond the life or death of particular individuals, imposing themselves in all the various sorts of social relations.'[15] The plethora of exchanges going on in a village every day form and constantly renew a value-orientated matrix which at the same time is constitutive for the persons involved, including the dead and the spirits. "Subjects and objects

---

[13] M. Mauss, *op. cit,* p. 82.
[14] *Ibid.*, p. 65.
[15] C. Barraud, D. de Coppet, A. Iteanu and R. Jamous (eds.), *Of Relations and the Dead: Four Societies Viewed from the Angle of Their Exchanges* (transl. S. Suffern) (Oxford and Providence, USA: Berg Publishers, 1994) p. 110.

intertwine ceaselessly", they write, underlining one of the key insights of Mauss' essay on the gift, "in a tissue of relations which make of exchanges the permanent locus where these societies reaffirm, again and again, their highest values."[16] Exchange in this sense — not in a narrow economic sense, but as *symbolic* exchange, as a 'total social phenomenon,' with many, non-separated aspects, normative, economic, jural, religious — is, with what is probably the most well-known dictum from Mauss' *Essai*, 'one of the *human* foundations on which our societies are built'.[17]

The influential structuralist approach of Claude Lévi Strauss shares the Maussian presupposition of social order as a *human* imposition upon a relatively unstructured, chaotic, brute state of nature: "The social life of monkeys does not lend itself to the formulation of any norm ... (The) monkey's behaviour is surprisingly changeable. Not only is the behaviour of a single subset inconsistent, but there is no regular pattern to be discerned in collective behaviour."[18] In Lévi-Strauss' opinion, an animal became human and social organisation came into being only by the prohibition of incest. "[Mankind] has understood very early", he states in *The Elementary Structures of Kinship*, "that, in order to free itself from a wild struggle from existence, it was confronted with the very simple choice of either marrying-out or being killed-out. The alternative was between biological families living in juxtaposition and endeavoring to remain closed, self-perpetuating units, overridden by their fears, hatreds and ignorances, and the systematic establishment, through the incest prohibition, of links of intermarriage between them, thus succeeding to build, out of the artificial bounds of affinity, a true human society ..."[19] Social, political and economic order, in this view, comes about by giving; it is a consequence of the exchange — giving and receiving, giving and giving-in-return — of women between male-dominated descent groups, whereby the 'state of nature' is transcended. Similarly, another influential ethnologist, Marshall Sahlins sees the gift, as does Mauss, as "the primitive analogue of the social contract ... the primitive way of achieving the peace that in civil society is secured by the State".[20]

This particular way of conceptualizing the relation between society and nature reminds one of Thomas Hobbes' social contract theory. 'The finall

---

[16] *Ibid.*, p. 105.

[17] M. Mauss, *op. cit*, p. 4.

[18] C. Lévi-Strauss, *The Elementary Structures of Kinship* (transl. and ed. J.H. Bell, J.R. von Sturmer and R. Needham) (London: Eyre and Spottiswoode, 1969) pp. 6-7.

L. Rodseth, R. Wrangham, A. Harrigan and B. Smuts, 'The Human Community as a Primate Society', in *Current Anthropology*, 32:3 (1991) pp. 222-233.

[19] C. Lévi-Strauss, 'The Family', in H. L. Shapiro (ed.), *Man, Culture and Society* (New York: Oxford University Press, 1956) pp. 277-278.

[20] M. Sahlins, 'The Spirit of the Gift', in M. Sahlins, *Stone Age Economics* (New York: Aldine de Gruyter, 1972) p. 169.

Cause, End or Designe of men,' Hobbes wrote in the first part of *Leviathan*, "... in the introduction of ... restraint upon themselves, ... is the foresight of their own preservation, and of a more contented life thereby; that is to say, of getting themselves out from that miserable condition of Warre, which is necessarily consequent to the natural Passions of men, when there is no visible Power to keep them in awe ..."[21] Social order is not in man's nature, but is installed by a social contract that constrains the natural state of mankind as well as the solitary individual's natural tendencies. Here the analogy stops, for while in Hobbes' thought, the state is — according to some interpretations at least — an instrument of selfish individuals, for the Durkheimians, the social fabric that comes about through exchange is a moral and religious order. Their approach was critically pitted against the liberal, in their view, too individualistic, voluntaristic, and utilitarianist *homo economicus* approach to the foundations of society of Hobbes and the other great social theorists of the Enlightenment.[22]

The view of man — and nature — underlying Mauss' analysis of the gift is the Durkheimian one of *homo duplex*, which was formulated succinctly by Emile Durkheim in an article on that subject written 1914. The individual, Durkheim wrote, has "a double existence ... the one purely individual and rooted in our organisms, the other social and nothing but an extension of society."[23] A deep antagonism between the demands of the individual organism and those of social order is postulated, a conflict in which Durkheim and Mauss are firmly on the side of the 'morals of reciprocity', which triumphs over the 'personal interests'. Man becomes human phylogenetically, ontogenetically, and ontologically through inculcation in a different order of existence, the spiritually, morally, and intellectually superior world of society, language, and culture, thus rising above his naturally selfish animal individuality which is directly rooted in his biological organism. Such Durkheimian or similar dualistic views of man and society, culture, and nature determine how many, probably most, ethnologists conceive of their discipline — as a *human* science.

According to Mauss, in traditional non-state societies not only social order but also personal identity, what Mauss calls 'le personnage', is constituted through gifts and exchange. Persons are not primarily particular biological

---

[21] T. Hobbes, *Leviathan* (Harmondsworth: Pelican, 1972) p. 223.

[22] T. Lemaire, 'De *homo economicus* tussen ruil en uitwisseling' ('The Homo Economicus between Barter and Exchange'), in *Antropologische Verkenningen*, 2 (1985) pp. 77-106.

[23] É. Durkheim, 'The Dualism of Human Nature and its Social Conditions', in K. H. Wolff (ed.), *Emile Durkheim, 1858-1917* (Columbus: Ohio State University Press, 1960) p. 337; M. Sahlins, 'The Sadness of Sweetness: The Native Anthropology of Western Cosmology', in *Current Anthropology*, 37 (1996) p. 402; N. Rapport, 'Individualism', in A. Barnard and J. Spencer (ed.), *Encyclopedia of Social and Cultural Anthropology* (London and New York: Routledge, 1996) pp. 298-302.

organisms, but come about and are transformed — for instance, from living to dead — by ritually and intergenerationally bestowing souls, names, titles, rights, and duties that are part of the family clan upon each other. This happens not only in birth ceremonies, marriages, funerals, and other important rituals that punctuate the life cycle, but also in the context of subsistence activities such as hunting and horticulture, usually conceived of as an exchange with spirits inhabiting the landscape, and in the context of such seemingly trivial everyday activities as greeting, gossiping, and sharing food. In Durkheimian terminology: raw organic nature is incorporated into the sociocosmic hierarchy of ideas/values. A person is not primarily a living being in the sense of behavioural ecology or ecological anthropology, but a moral subject.

In his essay 'Notion de personne',[24] Mauss has traced the historical development of personal identity in the western world. The tribal *personnage* is replaced by the Classical *persona*, the free and responsible state citizen; then comes the Christian *personne*, with its interior spiritual life associated with a unique soul and, for the first time in history, a full-blown personal conscience; in modern times, the *moi* appears as an independent rational agent. This line of analysis has subsequently been continued brilliantly by Louis Dumont and his followers, who focussed on differences between the modern and the non-modern (non-state, 'archaic') personal identity and the epistemological consequences of these differences for researchers from western cultures with western type personal identities trying to understand the rather different tribal worlds.

I would now like to address not the relatively well-known discussion on differences in personal identity between non-modern and modern societies, but — in line with Mauss' 'archaeological' intentions, and stretching these further back than the master himself — those between non-modern and earlier forms of social life, extrapolating them to how we *became* human in the first place. Here again, as in the case of the Maussian view of the coming about of social order, ontological assumptions as to how personal identity is constituted determine empirically directed research into its phylogeny. Mauss' idea of the gift as 'one of the human foundations on which our societies are built' as one of its many treasures holds a key to the periodization of human evolution.

## 3. The release from proximity

Looking at what we know about human evolution on the basis of recent research in a number of disciplines — archaeology, primatology, linguistics,

---

[24] M. Mauss, *Sociologie et anthropologie (Sociology and Anthropology)* (Paris: PUF, 1995) pp. 331-362.

anthropology — I think that part of the divide between nature and society which governs the Maussian approach to social order and personal identity is kept up.

One of the most salient developments in the course of human evolution and a distinctive feature of human social organization, setting humans apart from other primates and other animals, is "the fact that a full range of consanguineal and affinal ties, as well as exclusive sexual relationships, is maintained by humans, even in the absence of spatial proximity ... This release from proximity is a hallmark of human social organisation, [tying] together many varied aspects of human sociality, from the daily routines of the community to the pomp and circumstance of political alliance."[25] This release from proximity, the capacity to sustain relationships *in absentia*, stretching them across time and space, is mediated by symbolic, syntactic language, enabling humans to refer precisely and extensively to things in other times and places and even to possibilities and counterfactuals. It makes possible and necessary relationships and alliances, including affinity or marriage, between individuals and groups in the absence of spatial proximity, kept up through the reciprocal exchange of Maussian gifts, embedded in moral views and rules, with the concomitant threefold obligation of giving, receiving, and giving-in-return. At the same time, personal identity gets an additional dimension when individuals are vested with names and titles related to linguistically expressed mythical convictions, and correspondingly come to conceive of themselves — their past and future, rights and duties — through a permanent narrative synthesis or *mise-en-intrigue*, expressing their identity in terms of their past, present, and future reciprocal exchanges with significant others, including spirits and ancestors.

The release from proximity is something that took place in the course of hominid evolution, but at the same time is a permanent constituent feature of human social order — it is an aspect of both becoming and being human. It shares this double focus with an influential view of man elaborated during the 1920s by two German philosophers, Max Scheler and Helmuth Plessner. Scheler especially contrasted the ape's *Umweltbann*, its being enclosed in a milieu of species-specific, biologically relevant meanings to which it reacts quasi automatically, with the human *Weltoffenheit* (openness-to-the-world) that comes about by taking distance from and control over one's own impulses, thus getting access to one's environment more fully. Scheler, however, underestimated the germane role of symbolic resources and hardly paid attention to the social dimension of human existence in the sense Mauss and Durkheim were wrestling with it in those same years and in the way we are dealing with it here.

---

[25] L. Rodseth, R. Wrangham, A. Harrigan and B. Smuts, 'The Human Community as a Primate Society', in *Current Anthropology,* 32:3 (1991) p. 239.

The foregoing analysis of human sociality and identity permits us to formulate the empirical question where and when we became human more precisely: where and when do we see the first unambiguous signs of social life through interaction, not in co-presence but *in absentia*, with the help of symbolic resources? Upper Palaeolithic societies of hunters and gatherers show strong indications of elaborate symbolic communication; intergroup alliances over large regions cemented by ceremonial reciprocal exchange of gifts, goods, services, and partners; ritual exchanges with entities in nature; death rituals, and so on. For these societies, only the most recent and a very small — approximately a half percent — timeslice of the total evolution of hominids, there are also archaeological indications, although not altogether uncontested, of periodical, partly ritual reunions in the context of mostly seasonally bound 'fission/fusion' social patterns.

The status of the Neanderthals, who immediately preceded the Upper Palaeolithics in Europe, is less clear. There is much discussion about whether they had a full-blown syntactic language of the modern type, and to what extent they buried their dead ritually. It has often been suggested that their lack, or relative lack, of the kind of resources just described for their successors has ultimately led to their demise. Unlike the newcomers who replaced them, they could not fall back on the ecological safety network, kept up by gift exchange, that is provided by distant friends and relatives. There are strong, but again not uncontested, indications that earlier hominids — pre-Neanderthals, the earliest *Homo sapiens*, *Homo erectus*, and so on — lacked extensive, syntactic symbolic resources and the kind of sociality and personal identity such resources make possible. At the same time, these 'missing links,' bipedal, with large brains, complex tool technology, and control of fire, were quite different from our earliest, ape- or chimpanzee-like ancestors. This will be dealt with below.

### 4. Culture and human nature

Ironically, the *homo duplex* view which is at the basis of the valuable Maussian approach to social order and personal identity is at odds with Mauss' own programmatic heuristic of total social phenomena and total human beings. We hardly ever find man divided into several faculties ('l'homme divisé en facultés'), he wrote in 1924;[26] we always come across the whole human body and mentality, given totally and at the same time, and basically, body, soul, society, everything is mixed up here ("Au fond, corps, âme, société, tout ici se mêle"). One of the best examples of a total social phenomenon (*fait social total, prestation totale*) is the 'archaic' gift.

---

[26] M. Mauss, *op. cit.*, p. 303.

Given what was known in his day about behavioural genetics, inclusive altruism, gene-culture coevolution, the neurological basis of cultural behaviour, and epigenetic development, it may not be held against Mauss that he did not entirely live up to this valuable methodological adage as far as corporeality and the biology of behaviour were concerned. It may, however, be held against Durkheimian-orientated authors from recent decades, for example, Lévi-Strauss', who never gave up his conviction, germane to his structuralist approach, that, as cited already, the state of nature was one of 'a wild struggle for existence' in which biological families lived in "fears, hatreds and ignorances"; that "[the] social life of monkeys does not lend itself to the formulation of any norm ... [the] monkey's behaviour is surprisingly changeable. There is no pattern to be discerned in its collective behaviour." Over the last few decades, a wealth of primatological and ethological research has taught us otherwise.

In fact, as we now know, and as quite a few theoreticians on exchange fail to realize, human nature results from the co evolution of genetic make-up and cultural as well as social behaviour. Our hands, for example, were shaped while wielding Oldowan chopping tools and Acheulean handaxes; parts of our brains and respiratory tract developed when our ancestors started to manipulate arbitrary symbols. Similarly, the acquisition and intergenerational, partly symbolic transmission of cultural and social abilities in humans is crucially dependent upon a whole gamut of cognitive and motivational capabilities that are part of our specific biological equipment. A complex, subtle, and well-timed interaction of these capacities with social environmental influences is of vital importance, and these interactive processes can also be described on the level of epigenetic neuronal development.

Our nature thus was, and is, social and cultural from its very beginning. That there is a brutish, impulsive animal nature at our phylogenetic roots as well as, ontologically, deep within us, in the need of being restrained and subdued in order to make civilisation and social order possible, is a conviction that does not hold in the light of recent insights, at least not in this form. In fact, it corresponds to a typical European dualistic perception of man and reality that at least partly issues from Christian and Platonic ideas on the spirit and the flesh, redemption and sin. Much of what is social does not come about through a symbolic contract that restrains the biological, but is biological, that is, natural, itself. How much the Maussian perspective underestimates the role of that purportedly 'raw' organic nature, again both phylogenetically and ontologically, is illustrated forcefully by recent work on sociality, individuality, politics, motivation, and communication in nonhuman primates, for example, chimpanzees.[27]

---

[27] L. Rodseth, R. Wrangham, A. Harrigan and B. Smuts, 'The Human Community as a Primate Society', in *Current Anthropology,* 32:3 (1991) pp. 221-254; D. Quiatt and V. Reynolds, *Primate Behaviour: Information, Social Knowledge, and the Evolution of Culture* (Cambridge

Marcel Mauss' stimulating views of exchange can be put to good use in confrontation and concurrence with recent scientific insights such as those mentioned, going beyond what he intended where that is necessary, but remaining faithful to his heuristic principle of a 'totalizing' approach which must take the natural into account too; faithful as well to his program of an archaeology of exchange. I do not necessarily want to imply an ontological naturalism, but at least a methodological, pragmatic one, which helps us to think against the grain of *homo duplex* approaches. It is worthwhile to try and bring *homo symbolicus*, constitutive of much of cultural anthropology as a discipline, back down to earth, to nature, by bringing the whole riches of recent insights into human nature to bear upon the idea of man, the cultural animal.

The Maussian paradigm, valuable though it is, is seriously flawed by its too radically dualistic view of man, and it stands in the need not so much of being overthrown, but of being rethought and updated. More can be learned by asking how the symbolic behaviour that makes human societies and identities possible may be rooted in nature than by asserting that it is the difference that sets humans apart from nature.[28]

## 5. An intermediary stage

A number of palaeolithic archaeologists tend to dichotomize the Palaeolithic into animal-like 'Ancients' and behaviourally and cognitively modern 'Moderns', taking the release from proximity as the critical watershed.[29] However, our hominid ancestors probably did not develop directly from a generalized nonhuman primate mode of functioning — similar to that of extant apes — to complex relationships and identities transcending physical and temporal proximity by linguistically mediated relationships of exchange. At least part of the recent work on human origins, from various quarters, seems to converge on postulating an idiosyncratic mode of functioning in between the apelike earliest hominids and cognitively and linguistically modern humans — a behavioural and cognitive missing link of sorts. It is useful to take a closer look at this stage, for it is the closest empirical pendant for the notions

---

University Press: Cambridge, 1993); A. Ducros, J. Ducros and F. Joulian, *La nature est-elle naturelle? Histoire, épistémologie et applications récentes du concept de culture (Is Nature Natural? History, Epistemology and Recent Applications of the Concept of Culture)* (Paris: Éditions Errance, 1998).

[28] D. Quiatt and V. Reynolds, *Primate Behaviour: Information, Social Knowledge, and the Evolution of Culture* (Cambridge University Press: Cambridge, 1993) p. 265.

[29] W. Noble and I. Davidson, 'Tracing the Emergence of Modern Human Behavior. Methodological Pitfalls and a Theoretical Path', in *Journal of Anthropological Archaeology*, 12 (1993) pp. 121-149. R. Corbey and W. Roebroeks, 'Ancient Minds', in *Current Anthropology*, 38 (1997) pp. 917-921.

of a primeval 'natural state' of mankind that have been so crucial to much social thought.

A number of current approaches criticize the weight which is given to language and symbolic thought in the study of present-day humans — not least by Durkheimian-orientated researchers. Their symbolic capacity certainly makes for vast differences between humans and other animals with respect to certain aspects of sociality and identity. However, the similarities between both categories are as important, and symbolic behaviour, with its neurofysiological basis, can easily be interpreted as part of human biology as it results from evolutionary processes. Dunbar[30] points to the fact that most of the linguistic communication going on between humans cements their relationships as a kind of verbal grooming. Many social scientists somehow stress not so much mental representations as incorporated, bodily routines, habits, and skills as a way of dealing with reality; not so much cognition and language as the active engagement of humans with their environment. Some of these social scientists use Pierre Bourdieu's categories of the *habitus* and the *sens pratique* (the practical sense), which were influenced by Maurice Merleau-Ponty's ideas of *expérience vécue* (lively experience) and the *corps-sujet* (body-subject); others follow the anti-mentalism of Ludwig Wittgenstein and Gilbert Ryle, still others, for example Tim Ingold,[31] take their cues from J.J. Gibson's ecological theory of perception, or from André Leroi Gourhan's pioneering work, influenced by vitalistic philosophy, on the evolution of hominid technical acts as social behaviour.

I think this type of approach has considerable heuristic value with respect to a mode of functioning which was intermediate between our earliest hominid ancestors and modern human behaviour, and still constitutes an important dimension of the latter. In his most recent work, the British palaeolithic archaeologist Clive Gamble has elaborated the ideas of, among others, Gibson and Leroi Gourhan in this sense. "The rhythms and gestures of the body during the performance of social life," he writes, "the habitual actions of living, mean that social memory is passed on in non-textual, non-linguistic ways. ... [The] rhythms of encounters, seasons, hunting, growing up, sleeping and eating around hearths and under rock abris ... established an hourly, daily, annual and generational pace. They produced forms of doing and adapting which recurred and persisted through repeated gatherings and social occasions over many millennia".[32] This is in tune with ideas of the Canadian psychologist

---

[30] R. Dunbar, *Grooming, Gossip and the Evolution of Language* (London: Faber & Faber, 1996).

[31] T. Ingold, 'People Like Us: The Concept of the Anatomically Modern Human', in R. Corbey and B. Theunissen (ed.), *Ape, Man, Apeman: Changing Views since 1600* (Leiden: Dept. of Prehistory of Leiden University, 1995) pp. 241-262.

[32] C. Gamble, 'Palaeolithic Society and the Release from Proximity: A Network Approach to Intimate Relations', in *World Archaeology,* 29:3 (1998) pp. 429-439.

Merlin Donald[33] on mimetic culture as an intermediate stage between our earliest apelike and our most recent hominid ancestors. Mimesis, in this view, was a conscious, intentional, self-initiated but *pre-* and *non*linguistic mode of imitation, representation, and communication, and as such a formidable survival strategy that enabled the mastery and highly flexible use of hundreds of cultural routines.

At this stage, before the release from proximity by the use of symbolic resources, gifts in the 'total', Maussian sense were not possible yet, nor were the complex, symbolically based social constellations and personal identities constituted by that kind of exchange. Social life and individual identity were local, face to face, and probably did not stretch much beyond the primary group, the here, and the present, although communication by means of simple arbitrary symbols — in the sense of Donald Bickerton's[34] 'protolanguage' — may have already been available. Much of the group's solidarity and the individual's identity was undoubtedly biologically and epigenetically based in genetic altruism, patterns of hierarchy, grooming behaviour, and the like, while another part of it was probably constituted by the specific roles of the individual in the group's activities. The 'Maussian' dimension did not so much replace what went on at these levels as — *pace* the Maussians — add to it and incorporate it into more complex processes.

Much ongoing work on matters of social origins is utilitarian in orientation. Gamble, for example, stresses the survival value of symbolically based alliance networks kept up by exchange. To a considerable extent, that would seem to be justified, for utility is a powerful evolutionary factor, but is that all there is to be said, philosophically speaking? The underlying view of man here would seem to be that of a *homo oeconomicus* or *oecologicus*. However, many philosophers, especially those with a continental European background, are interested in the earliest origins of not only such aspects of human agency and society, but also, and especially, in normative and rational dimensions of being and becoming human. In their eyes, the challenge is to try and assess the limits of any strictly utilitarian perspective. Can it indeed, as it pretends to do in the hands of many, if not most authors in this field, give an exhaustive account of normativity, subjectivity, and rationality as those dimensions of human existence have been explored by the great European thinkers?

The most elaborated and probably most sophisticated effort to reconstruct the evolution of human identity and society in terms of a broad, nonreduction-

---

[33] M. Donald, *Origins of the Modern Mind: Three Stages in the Evolution of Culture and Cognition* (Cambridge, MA: Harvard University Press, 1991).
M. Donald, 'Origins of the Modern Mind: Three Stages in the Evolution of Culture and Cognition', in *Behavioral and Brain Sciences*, 16 (1993) pp. 737-791.

[34] D. Bicketon, *Language & Species* (Chicago and London: The University of Chicago Press, 1990).

istic view of agency is that of Jürgen Habermas in his *Theorie des kommunikativen Handelns*[35]. It is hard to overestimate the importance of this work, for, whatever one may ultimately think of the specific philosophical stance it develops, it is where European philosophy tries to come to terms with what is now known on human origins, with an open mind to philosophical perspectives from the English-speaking world and to the empirical sciences, and, moreover, critically building on Durkheimian insights. One of the ways in which it can be read is as a reflection on what the 'release from proximity' means philosophically, trying to account for human agency as fully as possible.

Habermas reconstructs the evolution of full-blown, linguistically mediated and normatively orientated interaction in terms of four aspects of human agency that are intricately intertwined but irreducible to one another: instrumental-teleological, normatively regulated, dramaturgical, and communicative. Independently of the aforementioned authors who stress bodily routines but in considerable convergence with them, he traces the origin of these aspects of human behaviour to a prelinguistic evolutionary stage which is intermediary between animal and human linguistic communication. In this stage, that of 'ritual practices as the archaic kernel of the normative'[36] elaborated in discussion with both George Herbert Mead and Emile Durkheim, hominid interaction is no longer primarily steered by genetically determined tendencies, but by a prelinguistic consensus which comes about through shared sacred symbols. In Habermas' view, we became human when linguistic communication on the various types of validity claims — 'true,' 'just,' 'sincere' — became possible, along with the various types of agency, which only then became differentiated. From that moment onwards, agents agreed by explicit conscious choice instead of quasi automatically as formerly, still under the constraints of biologically based ritual routines and complying with a normative consensus which was established by those routines. In the new phase, the routines persist, but are now permeated by language. This is the first manifestation of rational moral agency in human evolution; linguistically mediated intersubjectivity now becomes an additional constituent of social order.

These processes which Habermas analyzes in laborious detail in his grand effort to reconstruct the origins of normativity, rationality, and society can only be touched upon here. While the Durkheimian-Maussian view of moral agency and social order tends to sociological determinism, Habermas, better in touch with the main concerns of European thought, stresses that the acting individual always has some reflexive distance to the ideas and values that

---

[35] J. Habermas, *Theorie des kommunikativen Handelns*, two vols. (Frankfurt a. M.: Suhrkamp, 1987).
[36] *Ibid.*, Vol. 2, pp. 69 ff.

influence its behaviour, thus providing an alternative to one-sided holistic and/or utilitarian scenarios for how we became human. What the Maussians, with their decidedly holistic and relational approach to persons and societies, can offer him are their insights with respect to the constitutive role of exchange in the evolution of society and personal identity.

## 6. Conclusion — 'de quelque sorte archéologique'

In the foregoing, we have investigated what the Maussian approach to social order and personal identity in terms of symbolic exchange can contribute to a better understanding of human evolution, in line with Mauss' own 'archaeological' intentions. Although his *Essai sur le don* is primarily a contribution to sociology and ethnology, a philosophical view of what it means to become and to be human is germane to its argument. Social order and personal identity come about when through giving, a rupture is brought about with Hobbesian raw nature, both structurally, at any moment, as a constitutive moment of humanness, as well as at a certain moment in time — when natural history became human history.

Taking Mauss' views not so much as the definitive reconstruction of how we became human but as a potent heuristic strategy, I have argued for two lines of further research. The first is to try and take the natural dimensions of social order and personal identity into account in a less dualistic way than the Maussians do; the second is to try and avoid a too reductionist view of human agency. The considerable tension between these two requirements reflects how much the study of things human — including, as I am painfully aware, the present analysis itself — is dominated by the two types of metaphysical positions that western civilisation has brought forth: those posing the primacy of mind and those posing the primacy of nature. The divergence between human science types of approaches and natural science types of approaches between as well as within disciplines is one of the manifestations of that metaphysical watershed. Human origin studies in particular are plagued by a proliferation of paradigms, even within each of the two main types of approaches. Philosophical analysis and criticism of the most basic assumptions made in each case, as exemplified in the foregoing, is therefore much needed.

With respect to the periodization of the evolution of exchange, social order, and personal identity, the symbolically based release from proximity has very probably been a turning point. This is where the Maussian gift must have come into play. Three caveats, however, have been given in the foregoing. First, this transition should, if only for pragmatic reasons, not be reconstructed too dualistically in the sense of a rupture with nature. Secondly, it should not, again, if only for pragmatic reasons, be interpreted too dualistically in a slightly different sense, namely as a shift from the one to the other of two basic modes of existence — animal to human, nature to culture. There may have been an idiosyncratic mode of existence, a behavioural and cognitive missing link, in between. And last but not least, more faithful to Mauss' own methodological heuristic of 'total' facts than even the master himself, the rational dimension of human agency and existence should be accounted for.

More research along these particular lines is required in order to develop a sophisticated, critical update of the idea of a primordial 'natural state' of mankind that has played so substantial a role in the social thought of Hobbes, Rousseau, and Mauss, among others.

**References**

C. BARRAUD, D. DE COPPET, A. Iteanu & R. Jamous (eds.), *Of Relations and the Dead: Four Societies Viewed from the Angle of Their Exchanges* (transl. S. Suffern) (Oxford and Providence, U.S.A.: Berg Publishers, 1994).

J. BAZELMANS, *Een voor allen, allen voor een: Tacitus' Germania, de oud-Engelse Beowulf en het ritueel-kosmologische karakter van de relatie tussen heer en krijger-volgeling in Germaanse samenlevingen*, Doctoral Dissertation (Leiden, 1996).

D. BICKETON, *Language & Species* (Chicago and London: The University of Chicago Press, 1990).

M. BOULE, *Les hommes fossiles: Éléments de paléontologie humaine* (Paris: Masson et Cie., 1920).

M. CARRITHERS, 'Nature and Culture' in A. Barnard & J. Spencer (eds.), *Encyclopedia of Social and Cultural Anthropology* (London and New York: Routledge, 1996) pp. 393-396.

G. CLARK & C. WILLERMET, *Conceptual Issues in Modern Human Origins Research* (New York: Aldine de Gruyter, 1997).

R. CORBEY, 'Freud et le sauvage' in C. Blanckaert (ed.), *Des sciences contre l'homme II: Au nom du Bien* (Paris: Editions Autrement, 1993) pp. 83-103.

R. CORBEY, 'Gift en transgressie: Kanttekeningen bij Bataille', in *Tijdschrift voor Filosofie* 56 (1994), pp. 272-312.

R. CORBEY, 'De l'histoire naturelle à l'histoire humaine: Comment conceptualiser les origines de la culture?' in A. Ducros, J. Ducros & F. Joulian, *La nature est-elle naturelle? Histoire, épistémologie et applications récentes du concept de culture* (Paris: Éditions Errance, 1998) pp. 223-238.

R. CORBEY & W. ROEBROEKS, 'Ancient Minds', in *Current Anthropology* 38 (1997) pp. 917-921.

M. DONALD, *Origins of the Modern Mind: Three Stages in the Evolution of Culture and Cognition* (Cambridge, MA: Harvard University Press, 1991).

M. DONALD, 'Origins of the Modern Mind: Three Stages in the Evolution of Culture and Cognition', in *Behavioral and Brain Sciences* 16 (1993) pp. 737-791.

A. DUCROS, J. DUCROS & F. JOULIAN, *La nature est-elle naturelle? Histoire, épistémologie et applications récentes du concept de culture* (Paris: Éditions Errance, 1998).

R. DUNBAR, *Grooming, Gossip and the Evolution of Language* (London: Faber & Faber, 1996).

É. DURKHEIM, 'The Dualism of Human Nature and its Social Conditions', in K. H. Wolff (ed.), *Emile Durkheim, 1858-1917* (Columbus: Ohio State University Press, 1960) pp. 325-340.

R. FOX, *The Search for Society: Quest for a Biosocial Science and Morality* (New Brunswick and London: Rutgers University Press, 1989).

R. FOX, 'Comment' (on Rodseth et al. 1991), in *Current Anthropology*, 32:3 (1991), pp. 242-243.

C. GAMBLE, 'Palaeolithic Society and the Release from Proximity: A Network Approach to Intimate Relations', in *World Archaeology*, 29:3 (1998) pp. 426-449.

J. HABERMAS, *Theorie des kommunikativen Handelns*, two vols. (Frankfurt a. M.: Suhrkamp, 1987).

T. HOBBES, *Leviathan* (Harmondsworth: Pelican, 1972).

T. INGOLD, 'People Like Us: The Concept of the Anatomically Modern Human', in R. Corbey & B. Theunissen (eds.), *Ape, Man, Apeman: Changing Views since 1600* (Leiden: Dept. of Prehistory of Leiden University, 1995) pp. 241-262.

T. LEMAIRE, 'De *homo economicus* tussen ruil en uitwisseling', in *Antropologische Verkenningen* 2 (1985) pp. 77-106.

C. LÉVI-STRAUSS, 'The Family', in H. L. Shapiro (ed.), *Man, Culture and Society* (New York: Oxford University Press, 1956).

C. LÉVI-STRAUSS, *The Elementary Structures of Kinship* (transl. and ed. J.H. Bell, J.R. von Sturmer & R. Needham) (London: Eyre & Spottiswoode, 1969).

M. MAUSS, 'L'Homme fossile', in *Le Populaire*, 11 April (1921) p. 2.

M. MAUSS, *The Gift: The Form and Reason for Exchange in Archaic Societies* (transl. W.D. HALLS) (London: Routledge, 1990).

M. MAUSS, *Sociologie et anthropologie* (Paris: PUF, 1995).

W. NOBLE & I. DAVIDSON, 'Tracing the Emergence of Modern Human Behavior. Methodological Pitfalls and a Theoretical Path', in *Journal of Anthropological Archaeology*, 12 (1993) pp. 121-149.

N. RAPPORT, 'Individualism', in A. Barnard & J. Spencer (eds.), *Encyclopedia of Social and Cultural Anthropology* (London and New York: Routledge, 1996) pp. 298-302.

L. RODSETH, R. WRANGHAM, A. HARRIGAN & B. SMUTS, 'The Human Community as a Primate Society', in *Current Anthropology*, 32:3 (1991) pp. 221-254.

M. SAHLINS, 'The Spirit of the Gift', in IDEM, *Stone Age Economics* (New York: Aldine de Gruyter, 1972).

M. SAHLINS, 'The Sadness of Sweetness: The Native Anthropology of Western Cosmology', in *Current Anthropology* 37(1996) pp. 395-428.

D. QUIATT & V. REYNOLDS, *Primate Behaviour: Information, Social Knowledge, and the Evolution of Culture* (Cambridge University Press: Cambridge, 1993).

A. STRATHERN, *The People of Moka: Big-Men and Ceremonial Exchange in Mount Hagen, New Guinea* (Cambridge: Cambridge University Press, 1971).

# THE PHILOSOPHY OF THE GIFT

# Transpositions of Mauss' theory of the gift in the Personalist Social Critique of Arnaud Dandieu (1897-1933)

Christian ROY

My research in intellectual history has focused on the inter-war origins of French personalism, a philosophy that has had a considerable impact in Christian intellectual circles through such figures as Emmanuel Mounier and Jacques Maritain among Catholics, Denis de Rougemont and Jacques Ellul among Protestants, Nikolai Berdiaev and Olivier Clément among the Orthodox. Yet I have made the surprising discovery that, around the enigmatic figure of Arnaud Dandieu, there has been what may almost be termed a common source to this mostly Christian personalism and to a philosophy of difference and desire inspired by Nietzsche that leads up to post-modernist thought. For I have established that personalism did not originate, as generally assumed, among the Catholic founders of Mounier's influential review *Esprit*, launched in 1932 and still in existence, but in a group formed in 1930 under the name *Ordre Nouveau*, whose legacy was to live on after the war in a wing of the European federalist movement. Its initiators were a mixed bag of believers and agnostics, be they committed neophytes of different creeds or Nietzschean free-thinkers close to Surrealism, whose only common ground was personalism as a philosophy, defined therefore in anthropological rather than theological terms. On the basis of a definition of the spirit as the violence of heroic self-overcoming in the creative act, the group's founding members would soon work out the precise socio-economic principles and plans of an original personalist revolutionary project. It left behind the political categories of Left and Right along with what they saw as the outworn framework of the nation-state, and aimed at a continental — and eventually world-wide — federation of self-managed regional entities, in the name of the necessary tension between local rootedness and the universality of the person, conceived as a mind-body unity whose involvement in his/her environment demanded expression in the proper socio-political framework of flexibly interlinked small-scale communities.

*Ordre Nouveau*'s doctrine was formed under the impetus of its leading thinker Arnaud Dandieu (1897-1933). In the course of the 1920s, Dandieu had evolved a philosophy of the person and a novel critical theory on the basis of a bold application to all areas of human experience — from religion and literature to economics and politics — of insights largely gleaned from anthropologists like Lucien Lévy-Bruhl and Marcel Mauss, and from psychologists like William

James, Sigmund Freud, Jean Piaget, and Eugène Minkowski. In substantial unpublished manuscripts, his search for a new non-essentialist "Moral of Becoming" based on pleasure as opposed to duty assumed an impulse to give spontaneously, of the kind put forward by Jacques T. Godbout to dispute the holist paradigm by pointing out at the Leuven conference that "a gift made out of obligation, in obedience to a norm, is considered of lesser quality." As if out to prove Godbout's point in *"Homo Donator Versus Homo Oeconomicus"* that "the model of the gift is the only action system that incites its members to increase the freedom of others", Dandieu translated it into economic concepts appropriate for the post-industrial era of automation in a series of articles co-written with Antonin Artaud's former manager Robert Aron on the political economy of international finance at the onset of the Depression, that appeared in Romain-Rolland's review *Europe* and in dissident Surrealist publications: Georges Bataille's *Documents* and Georges Ribemont-Dessaignes' *Bifur*. Their themes were to be developed in books published under the banner of the *Ordre Nouveau* group: *Décadence de la Nation française* (1931), *Le Cancer américain* (1932), *La Révolution Nécessaire* (1933, reprint 1993). In the last one, Arnaud Dandieu's psychologically based "dichotomic method" allowed him to distinguish a personal sphere of creative work from the impersonal realm of repetitive labour, which ought to be automated as much as possible, leaving a decreasing residue to be spread out over the whole of society through a "civilian service" in exchange for which every citizen would receive a guaranteed basic income.

This is an economy of the gift where accumulation is subordinated to sacrifice, insofar as sacrifice is related to creative pleasure, and distinguished not only from Judaeo-Christian asceticism, but also from the nihilistic sovereignty of destruction implied in the notion of *dépense* that Georges Bataille came up with in his parallel reflection on similar themes in the same range of disciplines. Formed in the midst of their daily intellectual exchanges at the Bibliothèque Nationale where both men were employed, Dandieu's thought is as rich and provocative as Bataille's in its questioning of the rationalist assumptions of utilitarian social thought. Having long been inspired by the religious scholar Alfred Loisy's *Essai historique sur le sacrifice* (1920), Dandieu later turned his attention to drawing the socio-political implications of Mauss' *Essai sur le don* (1924), albeit in a more constructive — "personalist" — key than his dialogue partner Georges Bataille, whose crucial article "La Notion de dépense" appeared in *La Critique sociale*[1] shortly before Dandieu's testament, devoted wholly to this task, *La Révolution Nécessaire*, was completed on the eve of his death on August 6, 1933. Whereas Bataille would only develop his ideas into

---

[1] G. Bataille, La Notion de dépense (The Notion of Expenditure), in *La Critique Sociale*, 7 (1933) pp. 7-15, reissued in G. Bataille, *La Part maudite* (précédé de *La Notion de dépense*) (The Cursed Part, preceded by The Notion of Expenditure) (Paris: Minuit, 1967).

a "general economy" of the unproductive and wasteful "accursed share" after the war, and then fitfully apply them to current financial developments, Dandieu worked out his related insights in a sustained analysis of the emergence and dramatic collapse of an international financial system between the wars. He never loses sight of it when he insists in *La Révolution Nécessaire* that, in order to properly understand exchange and credit, we have to take into account, aside from "measurable and purely economic elements, irrational ones of confidence and action"[2] (again like Godbout in his critique of recent economic literature on confidence such as Cordonnier's writings). Referring to Mauss' paradigm of competitive ceremonial giving drawn from the winter festivals of Northwest Pacific coast Amerindians, Arnaud Dandieu reveals the theoretical ambition moving him to write this book that would become *Ordre Nouveau's* reference for personalist policies:

> "The study of the potlatch has only been done up to now from a historical standpoint, and the very sociologists who have attempted it seem to have deliberately kept away from the political ramifications that their discoveries could have. And yet, these may be as staggering for the evolution of modern societies as for our knowledge of primitive societies: and the study of the potlatch turns out to be extremely fertile in lessons concerning the genuine nature and the essential source of so-called economic phenomena."[3]

One of these lessons is that the social time of ritual gift and counter-gift precedes the disembodied atemporality of quantifiable material exchange in view of individual profit, that credit precedes both barter and cash[4]. "But we should not think that this modern term covers new operations without historical precedent: far from raising as they believe above the laws of morals and history," people like Herbert Hoover who would make credit out of nothing "suddenly return, through the abstract figures of the balance-sheets of their pyramidal trusts, to the region of ritual gift, of the assertion of power characterising the primitive magician's naiveté."[5] Building financial empires on the psychological projection of confidence, "credit is the most developed modern form of suggestive magic. Far from returning to the exchange of concrete objects, of identical values, we now only exchange fictitious papers, odourless and weightless, signs at the most: we are in the realm of pure abstraction where the prestige of the sign abolishes real values"[6] — a point reiterated about today's electronic environment in Jean Baudrillard's economy of the

---

[2] R. Aron & A. Dandieu, *La Révolution nécessaire (The Necessary Revolution)* (Paris: Bernard Grasset, 1933), reprint with an introduction by N. Tenzer (Paris: Jean Michel Place, 1993).

[3] *Ibid.*, p. 97.

[4] *Ibid.*, p. 98.

[5] *Ibid.*, pp. 105-106.

[6] R. Aron & A. Dandieu, 'De Wall Street à La Haye (Essai sur le crédit)' ('From Wall Street to the Hague: An Essay on Credit'), in *Europe*, 22:88, April 15 (1930) p. 587.

sign in symbolic exchange. Dandieu however constructively qualifies it; all he wants is to give credit where credit is due — and only there.

> "No doubt is it good that in life's daily and standardised exchanges, money no longer be any more than a purely economic and abstract sign, devoid of any capacity to proliferate, of all energy and efficacy: but it is indispensable that beside this sign money may freely be born, within spontaneous, corporative and productive groupings, dynamic credit, necessary for great human adventures, similar in almost every respect to that which the clan chief has at his disposal on the day of the potlatch."[7]

Just as for Dandieu psychological needs cannot be assimilated to physiological, economic needs, since "human work is neither purely spiritual nor simply material (...), the credit that animates it should function differently according to whether it applies to quantitative and undifferentiated labour or to qualitative and creative work. On the one hand credit is organised, that is to say psychically annihilated, on the other credit is liberated."[8] In the meantime, even in an ostensibly materialistic society, by its magical procedures, "credit, as it expands, becomes idealised. Formerly corresponding to factual realities (individual value, collective value, prosperity, fertility, gold reserve ...), it now results from compliance to a certain number of theoretical rules and the establishment of some purely technical relations."[9] Dandieu sees what he calls the American "religion of credit" conquering the world with its spirit and organisation in individual as in collective life; for such American innovations as investment trusts and the Federal Reserve System needed to become universal in order for the system to be complete. Devised on an American model, effectively under American control as a powerful hegemonic tool, "the Young Plan and the Bank for International Settlements thus constitute the crowning of the abstract edifice that rationalism has been busy building on the financial plane since the XVIth century. Thanks to them, financial operations take place from now on in a closed circle, where no external contingency is provided for. It is easy to understand why the most important men of the business world, delighted to find themselves amongst each other in a well stopped up cave, strike up a triumphal tune before such a result."[10] Current secret negotiations for the Multilateral Agreement on Investment at the OECD in Paris somehow come to mind, not to mention the World Bank. Then as now, "the merchants are in the temple. They have made of it a cave of thieves. But it is a magical cave where the sacred odour still wafts,"[11] since "all efforts, American or oth-

---

[7] R. Aron & A. Dandieu, *La Révolution nécessaire,* p. 141.
[8] *Ibid.,* pp. 145-146.
[9] R. Aron & A. Dandieu, 'De Wall Street à La Haye (Essai sur le crédit)', in *Europe,* 22:88, April 15 (1930) p. 586.
[10] *Op. cit.,* pp. 588-589.
[11] R. Aron & A. Dandieu, *La Révolution nécessaire,* p. 132.

erwise, to rationalise credit and separate it from its real bases, cannot prevent it from being an essentially psychological fact, exposed to the risks and hazards of affective operations," as demonstrated by the Crash of October 1929 and the close call of October 1997. Dandieu was however no less critical of the attempts of economists like Jacques Rueff (whose face appears on a recent French coin!) to integrate psychological factors that cannot be eliminated, but only to neutralise or regulate them by resorting to probabilistic calculations,[12] "the last empirical weapon they have to defend their abstract and rational conception of trading operations: it is a way to abstractise the concrete, to mechanise the individual: under the guise of giving him his place, he is destroyed and eliminated."[13]

To fight this creeping depersonalisation of all exchange, Dandieu resorts to two notions characteristic of the potlatch as seen by Mauss. "These are the notion of credit, of the time limit placed on it, and also the notion of honour."[14] If "to grant a credit is to colonise the future" on the strength of an accumulation of confidence (such as in the medieval crucible of capitalism[15]: "festivals and fairs, in which economic transaction is only one element" according to Mauss)[16], "neither confidence, nor the sun let themselves be rationalised, even though the course of the seasons and the needs of consumption can, in a normal period, and within certain limits, seem to conform to laws"[17], of the kind presupposed by the recent financial development of "futures trading"; Dandieu would have had a lot to say about this systematic colonisation of the unpredictable spontaneity of time by the abstract space of quantifiable reversibility — the element where utilitarian exchange proliferates. For credit to be freed from its grip, Dandieu maintains, "it must first wholly die, under its etatist figure just as much as under its liberal guise, in order to rise again under its genuine aspect, which is spiritual. It is only by going through this ordeal that it will find again all the complexity and efficacy of the potlatch, adapted to a society that has reached a peak of industrial evolution." On the "turf of the regional or creative economy" set aside for the self-managed or co-operative enterprise, "it should take, thanks to appropriate forms, the dynamic role of binding agent uniting just as much people and things as people with each other"[18] — a lot like the rules of generosity of the Andaman Islanders as described by Mauss in the first section of his second chapter on "Liberality, honour, money": "Lives are

---

[12] *Ibid.*, pp. 114-118.
[13] R. Aron & A. Dandieu, 'Les misères de la prospérité' ('The Misery of Prosperity'), in *Europe*, 22:93, September 15 (1930) p. 133.
[14] M. Mauss, *The Gift: the Form and Reason for Exchange in Archaic Societies* (London: Routledge, 1990) p. 35.
[15] R. Aron & A. Dandieu, *La Révolution nécessaire,* pp. 103-105.
[16] Mauss, *op. cit.*, p. 5.
[17] *Ibid.*, p. 142.
[18] *Ibid.*, p. 146.

mingled together, and this is how, among persons and things so intermingled, each emerges from their own sphere and mixes together. This is precisely what contract and exchange are"[19], so that Dandieu can conclude his own chapter on "Exchange and Credit" with a vision of the potlatch "taking back its fruitful role as divider of risks and catalyst of efforts. Thus exchange will again become what it should never have ceased to be, an adventure and an act."[20] Even capitalism started out this way, and still runs on the prestige and confidence associated with far-flung enterprise, blowing them out of all proportion even as it methodically dispenses with most actual involvement in adventurous acts — speculating instead; but if we just took them seriously once more, Dandieu seems to be saying, it might be possible to wrest an authentic personal existence from their mass-produced shadows, and to shun "risk-free investments" that end up putting everybody at risk.

Central to Dandieu's thought, "*the human act can only be seized in its totality,* taking into account its psychological factors as well as its material factors."[21] On the type of Loisy's "sacred action", and "in conformity to the *law of participation* established by M. Lévy Bruhl [sic]", as a "ritual act, which implies at once war and alliance, interested commerce and sumptuary feast, the potlatch constitutes a totality where economic elements are tightly bound up, or more precisely fused with mystical and affective elements"[22] such as considerations of prestige and honour, "in an unstable state between festival and war"[23]. " Now, the gift necessarily entails the notion of credit"[24], says Mauss, so that for Dandieu, "we have to take back from the merchants the privilege they have stolen, and which they unduly monopolise, the privilege of credit." "The element of risk and credit, which characterises genuine exchange and makes it irreducible to barter, has been fraudulently captured by them under cover of materialist theories that deny it its normal field of application by reducing exchange to purely arithmetic equality."[25] Not that barter does not have its place; Dandieu would have assigned it to a kind of state-free "anti-productivist communism" where planned exchanges would provide for a vital minimum available through a citizenship income as a starting base for entrepreneurial or creative risk. Dandieu's dichotomic method sharply demarcates the utilitarian economy of barter in view of consumption from a prestige gift economy, following a distinction found by Mauss in all traditional societies — from Rome to the Trobriand Islands.[26]

---

[19] *Ibid.*, p. 20.
[20] R. Aron & A. Dandieu, *La Révolution nécessaire,* p. 146.
[21] *Ibid.*, p. 91.
[22] *Ibid.*, p. 101.
[23] Mauss, *op. cit.*, p. 82.
[24] *Ibid.*, p. 36.
[25] R. Aron & A. Dandieu, *La Révolution nécessaire,* p. 132.
[26] Mauss, *op. cit.*, p. 47.

If those characters of the potlatch — joining self-assertion and community-building in a single heroic act — have such a normative value for Dandieu, it is because he traces back to the individuation of the chief in relation to the clan, first intimated in its ceremonial, the origin, if not the essence of the human person. Aside from the totem and the masks evoking the ancestors, the *persona* of the distinguished host, that is his social recognition by debts of gratitude, was represented by copper shields bearing their owner's blazon; he showed them off at the potlatch but only reluctantly parted with them, unless it be on loan as a mark of trust. Similarly "the plates, the forks, the coppers, everything is emblazoned, belongs to the *persona* of the owner and of the *familia*, to the *res* of his clan", [27] as Mauss would insist in 1938 in his essay on "The Notion of Person", where he comes back "to the fact of the 'person' and his rights and duties and religious powers, on the succession of names, etc.", not having had the chance to dwell on them in his "Essay on the Gift" of 1924.[28] He had however already pointed out that, in Rome as among the Northwest Indians, "the individual found unable to repay the loan or reciprocate the potlatch loses his rank and even his status as a free man" [29], while Dandieu underlined that for ancient citizens, slaves "do not exist as human persons" since they do not have a *caput* — a public face[30]. Mauss purposely used Latin terminology about the Kwakiutl, because he found at its roots the same atmosphere among the Ancients as among the Amerindians. The word *persona* might have been borrowed by the Romans from the Etruscans — these natives of Italy who like those of the American Northwest "had a mask civilisation"; though they may have adapted it from the Greek, what is certain is that these two words originally refer to one and the same thing: the death mask of a clan's eponymous ancestor, whose *imago* preserved thus by patrician families gave his heirs the right to bear a surname or *cognomen*. It is as a decisive extension of the civic *persona* that Mauss saw "the revolt of the plebs, the full citizenship rights acquired — after the sons of senatorial families [in the original sense of "emancipation" — C. Roy] — by all plebeian members of the *gentes*", "all free men of Rome"[31]. He could have added that these funeral masks were to become, in Hellenistic and Roman Egypt, painted portraits of the deceased, in which it is impossible not to recognise the source of the Christian icon,[32] as a striking representation of the universalisation —

---

[27] M. Mauss, 'La Notion de personne' ('The Notion of the Person'), from the *Journal of the Royal Anthropological Institute*, vol. LXVIII (1938), in M. Mauss, *Sociologie et anthropologie (Sociology and Anthropology)* (Paris: Presses Universitaires de France, 1968) p. 344.

[28] *Ibid.*, p. 341.

[29] M. Mauss, *The Gift*, p. 35.

[30] R. Aron & A. Dandieu, *La Révolution nécessaire*, p. 226.

[31] M. Mauss, 'La Notion de personne', pp. 350-354.

[32] L. Bréhier, *La Civilisation byzantine* (The Byzantine Civilization) (Paris: Albin Michel, 1970) p. 233.

this time metaphysical instead of political — of a new vision of any human person as an *imago Dei*, to be restored in its primal glory by this new form of heroism that is sainthood. But it did appear to Mauss in the light of American ethnographic research "that we already see, among the Pueblo, all in all a notion of the person, of the individual, one with his clan, but detached from it already in the ceremonial, by the mask, by his title, his rank, his role, his property, his survival and his reappearance on earth in one of his descendants endowed with the same position, first names, rights, and functions"[33]. This idea formulated by Mauss in 1938 had already been arrived at by Dandieu in 1933 on the basis of his *Essai sur le don* and of his colleague Georges Davy's *La Foi jurée*[34], since he could state in *La Révolution Nécessaire*:

> "Thus, on the economic plane, the first exchange to be performed freed personal initiative from the collective and gregarious will of the clan: in the shape of patriarchy, and then of feudalism, these first individuals, freed from the group, exerted a virility and an aggressiveness that were at first undisputed and without any counterweight. But soon, with the contagion of individualism acting upon the masses, chiefs and subjects, masters and slaves opposed each other in an unceasing dialectical movement: rigid authority, having lost its creative power, saw a new form of individualistic thought rise up against itself: and the germ contained in the potlatch blossomed precisely into a movement of permanent revolution, made up of successive explosions, in the course of which the person affirms itself as ever freer and always more creative."[35]

Arnaud Dandieu had just greeted Georges Bataille and Raymond Queneau's reevaluation (based on the work of Nicolai Hartmann) of the master/servant dialectic in Hegel's thought in an article on "Marxist social philosophy", to turn it against a materialist bias that could not account for the dynamism of class struggle and revolution or any creative change of plane. "This theory which reduces exchange to an equation considers in value only a quantity, and, in work, but an average: it is thus profoundly *abstract* and *static*."[36] Over against the utilitarian assumptions shared by Marxism with the capitalist system,

---

[33] M. Mauss, 'La Notion de personne', *op. cit.*, p. 340.
[34] G. Davy, *La foi jurée* (Paris, Alcan, 1932).
[35] R. Aron & A. Dandieu, *op. cit.*, pp. 100-101.
[36] A. Dandieu, 'La Philosophie sociale marxiste' ('Marxist Social Philosophy'), in *Demain?*, 16-17, July-August (1933) pp. 24-26, referring to G. Bataille and R. Queneau, 'La Critique des fondements de la dialectique hégélienne' ('Critique of the Foundations of Hegelian Dialectic'), in *La Critique sociale*, 5, March (1932) pp. 209-214. See R. Queneau, 'Premières confrontations à Hegel' ('First Approaches to Hegel'), in *Critique*, 195-196, August-September (1963) pp. 694-700. Dandieu's article was reissued under the new title 'Théorie marxiste de la révolution' ('Marxist Theory of Revolution') in *L'Ordre Nouveau*, 41, June (1937) pp. 24-31, a review he co-founded, and which is available again since last year as a 5-volume reprint from Le Château Edizioni, Aosta, Italy, c/o C.I.F.E., 10 avenue des Fleurs, F-06000 Nice, France — as will soon be the edition by the C.I.F.E.'s Presses d'Europe of my history dissertation for McGill University on the context of Dandieu's social critique: *Alexandre Marc et la Jeune Europe 1904-1934: L'Ordre Nouveau aux origines du personnalisme*.

Dandieu saw the escalating dialectic of the potlatch in the proliferating personalisation of society, and drew from it his "dichotomic law", whereby each victorious expansion of the person's scope of heterogeneity through the freedom to give him/herself in creative acts results in a corresponding homogenisation of the social and natural environments thus "colonised", presenting new threats of absorption of the individual in impersonal processes that need to be met again more sharply on a subtler plane, in an endless spiral of particular acts of re-establishing dynamic tension between these opposite poles. Since change itself has become automatic with the methodical application of Descartes' creative discovery to make the world ever more uniform and predictable, human specificity can now be saved only by making the proper dichotomic distinctions within the activities of personal subjects, rather than by setting against each other social groups that are just all the more given over to the same standard processes, making all specificities obsolete or instrumental. That is why, instead of relying like Marxists on the dialectical role of the proletariat as a class, Dandieu starts from a psychological definition according to the kind of work spent — as an adequate outlet for creative energies where effort is not counted, or on the contrary as a chore demanding no personal involvement but to put in just the right amount of labour to get monetary compensation in exchange.

In the face of the inability of the utilitarian model of exchange to deal with the uncoupling of income and salaried work to which seems to lead the development of automation at the root of unemployment, Dandieu already saw the need in a post-industrial era to "*realize* for the benefit of the whole of the community, for the personal liberation of each of its members, the power saving that is blowing apart the old world."[37] For "to constant work, but at a variable salary, rationalisation would tend to substitute irregular work, but at a fixed salary. To the financial straits of the worker whose salary is reduced, it substitutes the distress of the unemployed, whose salary is nothing, and who no longer has in front of him a boss that he can make responsible for his misery."[38] "The boss, the so-called ruling class, endures the same fate as he. Closed factories, failed businesses, are the unemployment of the boss; but he, at the top of the ladder, cannot blame anyone but an abstract mechanism."[39] This sudden absence of an actual rival to face competitively affects every level of society and tears at its fabric of agonistic relations, making it ripe for massive scapegoating of the kind endemic to our closing century. As for the more obvious victim, the unemployed, "his is a peculiar status, entirely negative, that can only be compared to that of the dead in primitive societies."[40]

---

[37] R. Aron & A. Dandieu, *La Révolution nécessaire*, p. 88.
[38] *Ibid.*, p. 43.
[39] *Ibid.*, p. 47.
[40] *Ibid.*, p. 43.

Dandieu takes this comparison very far in the ethnologically inspired analysis of the ambiguous relations of non-reciprocal propitiatory giving maintained by technological society towards the "economic dead" he sees in the unemployed, put in the degrading position of receiving just enough to maintain a life that is no longer life, since nothing can be given in return; it is in the end only a matter of conjuring the threat of this "ghost who haunts our shining Babels" — in the shadows of their social circuits.[41] Insisting on the establishment of a guaranteed basic income that would not be aimed at them upon proof of need but unconditionally granted to all citizens, Dandieu no doubt realised that, as Jacques Godbout told us in his paper for the "Gifts and Interests" conference, "the passage from a gift to a right constitutes an essential improvement, every time the receiver is unable to give back."

However, even more than the stigma of unemployment, Dandieu had in mind the prestige of work, which he hoped to undermine. He took a cue from Marx's son-in-law Paul Lafargue in his *Éloge de la paresse* to point out that "the first mistake was to preach the love of work since it gives wealth its prestige."[42] Thus, "the central framework of present-day capitalism and imperialism is not so much economics as the prestige of economics. The real struggle is (...) between concrete and abstract, between live individuals and rationalised society: the revolution will thus come from a psychological reaction and not from a scientific determinism, which itself partakes of rational magic in what is most unreal and most inhuman about it"[43]: the prestige of a power that knows how to multiply to infinity as it by-passes the contingencies of lived experience — or rather shoves them down the line to those who do not have a choice. This may sound like the old master/slave relationship once more, except that the masters do not even come close to a degree of sovereign freedom, since they value servile work. But in Dandieu's thought of the gift, work is strictly speaking the opposite of freedom. "Among what comes from man, work alone is an evil. If work be a task devoid of beauty, let it be done as needed, but let it be cursed and not paid."[44] That is why, given the fact that "the progress of technology is currently hindered by the fear of unemployment, we have to envision an egalitarian distribution of all the parts of work made automatic by rationalisation, over the whole of the social body. If we want to be free men, we owe society a service."[45] Such a civilian service would be the cursed yet sacred pledge of a new aristocratic citizenship depen-

---

[41] *Ibid.*, p. 44.

[42] Dandieu papers, 108-IV Notes for a Book on Keats (Bibliothèque Nationale, copies at CIFE).

[43] R. Aron & A. Dandieu, *Europe*, 22:88, April 15 (1930) p. 595.

[44] Dandieu papers, 108-IV Notes for a Book on Keats.

[45] Dandieu's answer to a survey of intellectuals by the reactionary essayist Léon de Poncins on whether machinism is a good or a bad thing, among his papers at the CIFE in Nice.

dent on machines instead of slave labour; as this institution would give it unprecedented legitimacy in an exercise of freedom that does not curtail that of others, but instead expands it, by methodically spreading the time and resources freed up by creative investment in the labour-saving devices of technology. The ancient promise of the potlatch would thus be fulfilled by giving to all a chance to give of themselves freely, and thereby actualise their personhood, sharing in the prestige of a Round Table of noble yet general fellowship, as in the closing image, drawn from Breton folklore, of Mauss' *Essay on the Gift*.[46]

Arnaud Dandieu's imagery was even more eclectic in gathering all Western configurations of the gift at the common feast of a reborn potlatch — in a gesture reminiscent of what Jean-Luc Boilleau is doing nowadays. Nietzsche and Christ would be reconciled on this occasion under the totem of the lilies of the field: as in this parable against work used by Dandieu as a foundation myth, "the warrior toils not, neither does he spin, he fights for pleasure; such was the ancient aristocratic tradition. Such also the tradition of the French Renaissance: in Rabelais' work, society and human action have only joy as a criterion and honour as a wellspring (Gargantua, chapter LVII)." Arnaud Dandieu liked to point out that the same gospel verse: "*Lilia neque laborant neque nent*", provides the motto of the French royal house's blazon of lilies on a field of blue, and "has survived every change of regime".

> "For far from denying the value of the act, this motto expresses the properly Western heroic tradition of which not only France, but the Revolution were born. Aristocratic contempt for gold, trade, and servile labour had been founded on the spirit before being transmitted by bloodline. The silliness of castes, the racist nonsense cannot disguise to us this truth: the spirit that vivifies early feudalism is the same one as that of the Committee for Public Safety; neither the first feudal lord nor the first *comitard* consent to be soldiers nor workers, they are before everything else creators and warriors. Modern war and quantitative labour reinforce each other in the absence of any truly human élan of creative aggressiveness. Massacres of by-standers and slave labour, there is truly the formula of the modern world."[47]

In order to break out of it, following the logic of the gift, "there should not be any manual workers or else there should be slaves"[48] — as was required at the level of civilisation of Aristotle's Greece.[49] "For what is work if not the blood of slaves?" It cannot be paid for with a salary, which to Dandieu is literally blood money. "That is what stains all desires and all things — For the

---

[46] M. Mauss, *The Gift*, p. 83.
[47] R. Aron & A. Dandieu, *op. cit.*, pp. 238-239.
[48] Dandieu papers, 'Révolution personnaliste' (Personalist Revolution), Centre international de formation européenne, Nice.
[49] R. Aron & A. Dandieu, op. cit., p. 226.

wages of labour do not quench the blood of the worker", just as the thirty gold pieces given to Judas in return for betraying Christ could not — even by the all too human account of the priests — in any way make up for the superhuman self-sacrifice of divine freedom on the Cross; trading in the priceless backfires as a curse when giving of oneself —especially all of it — is involved. Dandieu sees in the same light the sacrifice of the worker's personal dignity — his ability to give what he alone can give — in impersonal processes where only raw labour force like that of animals or machines is demanded of him. "He believes it is worth a higher salary — No! Salary is the grindstone that he turns. He has to give up the idea of a salary", as it enslaves him to the closed cycles of utilitarian activity for biological survival, which Hanna Arendt defines as labour as opposed to work in *The Human Condition*. Dandieu would even prefer alms to wages, since they are at least a gift of man. "But salary comes from the devil", to rob him of the opportunity to give of himself as such — of his humanity. "Are there only devils and slaves left? bosses and workers?" asks Dandieu.[50] To him, "the blood we give has no price. There is no man rich enough to buy even a single drop. Workers sometimes forget it, bosses always do."[51]

And sociologists too: this is probably where Dandieu parts from Mauss, singling out for condemnation his theory "concerning the moral consequences of the potlatch (coming back to the potlatch, etc.)" in a hit list of ideas he was planning to attack that appears among his papers. It comes as a bit of a shock to find it there, when he so clearly believes like Mauss that "we can and must return to archaic society and to elements in it".[52] I can only make sense of this seeming contradiction by putting it in the context of the headings that surround it — mentioning Bergson, Durkheim, Davy, Lévy-Bruhl and others — on the same page under the general title: "On the notion of orientation in sociological and pedagogical studies".[53] Here as elsewhere, Arnaud Dandieu is out to question the reversibility and parallelism assumed as dominant models in various fields of knowledge and experience. His critique would apply to Mauss precisely on the point of the remuneration of labour that is raised first in the "Moral Conclusions", then in those "for Economic Sociology and Political Economy" of the "Essay on the Gift". When Mauss writes in the latter "that we cannot make men work well unless they are sure of being fairly paid throughout their life for work they have fairly carried out, both for others and for themselves", he seems to be submitting their activity wholly to private

---

[50] Dandieu papers, 'Révolution personnaliste'.
[51] Dandieu papers, 108-IV Notes for a book on Keats (Bibliothèque Nationale, copies at CIFE).
[52] M. Mauss, *op. cit.*, p. 69.
[53] Dandieu papers, 6-Bloc I, unpublished notes, p. 30 (Bibliothèque Nationale, copies at CIFE).

interest on the one hand and to social duty on the other — the two things Dandieu would have liked to offer them freedom from by calling upon his theory of the gift. For Mauss, the producer "is giving something of himself — his time, his life. Thus he wishes to be rewarded, even if moderately, for this gift"[54] — of his life's blood and precious time? Dandieu clearly had no time for such "a good but moderate blend of reality and the ideal" as the merely reformist "new morality" Mauss was putting forward.[55] He insisted on a strict dichotomy between the only real gift: the one a person makes with pleasure, and the obligation it carries to allow everyone this possibility of dignified living by sharing the burden of thankless utilitarian tasks needed, among other things, to give to all "a certain security in life, against unemployment, sickness, old age, and death" — though not because "the state itself, representing the community, owes it" to the workers for their troubles, as Mauss maintained,[56] but as a general citizenship right unrelated to actual need. To Dandieu, no amount of wages or workers' compensations could ever make employers or the state quits of the sacrifice of the gift of life to the necessities of survival. The personal act that is the gift cannot be converted into the currency of things or worse, their signs, unless it be through the law of participation entailed by the act itself in a social setting that is bound to be highly sensitive to scale and tempo. Mauss overlooks these crucial factors when he translates his findings from traditional societies to modern states.

Arnaud Dandieu denies such ready convertibility between the realms of quality and quantity, and cries foul when he sees mere quantities turning into qualities of their own, as Hegel seemed to allow, and current economics dictate. That is why for Dandieu there should not even be such a thing as "intellectual workers": "For there is no common measure between intelligence and money. What is needed is intellectuals."[57] What he meant is that thought is literally a free act, whereby critical theory immediately translates into action leading back to thought, so that without first "paying his dues" to academic respectability and institutional socialisation, he could take Mauss' theory of the gift in stride to transpose it to the late industrial society he lived in, through practical proposals to make of the act of the gift the fulcrum of social life once more. By the same token, Dandieu also made it clear that the sort of agonistic giving he wanted to restore would have to take on new — even revolutionary — forms, which neither sociological holism could fully account for, nor altruistic mysticism wholly discount, as he brought to light its ultimate source, at once spiritual and social, in the person it in turn creates.

---

[54] M. Mauss, *op. cit.*, p. 77.
[55] *Ibid.*, p. 69.
[56] *Ibid.*, p. 67.
[57] Dandieu papers, 'Révolution personnaliste'.

# Social Gifts and the Gift of Sociality
## Some Thoughts on Mauss' *The Gift* and Hobbes' *Leviathan*

Marin TERPSTRA (University of Nijmegen)

**Introduction**

In the early eighties, I was part of a small group of young scholars that discussed different aspects of the realm of 'guilt' and 'debt' throughout many years. The studies and reflections of our group clearly tended towards some kind of 'general theory of obligation', although our main interest was in practices which deal with failures to fulfill one's obligations. However, it was inevitable that at some time during this process Mauss' intriguing essay on the gift entered our thoughts.[1] So it did, having a great impact on my intellectual development. Before I turn to the specific topic I announced in the title, it might be of interest to say something more about this context.

First of all, one needs to know that in the Dutch language there is one single word expressing both 'guilt' and 'debt': *schuld*. So, we say "schuld hebben" (having debts) or "iets schuldig zijn" (being indebted), but also "het is mijn schuld" (it is my fault) and "schuldig zijn" (being guilty). The same goes for the German language, and maybe that is why Nietzsche could more easily make his statement that everything that has to do with 'bad conscience', with 'guilt' or 'guilt feelings' can be traced back to the economic relations between people, that is the relation between buyer and seller, creditor and debtor.[2] Here lies the connection with Mauss' essay. What made the thesis of Nietzsche so interesting for our group was his attempt to cross the borders of academic disciplines (law, economics, morals, history, anthropology, theology, philosophy), although he did this in a somewhat reductionist way. The same synthetic interest can be found in Mauss. Here, we can refer to the notion of 'total social phenomena' or 'total services' ('prestations totales').[3] With this

---

[1] M. Mauss, *The Gift. The Form and Reason for Exchange in Archaic Societies* (London: Routledge, 1990). The reference to a general theory of obligation is on p. 13.

[2] F. Nietzsche, *Zur Genealogie der Moral*, II, 4. "But how did that other 'somber thing', the consciousness of guilt, the 'bad conscience', come into the world? [...] I have already divulged it: in the contractual relationship between *creditor* and *debtor*, which is as old as the idea of 'legal subjects' and in turn points back to the fundamental forms of buying, selling, barter, trade, and traffic." (For an English text see *On the Genealogy of Moral/Ecce Homo* (transl. Walter Kaufmann and R.J. Hollingdale) (New York: Vintage Books, 1989) pp. 62-63).

[3] M. Mauss, *op. cit.*, pp. 3-6.

notion, Mauss indicated that in many cultural surroundings moral, economic, legal, religious and other aspects of human conduct are not seperated as they are in modern Western society. This might suggest that the Dutch and German language reflect much more of the 'total services' in this field than does the English or French language.

The comparison between Nietzsche and Mauss proved very fruitful. It led me to follow three lines of action. The first one was rereading Nietzsche's *Genealogy,* resulting in a text in which his reductionist approach to the world of human exchange relations is criticized.[4] For Nietzsche only one obligation counted: that of returning a gift, that of paying one's debts. I think this reductionist theory of obligation was due to 'Victorian morals', which were very strict on debts.[5] On the other hand, the most important thing that I learned from Mauss' essay was his observation that three obligations were involved: to give, to receive and to return gifts.[6] This was my second point: the design of a general theory of 'economies of obligations', as I called it.[7]

## Economies of Obligations

The first of these economies (EO1) was the one Mauss described: an economy in which human relations are based on the exchange of gifts, and in which giving and receiving was obligatory as much as returning a gift. Here, the economic aspect of exchange interrelated with religious and moral aspects: exchange was as symbolic as it was economic. In this system, guilt and debt could also be connected to failing to give or receive.

---

[4] 'Het recht op genoegdoening. De betekenis van de economische schuldbetrekking in Nietzsches kritiek van godsdienst en moraal' ('The Right to Restitution. The Meaning of the Economic Relation of Debt in Nietzsche's Appraisal of Religion and Morality'), in P. Van Tongeren (ed.), *Nietzsche als arts van de cultuur. Diagnoses en prognoses (Nietzsche as Physician of Culture. Diagnostics and Prognostics)* (Baarn: Ambo, 1990) pp. 165-183.

[5] On this subject, the work of J.M. Buchanan is especially useful, for example: J.M. Buchanan, *Liberty, Market and State - Political Economy in the 1980's* (Wheatleaf Books, Sussex, 1986), especially part four.

[6] Nevertheless, Mauss himself is a little ambivalent on this matter. His main interest also seems to be the question: "What rule of legality and self-interest, (...), campels the gift that has been received to be obligatorily reciprocated?" (p. 3). But on p. 13 he notes: "The institution of 'total services' does not merely carry with it the obligation to reciprocate presents received. It also supposes two other obligations just as important: the obligation on the one hand to give present, and on the other, to receive them.". For me and, I think, for Mauss too, this 'just as important' was most significant.

[7] That is to say: in the English translation. In Dutch the term was: 'schuldhuishouding' ('economy of guilt and debt'). See my article 'Zo spreken de schuldigen. Over schuldbetrekking en schuldhuishoudingen' ('Thus Speak the Guilty Ones. On relations of Guilt, Debt and Economies of Obligations'), in M. Terpstra (ed.), *Schuld en gemeenschap. Hoofdstukken uit een genealogie van de schuld (Guilt, Debt and Community. Chapters from a genealogy of guilt/debt)*, in *Annalen van het Thijmgenootschap*, 79 (1991).

In a second economy of obligations (EO2), which I think is typical of a commercial society in which *homo oeconomicus* rules, both aspects fall apart. Economics are differentiated from morals and religion. Obligation in the strict sense is reduced to an obligation to pay one's debts, which means that giving and receiving is no longer obligatory. In this, one can find two tendencies: (1) atomization and individualization, through which all exchange becomes the exchange of 'strangers' who have no obligations to each other, except for those in which they voluntarily engage themselves, and (2) separation of morals from the legal-economic world.[8] Here a social environment appears in which the idea of 'innocence', 'being without guilt or debt', is made possible: as long as one does not incur debts which one cannot pay, there is nothing to induce guilt. A person who is not generous or receptive is not guilty of breaking the social bond; he will be a sinner only when he continues to be an incorrigible debtor.

But there is a third economy of obligations (EO3), which seems to go along, in the Western world, with the second one. Mauss refers to this kind of economy in just a few words: the State has an obligation to those who offer their hard labour to society.[9] This new economy of obligation has been worked out

---

[8] I refer to the notion of 'Inschuld' ('debt and guilt') in H. Grotius, *Inleidinge tot de Hollandsche Rechts-Geleerdheid (Introduction to the Jurisprudence in Holland)*, in F. Dovring, H. Fischer, E. Meijers (eds.) (Leiden, 1965) pp. 194-195. This idea can already be found in Thomas Aquinas: see T.C. O'Brien, 'Legal Debt, Moral Debt', in *Summa Theologiae*, vol. 41 (London/New York) pp. 316-320. This separation of moral and legal debts is linked to an idea of a perfect society, in which some state of *innocence* is realized. In its ideal form, this society is a collection of individuals (citizens) who mind their own business. Their interaction must be organized in a way that does not interrupt the purity of the individual's self-reliance. Again, I can refer to Grotius, who, in the *Prolegomena* to his book on war and peace, gave a clear description of this ideal society. Here obligations are identified with those of the debtor, whose duty it is to repair the order he has disturbed. The interruptions of order, which Grotius described, are: loans, promises, injury and crime. Only by these kinds of actions, the individual becomes a debtor in a strict sense. His obligation is to restore his innocence — in the modern sense of being without debts. As soon as the obligation to return a gift, which is only an act of balancing or adjustment, has become the only one, interaction with other people no longer is obliged. So, it is one of my ideas, as odd as it may sound, that the appearance of self-interest has something to do with the quest for the state of innocence. However, in this kind of society the *gift of sociality*, or the political dimension of human interaction, is no longer present. The system is, so to speak, not self-organizing. The obligations to give and to receive would make the system work, because these obligations are simultaneously and continually creating social life and mutual dependence. The rules of the market concern the system of demand and supply. Therefore, they exclude free gifts and the acceptance of gifts. It only works if a gift is returned by an equal gift.

[9] M. Mauss, *op.cit.*, p. 65: "All over social insurance legislation, a piece of state socialism that has already been realized, is inspired by the following principle: the worker has given his life and his labour, on the one hand to the collectivity, and on the other hand to his employers. Although the worker has to contribute to his insurance, those who have benefited from his services have not discharged their debt to him through the payment of wages. The state itself, representing the community, owes him, as do his employers, together with some assistance from himself, a certain security in life against unemployment, sickness, old age and death."

by the nineteenth century legal theorists of *solidarity*.[10] Here, there is an obligation to give to a public body, which has the right to redistribute the gifts among its members, according to a number of specific criteria. Important, of course, is the fact that in this economy of obligations the obligation to return is specified and not the only one.[11] An interesting question is what problems are involved when both the second and the third economy of obligation are functioning together in society. The most important problem is a very obvious one: seen from the point of view of the second economy of obligations, each citizen will expect his gift to be returned on a basis of equivalence. To put it simply: the taxpayer wants his money back in the form of civil services. This is contrary to the principle of solidarity. The main point is that the original gift to society, the act of solidarity, is not an economic one in which it is evident or garantueed that an equal gift is returned, although such a return is not excluded either. It is even possible that the returned gift is greater than the original one. The third economy of obligations led me to reconsider the theory of social contract.[12] This is the third line of action. It is on this subject that I want to say something more in this paper. To me (and to Mauss), the social contract seems to be an interesting case showing how important it is to hide or to include economic self-interest into a symbolic exchange.[13]

Let me summarize this in order to make clear what this differentiation of economies of obligations can add to political philosophy. Essentially, we are faced with three main questions. Firstly, what brought about the reduction of the system of obligations to the single obligation of returning gifts and what are its consequences for society? In this context, we might compare EO1 to EO2. How does a market society relate to a redistributive system organized by

---

[10] See the work of F. Ewald, *L'État providence (The State of Providence)* (Paris, 1986) pp. 349-380.

[11] Specified are the rights of citizens concerning public services. The system supposes an obligation to give for all (an obligation to pay taxes). To some extent, there even is an obligation to receive, because a citizen without income, for example, remains responsible for his own life and therefore needs an income; the obligation to have an income involves an obligation to receive — an additional — one.

[12] A first attempt to clarify this problem was worked out together with a colleague who was also a member of our group, T. Dewit, 'Het maatschappelijk geschenk. De verlossing van de schuld in Hobbes' *Leviathan*' ('The Gift of Sociality. Redemption of Guilt in Hobbes' *Leviathan*'), in M. Terpstra (ed.), *Schuld en gemeenschap. Hoofdstukken uit een genealogie van de schuld (Guilt, Debt and Community. Chapters from a Genealogy of Guilt/Debt)*, in *Annalen van het Thijmgenootschap*, 79 (1991) pp. 45-78.

[13] One of Mauss' main interests is to understand or explain the peculiar fact that in what he called 'archaic societies', exchange of goods, services, women etc., although 'constrained and self-interested', was performed as if it was a voluntary exchange of gifts (M. Mauss, *op. cit.*, p. 3). This 'as if' brought us to Thomas Hobbes' observation of the social contract as a "covenant of every man with every man, in such manner, *as if* every man should say to every man" (italics are mine). See T. Hobbes, *Leviathan. The Matter, Form and Power of a Commonwealth Ecclesiasticall and Civil* (J.C.A. Gaskin (ed.)) (Oxford and New York: Oxford University Press, 1996) p. 114.

the state? Secondly, how does the principle of self-interest relate to the principle of solidarity? In this context, we might compare EO2 to EO3. And finally, is the welfare state, as Mauss suggests, a modern version of the 'primitive' total prestation? In this context, we might look at the relation between EO1 and EO3. Important is that, to some extent, all three imply the myth of the 'gift of sociality', which is returned in exchange for the social gifts of men in society — not by actual men but through the social process itself. That is why an economic act is symbolic and religious at the same time. EO1 has peace and honour as gifts, EO2 the 'invisible hand' that organizes public welfare, and EO3 stability through redistribution of welfare.

**The political dimension of exchange of gifts**

Mauss offers two theses that might be of great importance for our understanding of social and political life. The first thesis is: human relations cannot hold if people are only motivated by self-interest. Self-interest might lead them to a commercial practice of exchanging goods, or to calculating too much about their benefits, but will never assure stable human relations. It seems necessary to hide or sublimate self-interest and perform some ritual or symbolic practice. The second thesis is: when people are exchanging gifts, they do not only give, receive and return these goods, but they give themselves as well, so to speak, to society and, by doing so, receive 'sociality' in return. By this I mean that they receive a *confirmation* that the public body they gave themselves to is *real*. Society is only real in people's minds to the extent that the existence and reliability of social relations is constantly corroborated. One might call this 'trust' or, as Luhmann puts it, *"Systemvertrauen"*. Both theses are present in the only explicit reference to the State, cited above, where Mauss confirms that a worker does not devote a large part of his life and energy to society just to receive wages in return, but gives himself as well. As a worker in a factory, he is a member of a collective body, whose representative must reward him for his contribution. Working for money only is a reduction which will destroy society. I will call the two theses of Mauss the *political dimension* of the social gifts which people give when they interact.[14] Typical of modernity is the fact

---

[14] Mauss himself noticed the difference between gifts that are given, received and returned among men in society, social gifts as it were, and gifts to gods (or kings): the same kind of gifts, which now are returned by *a gift of sociality*: prosperity, safety, freedom or honour of the community. So the question involved is this: what should men give, in order to receive in return the society in which they really want to live? How much this question is interrelated with self-interest in modern times can be seen in the way Rousseau formulated this question, by suggesting that in a social contract, men will recover everything he has given away, that is: his freedom. But I will leave Rousseau aside.

that this political dimension is to some extent represented or institutionalized, be it that for some part it still is symbolic. If we jump from Mauss' 'primitive' society to modern society, it is inevitable to grasp this point. For this purpose and to keep things transparent, I will only concentrate on Hobbes' political philosophy as put forward in his *Leviathan*. Marshall Sahlins has made a comparison between Mauss and Hobbes as early as the seventies. To his analysis I will add a few notes concerning the relation between gifts and interests.

Mauss described the customs of small communities (families, clans, tribes) which do not have any institutionalized form of state. These communities do have leadership, however. The leader represents the community. He constantly has to perform symbolic acts to assert his leadership. The political dimension in this respect is implicit in Mauss' descriptive approach. He is primarily interested in human relations, as can be seen especially in his conclusions, where he stresses the social and moral qualities of the life of the presented communities in contrast to those of modern commercial society. But maybe this political dimension can remain implicit because it still is not a problem. On the other hand, the fact that this same dimension becomes the centre of an explicit discourse means that it has become a problem — as is shown in Hobbes' *Leviathan*. We must be aware of this great difference when we compare both authors: in his description of the 'state of nature', Hobbes confronts the reader with the collapse of the implicit political dimension in human interactions. It is because of the disappearance of this 'natural' political dimension of social life that political power must be established in an artificial manner.

In his own terms, Sahlins has made clear that between the discourses of Mauss and Hobbes there can only be an analogy, not a similarity.[15] Whereas Hobbes is focused on the offering of the natural liberty and rights of individuals for the establishment of a common power, Mauss described a political dimension that is inherent in the interaction of people. Nevertheless, the offering produces something that is comparable: *peace*.[16] And while "Mauss is much closer to Rousseau, as a political philosopher he is akin to Hobbes", Sahlins wrote. This is so because for both authors *war* was the real "understructure of society"[17]. This means that all social relations are fragile and can break down when people take recourse to violence or other forms of agression. In social interaction, especially in the exchange of gifts, a spirit emerges that compels peace from people — a spirit that can be of a magical order (like the *hau*) or of a rational order. In his famous chapter on the state of nature, Hobbes made clear that without a common power people will enter "the war

---

[15] M. Sahlins, *Stone Age Economics* (London: Tavistock Publications, 1981) pp. 168-183.

[16] Sahlins equates peace with 'alliance, solidarity, communion' — which is only to some extent what Hobbes had in mind.

[17] M. Sahlins, *Stone Age Economics* (London: Tavistock Publications, 1981) pp. 170-171.

of every man against every man". But in the next two chapters, Hobbes shows the tragic component of this failure of mankind: most people *know*, because they use reason, how they should behave to sustain a peaceful and agreeable society in which all kinds of culture can flourish. This knowledge includes the benefits of reciprocity in social life. But despite this analogy, Sahlins points out an important difference between Mauss and Hobbes, which I already referred to: in *Leviathan*, nothing exists between the state of nature and the commonwealth (or civil state).[18] So, the question is why for Hobbes the deals and exchanges between people in a state of nature could no longer provide enough ground for ending the state of war in which people naturally are involved, or at least for tempering its manifestations.[19]

Before entering into this question, it might be of interest to summarize the differences between *Leviathan* and *The Gift*. First of all, Hobbes seems to presuppose the progressive differentiation of aspects of social life, especially between politics and religion, which is one of the aims of *Leviathan*, and between morals and economics. In Mauss' primitive society there is little differentiation (total prestations). Secondly, for Mauss society is something in which people are born, something natural, whereas for Hobbes' society is something artificial.[20] The only natural thing in human affairs are man's passions and his striving for power, i.e. the means by which he keeps himself alive for the amount of time that nature has allocated to him. Thirdly, for Mauss' society exists only on a small scale (families, clans, tribes), whereas Hobbes already sees masses of individuals who do not seem to be bound by any communal ties. Fourthly, the perspective of primitive man is not power in the sense of possessed means to achieve one's goals in life and therefore the acquisition of those means, but power in the sense of honour, recognition, prestige, which can only be gained by an apparent lack of interest in 'private property'. The power of primitive man is a complex social fact, whereas for Hobbes power is something which seems to put social life in danger. Fifthly, because of this, primitive man is interested in the symbolic function of his

---

[18] M. Sahlins, *Stone Age Economics* (London: Tavistock Publications, 1981) p. 179: "But Mauss' resolution of Warre also had historic merit: it corrected just this simplified progression from chaos to commonwealth, savagery to civilization, that had been the work of classical contract theory. Here in the primitive world Mauss displayed a whole array of intermediate forms". On this point, however, Hobbes seems to be unique. For example Spinoza and Locke, a few decades later, recognized that in the state of nature, forms of society and reasonable life are already possible. Concerning Spinoza, see my article: 'An analysis of power relations and class relations in Spinoza's *Tractatus Politicus*', in *Studia Spinozana*, 9 (1995) pp. 79-105.

[19] M. Sahlins, *Stone Age Economics* (London: Tavistock Publications, 1981) p. 182. Claude Lévi-Strauss wrote briefly: "Exchanges are peacefully resolved wars and wars are the result of unsuccessful transactions". And according to Mauss, "primitive society is at war with Warre, and all their dealings are treaties of peace".

[20] In T. Hobbes, *op. cit.*, pp. 113 ff., Hobbes gives his reasons why man has no natural inclination towards living sociably, in contrast to bees or ants. Social life is the product of reasoning.

prestations, whereas Hobbes' man is goal-oriented: he calculates the best chances he has to achieve his goals.

These differences show why for Mauss the political dimension of social interaction could not become a problem, although he was aware of the fragility of society and the danger of violence that was always there. In the primitive societies Mauss described, society always seems to exist already: it is the opinion of other people which is important for primitive man, because it is in this light that he gains prestige and self-esteem. All these aspects of social life are present in Hobbes' image of man as well, but they have changed their meaning because all are imbedded in the *absence* of a natural social bond. For Hobbes, as I have said, the political dimension of social interaction is the real problem. So, in reading *Leviathan* we can discern what went wrong as soon as EO1 transforms into EO2.

**The crisis of covenant**

When we take Mauss' essay as a point of reference, we might interpret Hobbes' political philosophy as a construction based on the awareness of a double crisis: that of obligation and that of contract or *covenant*. The ground for any obligation seems to have disappeared and so has, of course, any economy of obligations. The only obligation that seems to be valid, the one that arises from a man's explicit will,[21] is in danger because the basis for "mutual transferring of rights" is void.[22]

According to Hobbes, there are two kinds of exchanges: a mutual transferring of rights, which is called a contract, and a one-sided transferring of rights "in hope to gain thereby friendship, or service from another, or from his friends; or in hope to gain the reputation of charity, or magnanimity; or to deliver his mind from the pain of compassion; or in hope of reward in heaven".[23] This is called "gift, free-gift, grace". In Hobbes' view, the exchange of gifts seems to form part of society, but no longer as 'total service' and as an economy of obligations, but as a means to receive gifts of any kind in return, in cases where a contract or a covenant does not seem fit. If we generalize Hobbes' notions in the direction of Mauss' essay, this means that there still is a common practice of exchanging gifts of which only a part, or even the greatest part, has taken the form of an explicit commitment between two parties to the obligation to give and the obligation to return. But in a situation where obligations no longer seem to have any ground, not only EO1 but also EO2 is in deep

---

[21] *Ibid.*, p. 114. I will revert to this point in the next paragraph.
[22] *Ibid.*, pp. 89 ff.
[23] *Ibid.*, p. 89.

trouble. The reason to stick to a generalized view on the exchange of gifts, of which covenants form a part, is given by Hobbes' idea of a cosmo-economy involving God and mankind.

Man's relationship with God is not completely contractual, but basically an exchange of gifts.[24] First of all, God freely gives land and sea, to be used by man. In return, he may worship God, but he is free to do so. Secondly, man gives his labour through cultivation of land and sea, and receives further gifts in return. For this practice, Hobbes uses the word *cultus*, by which he means a kind of contractual exchange in which labour is returned by a gift "as a natural effect", or by which it is only offered as a gift in the hope of receiving some kind of benefit: "this is properly *worship*"[25]. The connection between causality and covenance is not a new one[26]. Hobbes is fully aware of the theological background,[27] which is linked to the idea that returning a gift in exchange for a performance is not something that goes on automatically or even something that can be enforced. The giver can only hope for a return of gifts. In a covenant, however, which is a mutual transferring of rights, the returning of the gift can be enforced and therefore is an effect of the first gift, which is a cause. A contract can be seen as a way to make a machine of the exchange of gifts, to make it calculable and secure, and to guarantee equal benefits for all. Therefore, the contract itself can be seen as a crisis of the first economy of obligations. It already is a sign of distrust of the functioning of this economy. Hoping for benefit is not enough.

But let us return to the cosmo-economic point of view. In this sense, the *cultus* of mankind is a machine which man has to discover. God rewards his labour and his use of reason by giving him more commodities in return. And here, the real crisis occurs. The cultus becomes insecure, that is man's input increasingly becomes a free gift, without any real hope for a return of gifts, when the fruits of labour cannot be possessed any longer by those who have laboured for it or can no longer be exchanged for other things. In the natural condition of mankind, which is without any common power to give force to the obligations of man, man lives in misery: "there is no place for industry;

---

[24] *Ibid.*, p. 163: "commodities, which form (the two breasts of our common mother) land, and sea, God usually either freely giveth, or for labour selleth to mankind".

[25] *Ibid., op. cit.*, pp. 238 ff.

[26] See W.J. Courtenay, *Covenant and Causality in Medieval Thought* (London, 1984). Causality was seen as a covenantal process, directed by God. God promised that a cause, under 'normal circumstances', will be followed by a certain effect (*de potentia Dei ordinata*), but He is not obliged to do so, because He can do otherwise (*de potentia Dei absoluta*). Hobbes seems to go into another direction.

[27] See T. Hobbes, *op. cit.*, pp. 90-91 and Terpstra/De Wit, 'Het maatschappelijke geschenk', The point is that in case of a gift, the returned gift is only merited *ex congruo*, but not *ex condigni*. See also A.P. Martinich, 'Grace', in *A Hobbes Dictionary* (Cambridge/Oxford: Blackwell, 1995) pp. 131-133.

because the fruit thereof is uncertain; and consequently no culture of the earth; no navigation, nor use of the commodities that may be imported by sea" *etcetera*.[28] This also means that the relationship between mankind and God (culture and worship) is disrupted. The solution Hobbes offers for this crisis, as is well known, consists in the creation of a *mortal God* whose function is to rebuild the machinery, or better: to enforce its perpetual functioning.[29] This is done "by mutual covenants one with another" in which rights are transferred, but not from one man to another and *vice versa*, but from every man to one man in particular or an assembly of men. By this act, the chosen man or assembly of men becomes sovereign. Moreover, this is done under the condition that all men do the same — or at least a great majority of them.

Thus the *scene* of what is known as the 'social contract', although this notion is never used by Hobbes, is as follows. There is no contract, because there is no giving and returning. It is a covenant between men, because every man has agreed and promised to give up his rights. In essence, what is happening here is a mere gift — be it a very symbolic one. The natural right of every man to govern himself, that is to decide what is best for his preservation, is the thing transferred. Every man sacrifices his freedom, so to say, and becomes subject. It is a decision to *obey* whatever the sovereign dictates. The scene says nothing about the party that receives this gift of every man or the great majority of men. The symbolic meaning, however, is clear: in this act of submission, the chosen man or assembly of men observes a recognition of his or its power. Now the laws this sovereign power will enact are legitimized beforehand. In this sense, the gift of the people seems to be the opposite of a *potlatch*: the gifts are made to honour and accept the power of another man or an assembly of men, not to defy them by showing one's own power. But in effect, the responsibility is now in the hands of the sovereign and every man expects a gift in return — the sovereign's true and full attachment to the *salus populi*.

For Hobbes, the essence of this scene is "the mutual relation between protection and obedience".[30] The mutuality of this relation, however, is not a contract, but is only present in the minds of the subjects: they obey in order to be protected. In the state of nature, every man "may seek, and use, all helps, and advantages of war".[31] His obligation to "endeavour peace" is only *in foro interno*.[32] Obedience, after all, means that every man has given up the right to decide between seeking peace or war: he does not have to protect himself any longer. But the protection is not a result of the obedience, as Hobbes seems to

---

[28] T. Hobbes, *op. cit.*, p. 84.
[29] The only exception is force from outside: *Ibid.*, p. 212.
[30] *Ibid.*, p. 475.
[31] *Ibid.*, p. 87.
[32] *Ibid.*, p. 105.

suggest in his *Review*. Therefore, the decision of most men to submit themselves to the sovereign power cannot be based purely on calculation. There is an element of gambling; there is an element of believing in the *magic* of the gesture of submission. Is this element not similar to the sublimation of self-interest into the exchange of gifts, which under normal circumstances indeed leads to results that are the same as they would be in the case of contracts? I will go further. The submission is not just a matter of hiding self-interest, but also of giving it up. The subject stops calculating the best chances for his preservation, because if he went on calculating, he would still make his own decisions.[33]

The sovereign himself is not part of the covenant. He just receives the gift from his subjects: their submission. And with this, he receives the right to command. For Hobbes, it seems almost evident that the sovereign power will act as it ought to: as the protector of the commonwealth and of its citizens. He even writes: "the good of the sovereign and people, cannot be separated".[34] In the end, the laws of nature (the precepts of reason) and civil laws are the same[35], and these laws even coincide with the laws of God.[36] But there is no guarantee. For example, the sovereign must create equality before the law. Every subject has an equal right to protection by the law. Partiality would mean the "ruin of the commonwealth".[37] This is the responsibility of the sovereign, but he has to respond to no one (except for God).[38]

This point needs not to be discussed any further here, because what matters is not Hobbes' political theory as such, but the thought that is expressed here: there is an unavoidable end to all 'contractualization'. The exchange of gifts cannot be completely rationalized in order to fully secure the *interests* of the contracting parties. Even in a normal contract, an element of uncertainty remains, which makes this "mutual transferring of rights", and later on the mutual transferring of the things promised, an exchange of gifts haunted by a magical spirit: faith in 'normality'. This political dimension of the exchange of gifts in human interaction is symbolic in itself and in essence non-contractual,[39] and this political dimension is an exchange of gifts between subjects

---

[33] Hobbes is not consistent on this point. The exception to this rule is very important: if the life (i.e. physical existence) of a subject is threatened by the state itself (for example, when he is caught for a crime), he is no longer obliged to obey, exactly because he would then not be protected any longer. I will return to this point soon.

[34] *Ibid.*, p. 230.
[35] *Ibid.*, p. 177.
[36] *Ibid.*, p. 235.
[37] *Ibid.*, p. 229.
[38] Hobbes makes this very clear in chapter 18 on "the right of sovereigns by institution": T. Hobbes, *op. cit.*, pp. 115 ff.
[39] This would exclude Hobbes' political philosophy from the social contract theorists. This might be less unfamiliar for those who know that Spinoza abolished the whole idea of a social contract and replaced it by a notion of 'political practice', in which people and politicians seek to

and the sovereign in itself, or between citizens and politicians. As Hobbes seems to indicate, contractualization and rationalization of this exchange, involving the introduction of self-interest and with this a fundamental *reservation*, would destroy the political dimension — and in the long run the state itself. The scene, instituting that great Leviathan, is even a *religious* gesture, an act of worship — giving in the hope of regaining peace. The gift of sociality itself, which is expected, can be seen as *grace*, because the sovereign has no contractual obligation to give. To this extent, Hobbes political theory is a *political theology*.[40]

### The crisis in the economy of obligations

More profound than the crisis in culture and commerce seems to be the crisis in the field of obligations. And the clearest sign that there is a crisis in the economy of obligations is perhaps the fact that Hobbes himself is ambivalent in this matter. Of course, there is this manifest doctrine of Hobbes according to which an individual man has a natural right to do what he thinks fit for the preservation of his life and has no other obligation than to do so. This may lead to the war of every man against every man. But this reign of self-interest is not the only and not even the last word on obligation in Hobbes' political philosophy. In fact, Hobbes seems to have three different theories of obligation, although in all three the 'right of nature' is the indication for its crisis. First of all, there is a *voluntarist* theory of obligation. Secondly, we can find a *social* theory of obligation in the exchange of gifts. Thirdly, there is a *moral* theory of obligation, which starts from the precepts of reason.

Let us start with the first theory. The axiom of this theory is a very simple one: "there being no obligation on any man, which ariseth not from some act of his own; for all men equally, are by nature free".[41] The act referred to is a "declaration, or signification" of this man, in which he admits his obligation. In this case, man is bound to his obligation by the fact that it is absurd — in the eyes of Hobbes — "to contradict what one maintained in the beginning: so in

---

find a balance of power. See my article 'Analysis of power relations'. And: A. Matheron, 'Le problème de l'évolution de Spinoza du *Traité Théologico-politique* au *Traité Politique*' (The Problem of the Evolution of Spinoza between the Tractatus Theologica-Politicus and the Tractatus Politicus), in *Spinoza. Issues and Directions. Proceedings of the Chicago Spinoza Conference* (E.Curley/P.F.Moreau (eds.)) (Leiden: E.J. Brill, 1990) pp. 258-270. See also O. Ueno, 'Spinoza et le paradoxe du contrat social de Hobbes. "Le reste"' (Spinoza and the Paradox of Hobbes' Social Contract), in *Cahiers Spinoza*, 6 (Paris: Ed.Réplique, 1991) pp. 269-295.

[40] C. Schmitt, *Politische Theologie. Vier Kapitel zur Lehre von der Souveränität* (1922) (Berlin: Duncker & Humblot, 1985[4]) p. 49: "All succinct concepts of modern theory of state are secularized theological concepts".

[41] T. Hobbes, *op. cit.*, p. 114.

the world, it is called injustice, and injury, voluntarily to undo that, which from the beginning he had voluntarily done". A declaration of will is the sole ground for obligation. These kind of social bonds, however, "have their strength, not from their own nature, (for nothing is more easily broken than a man's word) but from fear of some evil consequence upon the rupture".[42] This shows that a voluntarist theory of obligation is not a theory of obligation, but of its crisis. Man is bound by his declaration of will only on logical grounds — to prevent absurdity. But why should he be bound to act according to logic? This voluntarist theory seems to provide only for the necessary condition of obligation, but not for its sufficient condition. The cause of obligation must be sought elsewhere: in the social practice of exchanging gifts on the one hand, in the precepts of reason that commands man to seek peace on the other hand.

I already indicated that, for Hobbes, contract is not the only way to exchange things or services: there is a voluntary exchange of gifts as well. In a chapter on the difference of *manners*, Hobbes confronts the reader with an interesting observation, which leads us to a social theory of obligation. Here the axiom is: "benefits oblige".[43] Goods are circulating, the exchange of gifts is proceeding, favours are done: this is a common ground for obligations, at least those of receiving and returning benefits or gifts. Hobbes wants to show where the danger is hidden in this practice and where a crisis could occur, when he continues: "obligation is thraldom; and unrequitable obligation, perpetual thraldom; which is to one's equal, hateful". Hobbes alludes to the rules that govern the practice of exchanging benefits. The main rule is: exchange between equals should be on an equal basis, meaning that a benefit given should not exceed the receiving party's means of returning the gift. Excepted from this rule are gifts from persons superior to the receiving party, because in that case the obligation is already present and not the result of the benefit.[44]

But among equals, unequal exchange of benefits is detrimental: "To have received from one, to whom we think ourselves equal, greater benefits than there is hope to requite, disposeth to counterfeit love; but really secret hatred; and puts a man into the estate of a desperate debtor, that in declining the sight of his creditor, tacitly wishes him there, where he might never see him more. [...] Also to receive benefits, though from an equal, or inferior, as long as there is hope for requital, disposeth to love: for in the intention of the receiver, the obligation is of aid, and service mutual [...]."[45]

---

[42] Here, it concerns the rights he transfers to others or which he simply renounces: *Ibid.*, p. 88.

[43] *Ibid.*, p. 67.

[44] *Ibid.*, p. 67: "But to have received benefits from one, whom we acknowledge for superior, inclines to love; because the obligation is no new depression: and cheerful acceptation, (which men call *gratitude*,) is such an honour done to the obliger, as is taken generally for retribution."

[45] *Ibid.*, p. 67.

I have quoted this passage almost *in extenso*, because it shows on what point EO1 is in crisis: excessive gifts, as in a *potlatch,* should only be given by superior men between themselves, but should be prevented in other cases. This means that EO1 cannot stand in an *egalitarian* society, which in fact is developing under Hobbes' eyes. The danger is the appearance of the *desperate debtor*, who is not grateful, but filled with hatred towards his benefactor. The gift is an insult, a wound, which forces to war.[46] Here is the ground for EO2, the 'Victorian morality' that says that one should be cautious of giving and receiving, because what counts most is the obligation to return. This obligation seems not contrary to human passions, but inherent in them. The only way to escape hatred and the resulting strive is to stay away from benefactors and to prevent too much charity. The exchange of gifts should be reduced to calculable forms: giving and receiving, buying and selling in a moderate, calculated or contractual manner. But the historical and anthropological question here is: from where comes this type of man who becomes distrustful of the exchange of gifts?

The question may be answered by turning to the third theory of obligation, which I called a moral one. The axiom is now: man is obliged to preserve his own life. The implications Hobbes attaches to this axiom are threefold. (1) The obligation involves that man is "by nature free" to seek the means by which he can fulfill this obligation. Therefore, man has a "right of nature [...] to use his own power, as he will himself, for the preservation of his own nature".[47] (2) Although the obligation is based on a natural inclination of man, like all living creatures, to preserve his life, the obligation includes seeking for the *best*, i.e. most effective, means to do so. Therefore, reason prescribes how a man should preserve his life. These prescriptions are called "laws of nature".[48] Above all, reason demands that man seeks peace: that would be the best for his preservation, provided that others act in the same direction. (3) The particular obligations, prescribed by reason, to which man is only bound *in foro interno*.[49] Man is not obliged to follow reason in his acts, when this would endanger him. The obligation involved in the precepts of reason oblige only *in foro externo*, i.e. in actual practice, if there is evidence that following reason is not contrary to the preservation of man's life.

The moral theory of obligation is oriented towards social reality,[50] and the analogy between Mauss and Hobbes, of which Sahlins has made us aware:

---

[46] M. Mauss, *The Gift,* p. 63: "Charity is still wounding for him who has accepted it.", and p. 72: "To accept without giving in return, or without giving more back, is to become a client and servant, to become small, to fall lower."
[47] T. Hobbes, *op.cit.*, p. 86.
[48] *Ibid.*, p. 86.
[49] *Ibid.*, p. 105.
[50] "For moral philosophy is nothing else but the science of what is *good*, and *evil*, in the conservation, and society of mankind": *Ibid.*, p. 105.

reason requires every man to seek for peace, if this endeavor is not detrimental to his life. Seeking for peace means 'sociality': trying to interact with other men without giving offence. The laws of nature, which in many variations all translate this endeavour, can be summarized as a very simple rule ("to leave all men inexcusable"): "Do not that to another, which thou wouldest not have done to thyself."[51] Here, reciprocity or equity is the main principle. I do not have to go into further details about these laws of nature — or reason. We have to find out in which sense this reciprocity is in danger.

The crisis is in the *krinein*, that is in judging whether man should pursue peace or should fall back on actions of war to protect himself. How should man decide? His condition is precisely that of uncertainty. Now he is on his own. Everything depends on his judgement. In this natural condition, every man is his own judge — and therefore innocent.[52] But because this is a miserable condition too, man decides to accept a person who will represent him exactly in this respect. The sovereign gives man his laws, which he has to obey: "civil law is an *obligation*; and takes from us the liberty which the law of nature gave us".[53] Man's conscience, doubting whether his obligation is only *in foro interno*, or also *in foro externo*, seems to be released from its troubles, the burden of natural freedom. Unfortunately, in the end, every man still faces the same problem: the obligation to obey the sovereign is not unconditional, as Hobbes makes clear in the chapter on the liberty of subjects.[54] And because this is so, man is drawn back into his original position, in which he has to be judge in his own case. The ambivalence of Hobbes becomes clear, when the question is asked whether a subject should protect his own life first or should try to save the commonwealth. On the one hand, Hobbes notes: "The obligation of subjects to the sovereign, is understood to last as long, and no longer, than the power lasteth, by which he is able to protect them".[55] On the other hand, every subject "is obliged (without fraudulent pretence of having submitted himself out of fear), to protect his protection as long as he is able".[56] The ambivalence has to do with Hobbes' own conception of what is happening in the transference of rights in the covenant that generates the commonwealth: is it a gift or is it a contract? If the people surrender to what then becomes their sovereign, it seems fit that they endeavour to protect their protector. If the people interpret their gift as the delivering of their contractual

---

[51] *Ibid.*, p. 104.
[52] *Ibid.*, p. 93: "in the condition of nature, where every man is judge, there is no place for accusation".
[53] *Ibid.*, p. 192.
[54] *Ibid.*, pp. 144 ff.
[55] *Ibid.*, p. 147.
[56] *Ibid.*, p. 221 (also pp. 468-469) and M. Terpstra, T. De Wit, 'Afschrikking en zelfopoffering. Thomas Hobbes en het nucleaire tijdperk' ('Deterrence and self-sacrifice. Thomas Hobbes and the age of the nuclear bomb'), in *Krisis,* 29, 7: 4 (1987).

obligation, they may withdraw their obedience as soon as the sovereign fails to deliver his part: protection. In any case, the difference between the two is determined by the question whether an individual is 'on his own' or feels part of society as a whole.

## Back to Mauss

Some preliminaries to a political philosophy are given by Mauss in the last chapter of *The Gift*: moral, political, ethical, sociological and ethical conclusions. These distinctions are less than clear, which is no surprise if we know that Mauss' main point is his preference for a 'total' viewpoint. His last words are that studies of the kind of *The Gift* could promote "the supreme art — *Politics* in the Socratic sense of the word". By this he means an approach that opposes "reason to feeling". Emotion leads to "sudden outbursts of insanity", to "war, isolation and stagnation", slaughter and sacrifice. Reason might lead to "alliance, gift and trade" and stabilizing contracts.[57] Of course, this is to some extent a commonplace. What seems of interest, is what reason has prescribed in Mauss' "primitive societies", so that it prevented war in a destructive sense.

What seems most important for Mauss is that capitalism, with its exclusive devotion to the *homo oeconomicus*, commercial thinking, utilitarianism, rationalism and so on, should be countered by the moral forces still present in everyday life in small communities or within other groups on the one hand, and by state solidarity on the other hand. Mauss' diagnosis seems to be that capitalism tends to aggravate social struggle between groups or classes,[58] but that this development can be stopped. Mauss is optimistic, so to speak. Modern society is just a historical deviation — although its roots lie in Greek and Roman Anciety, and feodalism seems to be part of the deviation — from a *political truth* that was already there in "primitive society" and still is. This political truth is in fact a moral truth, or rather, the truth of authentic morality.

The opening paragraph of his conclusions indicate that for Mauss modernity is a big mistake: Western man has gone astray. He has lost his roots, but he can find them back. In reality, "We possess more than a trademan morality",[59] people have more obligations to each other than those connected to a commercial contract,[60] there is need of a return to law or "to group morality", a

---

[57] M. Mauss, *The Gift*, pp. 82-83.
[58] *Ibid.*, p. 77: "The brutish pursuit of individual ends is harmful to the ends and the peace of all, to the rhythm of their work and joys, and rebounds on the individual himself."
[59] *Ibid.*, p. 65.
[60] *Ibid.*, p. 66. This corresponds to my conceptual opposition between EO1 and EO2.

resurrection of "a dominant motif too long forgotten",[61] and finally the need of a "return to the enduring basis of law, to the very principle of normal social life".[62] We can find a parallel for this in Hobbes' idea of 'natural laws', the precepts of reason. But whereas Mauss seems to expect a revival of social life, which cannot come from outside but only from within, for Hobbes modernity poses a more fundamental problem which cannot be dealt with by a return to reason. Reason itself seems to have lost its substance.

At first sight, the opposition between reason and emotion, and between peace and war, seems to justify an interpretation of Mauss' political philosophy as 'Hobbesian'. About the societies described by him, Mauss says: "In al the societies that have immediately preceded our own, there is no middle way: one trusts completely, or one mistrusts completely; (...) Two groups of men who meet can only either draw apart, and, if they show mistrust towards one another or issue a challenge, fight — or they can negotiate."[63] Is not this exactly what Hobbes said? In Hobbes' view, men can live in two conditions: that of war, which also consists "in a tract of time, wherein the will to contend by battle is sufficiently known",[64] and that of peace. There is no middle way. But I think the meaning of war is quite different in the two political philosophies.

If we look closely at the way Mauss' interprets war or rivalry within the social system, we see that it is understood as interruption, as a temporary crisis which does not affect the social system itself. The morality does not change after a war has been fought. For Hobbes, the crisis is much deeper. The war "of every man against every man" is not just the result of rivalry, but of a tragic and fundamental failure to find peace — although that is what man really wants. Modernity has thrown man into this condition of war, out of which he cannot escape by his own means. The fight does not end and people do not come together in peace again. The social system itself is destroyed and can only be resurrected artificially by "a common power". It seems as if the way back to the roots of "normal social life" has been lost, and that this normal life can only be reconstructed by an intervention: an independent and sovereign power. On this point, Mauss and Hobbes oppose each other as extremes: faith in social life versus faith in political power.

Everything now depends on the diagnosis of modernity. Has modernity destroyed social life by dividing society into individuals who cannot but act as "calculating machines"[65] and who cannot but interact as strangers, contracting each other under the watching eyes of the state? Or has modernity just inter-

---

[61] *Ibid.*, p. 68.
[62] *Ibid.*, p. 70.
[63] *Ibid.*, pp. 81-82.
[64] T. Hobbes, *op. cit.*, p. 84.
[65] These are the words of M. Mauss, *op. cit.*, p. 76, but could be those of T. Hobbes.

rupted the age-old morality of mankind, still rooted in everyday social life, and is it our task today to restore the old law of 'the gift'? Neither is really the case, I think. To Hobbes, one can respond that his picture of the condition of mankind was exaggerated. Hobbes did not have much faith in man as a social animal.[66] While Mandeville sharpened this picture as given by Hobbes,[67] another movement in political philosophy arose, starting with Spinoza and Locke, in which political power is understood as the strengthening of "normal social life" (reason), not as its only garantuee. This has become the main stream in political philosophy. On the other hand, Mauss underestimates the crisis which is essential for modernity: the individual is left to its own judgement because law and normality have lost their substance. There is a big difference between the surviving of all kinds of social obligations within — small — communities or family life and the fundamental structure of modern society. The first one can soften the effects of a depersonalized society of individuals, but cannot replace it. The war witnessed by Hobbes was not just an interruption of an ongoing social order, but the beginning of a new one. This seems to be a point of no return.

---

[66] Cf. his infamous appreciation of "the savage people in many places of America": T. Hobbes, *op. cit.*, p. 85.

[67] M. Mauss, *op. cit.*, p. 76: "One can almost date — since Mandeville's 'The Fable of the Bees' — the triumph of the notion of individual interest".

# Personal obligations in personal relations

Aldo De MARTELAERE (K.U.Leuven)

**Introduction**

It has often been observed that the primary sphere in which gifts are exchanged in a modern society is the sphere of personal relations, i.e. relations between members of a family, between friends, between lovers. These gifts have been studied by numerous sociologists, whose main concern is to analyze how gifts *function:*[1] what is the role they play in the creation and maintenance of personal relations? My concern in this paper is different. I will not examine *how gifts function* in personal relations; instead I will ask the philosophers' question *what they are*. Next to being interesting in itself, this question may also widen the sociologists' view on gifts, because in answering it, it will become clear that one can understand *virtually everything that happens in a personal relation* as a gift, and that includes, of course, *much more* than the *giving of material things* on which sociologists tend to focus.

In order to be able to define gifts in personal relations I will first of all define the concept of a personal relation. That will be the main object of the first section of this paper. Here I will elaborate on the intuition that what defines a personal relation is love, and more in particular, reciprocal love. Towards the end of the section I will give some reasons for understanding virtually everything that happens in personal relations as a gift. The main reason for this is that most things in a personal relation happen out of love: and love, as well as actions out of love, can be understood as gifts.

This paper, however, has another aim besides defining gifts in personal relations. Mauss and his followers often insist on the fact that gifts are not spontaneous but obligatory, or, in some way, spontaneous and obligatory at the same time. Hence Mauss' famous doctrine of the three obligations of the gift: the obligation to give, to receive and to return. Although I do not fully endorse this doctrine — certainly not when it comes to gifts in personal relations — I do think that there exists a kind of obligation in personal relations that can in some way be understood correctly as an 'obligation to give'. In the second section of this paper I will first try to describe this kind of obligation. After that I will summarily point out some interesting problems that one may encounter in trying to justify these obligations. Here I utterly reject all Maussian justifica-

---

[1] Two examples are D. Cheal, *The Gift Economy* (London and New York: Routledge, 1988) and J. Godbout, *L'esprit du don (The Spirit of the Gift)* (Paris: La Découverte, 1992).

209

tions in terms of 'the spirit of the gift'; instead, I will take a look at some classical ethical theories and the problems involved in them.

In the conclusion of this paper I will explicitly compare my conception of the gift in personal relations with one central aspect of Mauss' theory of the gift, namely his thesis that gifts are reciprocal and governed by the obligations to give, to receive and to return. I will try to show that reciprocity does not necessarily apply to gifts in personal relations and that the three obligations do not apply at all. This will lead me to nuance his theory a little bit: reciprocity and the three obligations do not necessarily apply to *all* kinds of gifts, even though they may be essential to *some* kinds.

**Personal relations**

Let me assume — obviously much too quickly — that there is one central thing that makes all kinds of personal relations personal: *love*. What is more, not just love, but *reciprocal* love. Love as well as the requirement of reciprocity must be studied a bit more closely.

Clearly love is an emotion. But what kind of emotion? A very short *cognitive* analysis of love[2] is needed here. Such an analysis understands an emotion as a complex intentional mental state that grasps and evaluates its object in a certain way and that furthermore consists of certain desires and attitudes towards this object. Surely this is not meant to denigrate the inner feelings of love. But what *distinguishes* love from other emotions are not those feelings but rather love's way of grasping and evaluating its object, as well as its characteristic desires and attitudes toward this object. Before starting the announced analysis I would like to introduce two abstract and rather impersonal creatures *A* and *B,* who will elegantly help me with my proceedings. Most of the time, A and B will be having a personal relation. Most of the time, however, is not always. As the attentive reader will be able to notice occasionally, at times they are trying to get involved in a personal relation, at other times they are momentarily falling out of it. But basically, yes, they have a personal relation.

A loves B. What does this mean? As to the way of grasping B, it means that A sees B *as a unique person*, different from all other persons. And as to

---

[2] The founding father of cognitive analyses of emotions is, of course, Aristotle. The locus classicus within contemporary analytic philosophy is Anthony Kenny's *Action, Emotion and the Will* (London: Routledge & Kegan Paul, 1963). Numerous analyses have followed since. The main competitor of a cognitive analysis of emotions is the theory that reduces emotions to inner feelings. A more comprehensive analysis of the emotion 'love' can be found in, e.g., I. Singer, *The Pursuit of Love* (Baltimore: John Hopkins University Press, 1994), R. Brown, *Analyzing Love* (Cambridge: Cambridge University Press, 1987), R. C. Solomon, *About Love* (New York: Simon and Schuster, 1989) and A. Soble, *The Structure of Love* (New Haven & London: Yale University Press, 1990).

the way of evaluating B, it means that A finds B *highly important*. Combining both aspects, it means that A finds B highly important as a unique person. This is almost as abstract as A and B themselves. To get a grip on it, let me contrast it with some other ways of grasping B. For instance, A could see B as a doctor, as a person in need, and even more basically, simply as a person. And these other ways of grasping B can ground other evaluations, like for instance, finding B a fine doctor, finding B badly in need, or finding B worthy of respect. In none of these cases one is directed to what makes a person unique and irreplaceable. And this distinguishes them clearly from love. At this point I must say one more thing about what is involved in finding B important as a unique person. It at least involves finding B's *well-being* important. The term well-being is to be understood here in its broadest possible sense, i.e. as a state that depends on the fulfilment of B's *desires*, whatever those desires are, and not just on the fulfilment of B's *needs,* as it might be understood in other contexts.[3]

Love contains not only a cognitive and evaluative aspect but also characteristic desires and attitudes. Let me mention five desires and one attitude. What does A, who loves B, want? First of all A wants to *be with* B. He wants to spend time in B's company. Second, A wants to *know* B. He wants to know B's character, desires, attitude toward things, opinion about things, and so on. Third, A wants to *reveal himself* to B. In a way this desire is complementary to A's desire to know B. Fourth, as A finds B's well-being important, he wants to *further his well-being*, and, typical of love, he wants to further it himself. And fifth, odd as it may be, A wants *B to love him*. He wants his own love to be returned by B's love. Consequently, he wants B to find him uniquely important, to want to be with him, to know him, etc. As to the characteristic attitude, let me just mention that A, who loves B, is disposed to give B a non-negligible part of his *attention*.

The ordinary examples of personal relations suggest that love is necessarily reciprocal *within* such relations. Nevertheless, this does not imply that love is necessarily reciprocal. It is not. Think of the rejected lover, or the fan who loves his idol. Both are examples of one-sided love, in which the love of one person is not accepted and returned by the other. Why then make reciprocal love a necessary condition for the existence of a personal relation?

To begin with, most of the time reciprocal love is much *better* than one-sided love. This is because one-sided love is inherently *frustrating* and *risky*. *Frustrating* because one's desires remain unfulfilled. This obviously holds for the desire that one's love be returned. But it also holds for the other desires.

---

[3] In impersonal contexts, like the context of justice, a much more restrictive conception of well-being tends to be implied.

Normally, one who does not love you will not allow you to be with him, to learn about him, to reveal yourself to him, and even to further his well-being. He will simply not *accept* this. And when he does accept it, he will probably do so for the wrong reasons. This brings us to the fact that a one-sided love can be risky. *Risky* because loving someone inclines one to do a lot of things that might be *misused* by the other. For instance, the other could easily use what you say in a self-revelation to make a fool of you, or accept your help simply because he needs it. This kind of risk fades away in a relation of mutual love. Persons who love each other indeed accept each other's love *and* they accept it for the right reasons: because they love each other and in doing so desire each other's love. This *prevents* them from misusing what the other wants to do out of love.

The fact that reciprocal love is better then one-sided love does, of course, not imply that one-sided love is impossible. On the contrary: it offers an additional reason for affirming the possibility of one-sided love. The *painfulness* of unanswered love precisely *shows* that this love *exists already*, *before* and *independently* of its being answered. *If* it would not exist already, its rejection simply would not be so painful.[4]

Next to the avoidance of frustration and risk, there is a positive reason for making reciprocal love a necessary condition for the existence of a personal relation. The reason is that some *values* can only be realized when love is reciprocal. And these values are so typical of personal relations that they cannot be left out. Think of certain forms of intimacy and intimate self-revelation, self-confidence, self-knowledge and self-fulfilment that are only possible within a relation of reciprocal love.[5]

Let me summarize. Persons who stand in a personal relation love each other and accept each other's love. They accept what the other person wants to do out of love and they accept it because they love him. Of course, loving someone does not imply accepting *everything* the other wants to do out of love. A may desire to be with B all the time. But A's constant presence might simply suffocate B who may need some time for his own, although he loves A very much. So even in a personal relation there is a limit to what can possibly be done out of love, the line being drawn at what the other *accepts* you to do.

---

[4] There is no universal agreement on love being necessarily reciprocal. I am convinced, however, that reciprocity is not necessary (although desirable), for the reasons offered in this text. An important philosopher who shares this conviction is H. G. Frankfurt (See for instance his 'Duty and Love', in *Philosophical Explorations*, 1 (1998)). Among Frankfurt's reasons may be the fact that he considers both love for a concrete individual and love for an abstract type as essentially of the same type (what is essential to them both is *caring*). And love for an abstract type cannot be reciprocal. Arguments for the opposite view can be found in A. Soble, *The Structure of Love* (New Haven & London: Yale University Press, 1990).

[5] The basic idea — which I cannot prove, but which seems intuitively right — is that in order to attain certain goods, a personal relation is a necessary condition, an indispensable means.

However, as the other loves you, he is at least *willing* to accept what you want to do out of love.[6]

After having defined what makes a relation *personal* I must consider briefly what makes a personal relation *valuable*. Here it is important to distinguish between two questions that are often confused.[7] First: what is the value of A's personal relation with B? And second: what is the value of this personal relation *for A who is part of it*? That these are two different questions can be most readily seen when looking at their respective answers. The core of the answer to the second question takes one letter: B. What is most valuable to A in his personal relation with B is very simply *B itself*. Of course we can elaborate this answer. As A loves B he finds it important that B loves him *and* that B acts out of love for him. This is a general truth about personal relations. People who have entered into such a relation value the other's *motivation* for action highly. They desire — or hope — that this motivation may be love[8].

In reply to the first question, however, this answer does not make sense. The reason for this is that it asks for the value of A's personal relation with B, *abstracting it from the point of view* of those engaged in the relation. What could be that value? Two kinds of value must be distinguished here. First, one might say that the personal relation between A and B has *intrinsic* value, in other words, that the fact that A and B love each other is a good *in itself*. Second, one might say that this personal relation has *instrumental* value, meaning that, in some sense, it causes A and B to have some goods that belong to either of them separately, goods that one might call *advantages* of the personal relation for those engaged in it. Various kinds of advantages can follow from a personal relation. Some of them are loosely bound up with a personal relation

---

[6] Kant believed that there is a tendency in love to disregard the *autonomy* of the beloved person that has to be *counterbalanced* by *respect* for that person. Respect requires and motivates us to keep an appropriate *distance* from a beloved person (See I. Kant, *The Metaphysics of Morals* (trans. Mary J. Gregor) (Cambridge: Cambridge University Press, 1797, 1991) p. 449). However, there might be a tendency *within love* to keep an appropriate distance from the beloved, a tendency that stems from paying attention to what he *wants*. If he wants to be on his own, then *love* requires and motivates you to let him be. A tendency from within love would explain better, I think, why the distance between loving persons is more flexible than the much more rigid distance between persons who merely respect each other.

[7] For this distinction see J. Hardwig, 'In Search of an Ethics of Personal Relationships', in G. Graham and H. Lafollette, *Person to Person* (Philadelphia: Temple University Press, 1989).

[8] In a by now famous article (M. Stocker, 'The Schizophrenia of Modern Ethical Theories', in *Journal of Philosophy*, 73 (1976), reprinted in R. Crisp & M. Slote (eds.), *Virtue Ethics* (Oxford: Oxford University Press, 1997)) Stocker uses this general truth in order to criticize modern ethical theories that require people to act out of duty in all circumstances. He gives the example of someone visiting a friend in hospital 'out of duty'. Other important contributions on the subject at hand are e.g. B. Williams, 'Persons, Character and Morality', in B. Williams, *Moral Luck* (Cambridge: Cambridge University Press, 1973), B. Herman, 'On the Value of Acting from the Motive of Duty', in *The Philosophical Review*, 3 (1981) and M. W. Baron, 'The Alleged Moral Repugnance of Acting from Duty', in *Journal of Philosophy*, 81 (1984).

in the sense that many other things could give those advantages. Fulfilling one's needs and providing a feeling of security are examples of this category. Other advantages are more tightly linked to personal relations. Here again I think of self-confidence, self-knowledge and self-fulfilment. The presupposition for the very existence of the latter seems to be that one is loved by a person whom one loves oneself. Consolation, for example, may restore self-confidence. But B's consoling words to A are consoling to A only because they come from B who loves A and who is, in his turn, loved by A.

That the values of a personal relation differ from the prime value it has for the persons who are involved in it can be seen in yet another way. Someone may desire to enter into a certain kind of personal relation. Such a desire is usually aroused by acknowledging the value of such a relation, be it its intrinsic or instrumental value (of course the latter is more likely). Such a desire may even take the form of a desperate need. But somehow the fulfilment of this desire is impossible, because the person who 'fulfils' it is likely to be seen *as someone* who fulfils the desire and *not* as a unique person. And this means that one does not *really* love this person and has no personal relation with him. The moral to be drawn from this is that love is the *only possible* motivation for a personal relation. Of course, it is possible that someone who is involved in a personal relation is *aware of* its intrinsic and instrumental values. And this awareness could ground someone's *gratitude* towards the other person. But it can never be the motivation for entering into a personal relation. That motivation must be love.[9]

It seems to me that *most of what happens* in a personal relation can be conceptualized as a gift. This is most surely the case for 1) what the parties involved in a personal relation do for each other to further each other's wellbeing, and for 2) what they reveal to each other, but it also holds for 3) the attention they give to one another. I have three main reasons for conceptualizing these things as gifts.

First of all, what is done in a personal relation *falls outside* the scope of *economics*, *morality*, and *law*. Let me explain this summarily. First — as far as the link with economics is concerned — what people do out of love is *uncondi-*

---

[9] This point has important consequences for the 'egoism-altruism' debate as applied to personal relations. It is clear that most personal relations are very advantageous for the parties involved in it. But when love is considered to be the only possible motivation for a personal relation, then these advantages *cannot* be what motivates people to get involved in a personal relation. To put it differently, personal relations *cannot* have egoistic motivations. If one combines this point with the intuition that there are certain kinds of goods for which a personal relation is a necessary means (see fn. 6), one ends up with Elster's *essential byproducts* (John Elster introduced this term in the second essay of *Sour Grapes* (Cambridge, Cambridge University Press, 1983). If a good can only be realized in the context of a personal relation, and if desiring that good makes a personal relation impossible, then the desire for that good is necessarily frustrated. That good will only be realized as the byproduct of another motivation, namely love.

*tional*. They do not do it under the condition of receiving something in return. Although they might hope for and even expect something in return, this is never their main motivation for what they do. That is simply their love. This distinguishes what people do here, even when it is reciprocal, from an ordinary *market transaction*, in which something is done in order to get something else. Second — as far as the link with morality is concerned — what people do in a personal relation can *not* be *obligatory*. And third — as far as the link with the law is concerned — what they do can *not* be *enforced*. The second and the third point should not be misunderstood. Of course, in principle, every action can be obligatory or enforced. But what cannot be obliged or enforced is acting *out of love*. And *without* this motivation the action simply loses its significance.

The fact that actions out of love are unconditional, not obligatory and unenforceable explains why *uncertainty* is at the core of a personal relation. One can never get a guarantee for someone else's love. Although actions in a personal relation may to some degree become *habitual*, love is essentially incompatible with habit. Deep down the relation an element of uncertainty must remain. Because without it there would be no love, and hence no personal relation.

A second reason for regarding what happens in a personal relation as gifts has to do with the way things are *viewed* in a personal relation. The parties involved *see* each other's actions as *personal things*, things that are essentially linked with the person who performs the action. Here it might help to take a closer look at the two types of action distinguished above. First consider what people do to further *each other's* well — being. Now this type of action surely has an altruistic, and consequently an instrumental ring. Suppose that A does something to further B's well-being. B will surely be happy because A has done something useful to him. But that is not what it is all about. B will also be happy because *A* has done it and because A has done it *out of love*. And for this he must *see* the action essentially as done by A. Next consider self-revelations. No doubt a self-revelation is personal in the sense that one reveals in it part of oneself. But again what is revealed might or might not be *seen* or even *treated* as highly personal. Suppose that A reveals to B that he has strong feelings for someone called C. Two days later at a party A hears B making a joke about this. People are laughing and A is upset. But why? Is it because his feelings for C must remain a secret? Maybe. But it may also be because A heard B *using* what he revealed to him for his own purposes, in this case for the quite insignificant purpose of making a joke.[10] This is an example of someone who does not see A's self-revelation to him as something highly personal.

---

[10] The example is borrowed from A. Baier, 'Trusting Ex-intimates', in G. Graham & H. Lafollette (eds.), *Person to Person* (Philadelphia: Temple University Press, 1989).

If he did see it that way he would have treated it with more caution. Let me note here the parallel with the distinction between *gifts* and *commodities*.[11] This distinction also has to do with the way things are viewed and subsequently treated.

To see an action as personal essentially means the same as seeing it as *expressive of* a certain kind of motivation. Is it precisely because the parties involved in a personal relation *value* each other's motivations highly that they *see* each other's actions as expressive of motivations. The motivation they value most highly is love. Likewise, the motivation that 'makes' an action personal is love. To act out of love and hence in a personal way is often equated with acting *spontaneously*.

The third reason for linking gifts and personal relation has to do with the *vague* and *implicit* character of the expectations in a personal relation.[12] Clearly people in personal relations have expectations about each other's behaviour. But *what exactly* they expect from each other or *when* they expect it is never clearly stated. Even the fact of having the expectation is seldom made explicit. Taken together, it is like admitting that you expect help from your best friend when you are in trouble without specifying what kind of help and what kind of trouble are involved. Contrast this with making a promise. Most of the time promises have a clear content. The promissee knows exactly what he may expect the promissor to do and when he will do it.

Conceptualizing almost everything that happens in a personal relation as a gift leaves us with a very *broad* conception of the gift indeed. What to do then with gifts in the *narrow* sense of material things that are given? Insofar as they have a place in a personal relation, they are just *part* of it and have the *same significance* as everything else that happens there. However, they add something to a personal relation. In some way they *concentrate on* the significance of a personal relation. Contrary to the many habitual actions of a personal relation, material gifts — at least sometimes — *explicitly affirm* someone's love. The best material gifts come as a *surprise* to the receiver, reminding him of the nonevidential (and unguaranteeable) character of the other's love. Of course one may put forward that many occasions for material gifts are highly *ritualized* (birthday, Christmas, etc.) and hence splendid occasions for 'giving out of

---

[11] The idea that gifts are seen as personal strikes me as similar to the concept of an inalienable possession that one finds in at least part of the anthropological literature on the gift (see, for instance, A. B. Weiner, *Inalienable Possessions, The Paradox of Keeping-While-Giving* (Berkeley: University of California Press, 1992) and M. Godelier, *L'enigme du don (The Enigma of the Gift)* (Paris: Fayard, 1997)): inalienable possessions are things that in some sense remain property of the giver even after having been given.

[12] See for example the article of McC. Barry, 'Adult Friendships', in G. Graham and H. Lafollette, *Person to Person* (Philadelphia: Temple University Press, 1989) about what he calls the 'informality of friendship rules'. Jacques Godbout emphasizes the same point in *L'esprit du don* (Paris: La Découverte, 1992) and in his article in this companion.

habit'. I have two replies here. First, there is obviously much room for spontaneity and surprise in a context of ritual gifts. And second, one may conceive of these ritual gifts as games in which the core of a personal relation (love, uncertainty) is, if not genuinely present, then at least explicitly 'replayed'.

**Personal obligations**

People involved in a personal relation value each other's motivations for acting highly. The only motivation they really appreciate is love. Actions out of compassion or out of duty occupy, at most, a marginal place in a sound personal relation. Nevertheless, people involved in a personal relation *do have* obligations towards each other. Of course most of the time these obligations are not their reason for acting; most of the time they act out of love. But sometimes, and for several reasons, love cannot motivate one's action because it is too weak and overpowered by other passions. In such cases these obligations can take over as the motivating source.

What exactly are those obligations? First of all there are the ordinary *moral obligations*. A and B are of course obliged to respect each other, not to kill each other and not to steal from each other. Apart from these obligations that one has to everyone, A and B have some *special obligations*, obligations they have to each other and not towards other people. I call the special obligations that the parties involved in a personal relation have towards each other the *obligations of love*. Because *the reason* why one has those obligations is love. To say it more precisely, the fact that one loves someone *grounds* those obligations.

Obligations of love are not the only special obligations. Think for example of the obligation *to keep a promise* or about *role-bound* obligations. An example of the latter is the obligation of secrecy a doctor has concerning his patients. These are also obligations one has to specific persons and not to everyone. What makes them different from the obligations of love is most of all their ground. For instance, what grounds the obligation to keep a promise is the fact that one has made the promise. And what grounds the obligation of secrecy is the fact that one has the role of doctor and the other has the role of patient. Before elaborating on the difference between those special obligations and the obligations of love I will try to specify the content of the latter.

Exactly *what* is one obliged to do out of love? The answer is fairly simple. One is obliged to do what one *would* do *if* one acted out of love. Now this sounds a little crazy. A has obligations of love to B only because he loves B. But given that he loves B it seems unnecessary to oblige him to do what he would do out of love, because he does it already *and* out of love. But one can see the point of these obligations if one realizes that there are a lot of circumstances in which A is *not inclined* to act out of love for B although he loves B. For instance, when A's love for B looses the battle against another passion that has greater motivating power and that would lead to an action that is in some way incompatible with an action out of love. Examples of this are numerous. Just think of someone who does not inform his best friend about an interesting and vacant job because he wants it for himself. As his best friend he should have informed him. Or think of a mother who, because of serious troubles at work that captivate her mind, is not inclined to give her child the attention that she would normally give it out of love. There is a chance however that she will give it out of a sense of obligation. The content of personal obligations *varies* from personal relation to personal relation. The reason is that the content depends on what one would do out of love, and what a certain person usually does out of love depends on many factors, like for instance, the nature of his love, the strength of the desires that are part of it, his own character, and, last but not least, what the other person accepts him to do out of love.

So much for the *content* of the obligations of love. Let me now consider their *object* in more detail. As mentioned before, obligations of love are special obligations that we have towards specific persons and not to everyone. They share this feature with some other obligations, like for instance the obligation to keep a promise or to do as a role requires. But behind this similarity in object lies a difference that comes to light when we ask *to whom exactly* the obligation is directed. For instance, if A makes a promise to B, then A has the obligation to keep his promise to B *as the one who* accepted the promise. In a similar vein, if A is a doctor and B a patient, then A has the obligation to remain silent about B *as a patient*. And this strikes me as different from the obligations of love because, if A loves B, then he has obligations of love to B *as a unique person*. That is why I call them *personal obligations*. Again, the idea that the obligations of love are personal obligations is some kind of intuition. Instead of trying to defend this intuition here, I will rather examine *how* it is possible that the object of an obligation is a unique person. Let me reverse the question to launch the answer. Why is the object of an obligation to keep a promise or to act as a role requires *not* unique? Obviously that has to do with the *ground* of those obligations. Take promises. A must keep his promise to B because he has made a promise to B. But he could as well have made *the same* promise to someone else. In that case he would be obliged to keep his promise to *that* person. Of course I do not mean that it is arbitrary to whom A makes his promise. I only mean that one, including A himself, could easily imagine circumstances in which it would make sense to make that promise to someone else. That is the reason why the object of the obligation to keep a promise is not B as a unique person. The same story could be told for role-bound obligations, but not for the obligations of love. In some way, it is impossible for A to love someone else in the way that he loves B. In some way, his love for B is so uniquely tied up with B that A simply cannot love someone else in the same way. Twice I said *in some way* because I don't know exactly how it works. The verb 'to be' might be too strong here. It is rather that from A's point of view, in his experience, it *seems* impossible to love someone else in the same way.

In order to complete this small conceptual map of the obligations of love I will distinguish them from moral obligations. Let me first say how I understand morality.[13] Morality is a system of rules that enables the peaceful coexistence of people with various and competing interests. Core examples of moral rules I mentioned before are the prohibition of murder and theft. These moral rules have the interesting feature that they have an equivalent in a legal rule. It is not only *morally* but also *legally* forbidden to murder or to steal. There are typically legal ways to enforce compliance with those rules.[14] It is obvious that some of the special obligations can be understood as moral obligations. Both the obligation to keep a promise and various role-bound obligations facilitate the peaceful coexistence of people with different interests. And, putting many complications aside, one can say that both kinds of obligations, or at least part of them, are legally enforceable. Besides, that is why those obligations have *corresponding rights*. None of this, however, holds for the obligations of love. First, it would be very weird to see these obligations as a means for enabling the coexistence of people with competing interests, because people who love each other positively care about each other's interests. And second. The obligations of love are surely not legally enforceable. That is why they have no corresponding rights. A previous example can illustrate this. Although your best friend has an obligation of love to inform you about a vacant job you cannot claim the right to be informed about it by your best friend. And you surely cannot press charges against him because he did not inform you. There are two more differences between moral obligations and the obligations of love that concern the way people react to a *violation* of those obligations. It has often been observed that people react with *resentment*, *indignation* or *contempt* to the violation of a moral obligation. These are at least their immediate emotional reactions. But it would simply be inappropriate to react likewise to the violation of obligations of love. They are much too heavy, too morally charged for that. A more common and appropriate reaction in this context is *pity*. We sometimes find it regrettable that someone did not fulfil his obligations of love and we pity the person to whom those obligations are directed. In these cases not only the *nature* of the reactions is different, so

---

[13] For one example, see the introduction to H. G. Frankfurt, *The Importance Of What We Care About* (Cambridge: Cambridge University Press, 1988).

[14] A classical statement of the relation between morality and law can be found in H.L.A. Hart, *The Concept of Law* (Oxford: Clarendon Press, 1961), ch. 8.

is their *extension*. In principle, everyone can react with, let us say, resentment to the violation of a moral obligation. Here 'everyone' *includes* the victims who suffered from the violation. Their resentment may even be stronger than that of others, because they are directly affected by the violation. But it will still be resentment and only differ in *degree* from the reactions of other people. This does not hold for the obligations of love. Again, in principle, everyone can react with pity to the violation of an obligation of love. But here, 'everyone' *excludes* the one to whom the obligation applied. This person's reaction will be different in *kind* from the reactions of other people. B for example will not simply 'find it regrettable' that A did not observe his obligations of love to him. He will be *personally hurt*. And that is, at least to my mind, something fundamentally different.[15] Obviously the fact that a *personal* obligation has been violated plays an important role in the explanation of this very personal reaction.

Most — if not all — classical ethical theories fail to justify the obligations of love, mainly because their justifications do not grasp the fact that these are obligations towards a unique person. Take for instance the various kinds of *ethics of rules*: by this I mean ethical theories that formulate rules that guide our actions (be it deontology, Kantian ethics, contract-theories or rule consequentialism in one or other version). In all these theories, the procedure that leads to the formulation of these rules simply overlooks most of people's individual features, and is left with some highly general features shared by all persons. As a consequence, these theories can only formulate obligations that one has to a person '*as the bearer of these highly general features*', and that means in fact to *anyone*. Virtue ethics fares no better. Consider for instance the idea that one ought to act out of love because it is virtuous to act out of such a motivation.[16] Now this seems to imply that one should try to act out of love as much as possible and to as many persons as possible. However, this recommendation, besides being somewhat unrealistic, cannot explain why A should

---

[15] In the debate between morality and virtue ethics it is quite common to distinguish between two types of evaluative terms (See for example M. Slote, *From Morality to Virtue* (Oxford: Oxford University Press, 1992), introduction and ch. 10). The central evaluative terms of a moral theory are *right* and *wrong* and they apply primarily to actions. The central evaluative terms of an ethics of virtue are *admirable* and *deplorable* and they apply primarily to the character traits of a person. The difference between these two kinds of evaluative terms is conceptually related to a difference between two kinds of 'oughts' or 'obligations' and between two types of reactions to their violation that I already mentioned in the text: *resentment* versus *pity*. By distinguishing a third kind of reaction (being personally hurt) I make room for yet another type of 'obligation' and 'evaluation'. It brings us close to a kind of obligation *to the self* (although, of course, the object of the obligation is another person) and to integrity, the violation of such an obligation being a kind of self-betrayal.

[16] For an account of the obligations in personal relations in terms of the virtuous character of acting out of love, see M. Slote, *From Morality to Virtue* (Oxford: Oxford University Press, 1992) ch. 9.

in particular act out of love *for B* whom he loves already. Or consider, finally, a type of virtue ethics that links virtues directly to the realization of certain goods.[17] A virtue is seen then as a quality in a person that makes the realization of those goods possible. I will further assume that a virtuous person's actions are implicitly guided by vague rules that help realize those goods. One can easily apply this scheme to the case at hand. For instance, one can see the maintenance of personal relations as a good, worthy to be realized (remember what I said about the values of a personal relation). And one can see the obligations of love as vague and implicit rules that help maintain those relations. So far so good. But this model cannot explain A's obligations of love to B as a unique person: what obliges A in this case is not B, but rather the realization of a good that differs from B; the maintenance of his personal relation with B. In other words: the obligations of love would be directed to the wrong thing.

## Conclusion

Mauss '*Essay sur le don*' offers a very rich and complex analysis of gift practices and unravels many of their key features. Among them are the ambiguity of motivations for giving (hovering between altruism and egoism, or between spontaneity and obligation), the personal character of a gift, the importance of uncertainty, and the sociological role of gift practices in constituting social relations. Mauss takes much interest in the link between gifts, the desire for power of the donator (honour, status) and the humiliation of the receiver. These features have received considerable attention in the literature on the subject. Most important, however, is Mauss' famous 'discovery' that practices of giving are reciprocal and in some sense governed by three obligations: the obligations to give, to receive and to return.[18] I will concentrate on this discovery in my conclusion. More specifically, I will investigate whether, and in what sense, reciprocity and the three obligations apply to love and acts out of love. This will lead me to modify Mauss' claim about the importance of reciprocity and the three obligations for the gift.

Although Mauss is never fully explicit about these matters, what he says comes closest to the following position: *both* reciprocity and the circle of

---

[17] The classical statement of this type of virtue ethics can be found in A. MacIntyre, *After Virtue* (University of Notre Dame Press, 1981), ch. 14.

[18] I deliberately use the qualification here '*in some sense*', being aware of the fact that it is not clear in *what* sense. I refer to the extensive debate on 'following a rule' that has followed Wittgenstein's remarks on this topic. For example: is following a rule a matter of having an *explicit representation* before the mind, or is it rather a matter of being *bodily disposed* to do certain things in certain circumstances (cfr. Bourdieu's habitus)? A very interesting paper on this topic is Ch. Taylor, 'To Follow a Rule', in *Philosophical Arguments* (Massachusets: Harvard University Press, 1995).

obligations are *necessary* conditions for the existence of a practice of giving, but *neither of them* is a *sufficient* condition.[19] I agree with Mauss that reciprocity and the circle of obligations are not sufficient conditions, but I doubt that they are necessary conditions. This doubt stems from an unsuccessful attempt to apply those requirements to love and acts out of love.

It is fairly clear why neither reciprocity nor the circle of obligations can be a sufficient condition for a gift. As far as reciprocity is concerned, it suffices to remember that *market transactions* are reciprocal too. As has been argued in several articles in this companion, exchanges of commodities differ substantially from gift exchanges. As far as the circle of obligations is concerned, Mauss is well aware of the importance of *spontaneity*. At various points he emphasizes the mysterious *mélange* of motivations that characterizes a gift: a purely obligatory gift is hardly a gift at all.

Before going on it is important to note a crucial difference between reciprocity and the circle of obligations. Reciprocity is something we can *observe*. The circle of obligations offers a possible *explanation* of that observation. Reciprocity *results* from the fact that people follow those obligations. But sometimes another explanation is required. Market transactions and exchanges of gifts, for instance, are both reciprocal. They differ in that the reciprocity involved is explained otherwise. The presence of the three obligations may be enough to rule out the possibility of a market transaction (the reciprocity of which obviously has a different explanation). That in itself, however, does not imply that the circle of obligations is a necessary condition for the gift.

Why are reciprocity and the circle of obligations no necessary conditions for love? As far as reciprocity is concerned, it will suffice to repeat a point made in the first section. *If* love would be necessarily reciprocal, it would be hard to understand why unanswered love is so *painful*. Obviously it is so painful precisely because it *exists already, independently* of its being reciprocated. It is a *fact*, however, that most *instances* of love are reciprocal. The explanation of this fact may again lie in the inherent painfulness of unanswered love: it seems wise to stop loving someone, or at least try to do so, if there is no hope of success. The reciprocity of most instances of love, however, does not imply that love must be reciprocal.

Clearly Mauss' circle of obligations *does not* apply to love. Imagine there would be an obligation to love, to accept someone's love and to love someone in return. That would be absurd. Let me take a look at these obligations in reverse order. First, the obligation to return someone's love seems the most far-fetched. The main reason is that a lover values the *sincerity* of his beloved

---

[19] I hope to do no injustice to Mauss in trying to capture what he says in terms of necessary and sufficient conditions (which he nowhere does). However, the important thing here is not so much to uncover Mauss' exact position, but rather, to have something definite to which I can contrast the distinctive features of loving and acting out of love.

(and that is precisely because he values his motivation so highly). If A loves B, then he desires that B *loves* him and not just that B pretends to love him.[20] The latter, however, would be very likely to happen if people were obliged to love in return for love. The idea of being obliged to love someone seems quite extraordinary, if not impossible.[21]

Second, there is no obligation to accept someone's love. In fact one *should* only accept someone's love *if* one loves that person in return. Otherwise one is *at best insincere* (if you give someone the impression that you love him) and *at worst immoral* (if you do so in order to take advantage of his love). Instead of an obligation to accept someone's love there may be an obligation to *consider* his love. B cannot simply *neglect* A's love for him. He is at least obliged to contemplate matters as: 'is A worth being loved?', 'does A in some way attract me?', 'will I give it a chance?', etc. Having this obligation is a matter of taking other persons *seriously*.[22]

Finally I will take a look at the obligation to love. It is important to distinguish here between two possible meanings. First, one might mean an obligation to love *a specific person*. This obligation is similar to the obligation to return someone's love which is also an obligation to love a specific person. Hence it is susceptible to the same criticism. Second, one might mean an obligation to further one's own *capacity* to love. This obligation does not specify which particular person must be loved. It is doubtful whether we have *that kind* of obligation. But at least it seems possible to oblige someone to further a general capacity to love as time goes by.[23]

---

[20] The actions of a lover normally *express* his love, and these expressions normally *reveal* his love to the beloved person. However, expressions can be sincere or insincere. One can deliberately 'wear an emotion on one's face' without experiencing the emotion. That is what actors do. For this distinction, see Alan Tormey's important *The Concept of Expression* (Princeton: Princeton University Press, 1971).

[21] It is extraordinary because most people would find such an obligation undesirable. It may be impossible because of the (much agreed upon) principle that *ought* implies *can*, and it is obviously impossible to love a specific person on demand.

[22] According to some theories of ethics this is a moral obligation (e.g. Kantian ethics). We can find an analogous reasoning in the contemporary analytic literature on Kant's moral theory. It sometimes claims that we have an obligation to take someone else's ends *seriously*. This is not an obligation to consider these ends as valuable. Neither is it an obligation to help someone else in pursuing those ends. It is rather an obligation to *consider* whether these ends are valuable and worth being pursued. That obligation is a moral one, stemming from the idea that this someone is a person, i.e. a being capable of setting his own ends. See for example B. Herman, 'Mutual Aid and Respect for Persons', in *Ethics*, 94 (1984).

[23] Most virtue ethics imply the obligation to promote in ourselves (and as time goes by) the character traits that are virtues. We have a similar obligation to further our capacity to love *in so far as love is a virtue*. I think that being capable of loving other persons *is* a virtue but loving *this* or *that* person *is not*; hence the latter can never be obligatory. Again, this does not mean that there are no obligations that are grounded in the love for a particular person (cf. the personal obligations of section two). But it shows that there is something awkward in trying to justify those obligations using the fact that (the general capacity to) love is a virtue (*see also footnote 20*).

These considerations show that Mauss' circle of obligations does not apply to love. The preceding section, however, showed an attempt to describe a kind of obligation that *does* apply to love: the obligations of love. It is important to elucidate the differences between these two kinds of obligations. First, they are both *special* obligations. And they are both *conditional* obligations (obligations one has *under the condition that* 'x' is the case). But the respective conditions differ. Mauss' obligations (especially the second and the third one) are dependent on a state of affairs that concerns *someone else*. A has an obligation to accept x and to return y because *B* has given x to him. Contrariwise, A's obligations of love towards B are dependent on a state of affairs that concerns *himself*, namely, *his love* for B. A second difference is congenial to the first one. Applying Mauss' circle of obligations to love would result in a set of obligations *to love* and *to act out of love*. The obligations of love, however, are obligations *to act as one would act if one acted out of love*. To put it more technically, love is not part of their content, it is only part of their ground: they do not entail an obligation to love someone. Hence the impossibility critique of the preceding paragraph is not applicable; neither is the insincerity critique, because the obligations of love *presuppose* that A loves B.

Let me take stock of the situation. It is one thing to say that reciprocity and the circle of obligations do not necessarily apply to love. It is another thing to say that they do not apply to gifts at all. The latter is too strong. The example of love shows *at most* that reciprocity and the circle of obligations are not necessarily applicable to *all kinds of gifts*. However, this does not imply that they are not necessary conditions for, or at least highly significant features of, practices to which they *do* apply. Let me pursue this train of thought. Are there any practices of giving to which reciprocity and the three obligations *do* apply?

At least one example immediately springs to mind: *gratitude*. In certain circumstances there is a clear obligation to be grateful and to act out of gratitude (analogous to the obligations to accept and to return). And this obligation is dependent on something that *someone else* has given to you. I do not intend to examine the precise conditions under which gratitude is owed or what exactly gratitude requires in these conditions,[24] neither to investigate in detail how and why love and gratitude differ. But the fact that the Maussian obligations at least roughly apply to gratitude and *not* to love suffices to mark their difference. And this difference must urge us to be careful in giving a place to gratitude in personal relations. Not that these emotions are utterly incompatible, in the sense that it is impossible to both love and be grateful towards the same person at the same time. But intuitively, there exists a kind of subtle tension between these emotions, which implies that gratitude must never get too firm

---

[24] The only comprehensive book on gratitude that has come my way is T. McConnel, *Gratitude* (Philadelphia: Temple University Press, 1993).

a foothold in a personal relation. Too much gratitude, I think, ruins love and hence destroys the personal relation.[25]

In a previous paragraph I cautiously posited that the example of love might *at most* show that reciprocity and the three obligations are not necessary conditions for the gift. One way out of this conclusion would be to deny that love and acting out of love *are* gifts: if they are not, then they cannot serve as counterexamples for whatever aspect of whatever theory of the gift. In order to refute this way out we need sufficiently strong and independent reasons for conceptualizing love and acts out of love as gifts. I hope that the first section of this paper has offered such reasons. If so, this short analysis of love and personal relations will have contributed a little to our conceptual map of the gift-giving.

---

[25] Some authors ground the obligations of children towards their parents in love (see for example J. English, 'What Do Grown Children Owe Their Parents', in O. O'Neil & W. Ruddick(ed.), *Having Children* (New York: Oxford University Press, 1979)). Others attribute an important role to gratitude in justifying these obligations (see for example, McConnel, op. cit., ch. 7). The fact that these rival accounts exist exemplifies the tension between love and gratitude.

PRINTED ON PERMANENT PAPER • IMPRIME SUR PAPIER PERMANENT • GEDRUKT OP DUURZAAM PAPIER - ISO 9706

ORIENTALISTE, KLEIN DALENSTRAAT 42, B-3020 HERENT